W.E. Fairbairn's Complete Compendium of Lethal, Unarmed, Hand-to-Hand Combat Methods and Fighting

Get Tough!
All-in Fighting
Shooting to Live
Hands Off!
Scientific Self-Defence
Defendu

The Naval & Military Press Ltd

Published by

The Naval & Military Press Ltd
Unit 5 Riverside, Brambleside
Bellbrook Industrial Estate
Uckfield, East Sussex
TN22 1QQ England

Tel: +44 (0)1825 749494

www.naval-military-press.com
www.nmarchive.com

*In reprinting in facsimile from the original, any imperfections are inevitably reproduced
and the quality may fall short of modern type and cartographic standards.*

W.E. Fairbairn's
Complete Compendium of
Lethal, Unarmed, Hand-to-Hand
Combat Methods and Fighting

CONTENTS

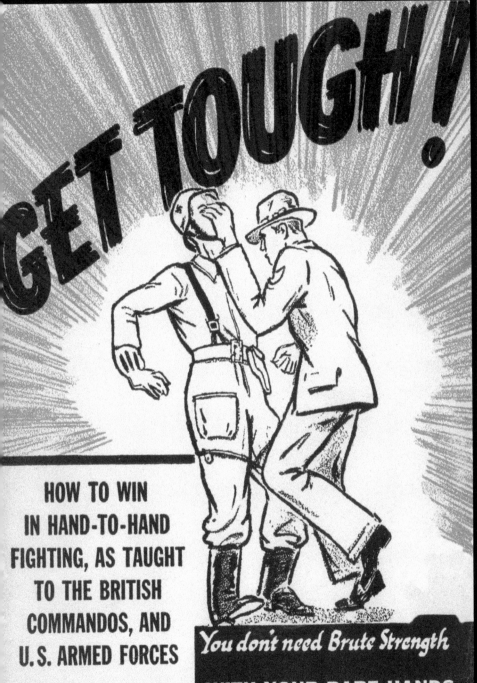

GET TOUGH!

HOW TO WIN IN HAND-TO-HAND FIGHTING, AS TAUGHT TO THE BRITISH COMMANDOS, AND U.S. ARMED FORCES

By MAJOR W. E. FAIRBAIRN

You don't need Brute Strength

WITH YOUR BARE HANDS YOU CAN BEAT THE MAN WHO WANTS TO KILL YOU

GET TOUGH!

HOW TO WIN
IN HAND-TO-HAND FIGHTING

AS TAUGHT TO THE BRITISH COMMANDOS
AND THE U. S. ARMED FORCES

By

MAJOR W. E. FAIRBAIRN

Illustrated by "Hary".

The Naval & Military Press Ltd

PREFACE

The method of hand-to-hand fighting described in this book is the approved standard instruction for all members of His Majesty's forces. The Commandos, and parachute troops, harrying the invasion coasts of Europe, have been thoroughly trained in its use. Britain's two-million Home Guard are daily being instructed in its simple but terrible effectiveness. The units of the United States Marine Corps who were stationed in China between 1927 and 1940 learned these methods at my own hands when I was Assistant Commissioner of the Shanghai Municipal Police.

There will be some who will be shocked by the methods advocated here. To them I say "In war you cannot afford the luxury of squeamishness. Either you kill or capture, or you will be captured or killed. We've got to be tough to win, and we've got to be ruthless—tougher and more ruthless than our enemies."

It is not the armed forces of the United Nations alone who can profit by learning how to win in hand-to-hand fighting. Every civilian, man or woman, who ever walks a deserted road at midnight, or goes in fear of his life in the dark places of a city, should acquaint himself with these methods. Once mastered, they will instil the courage and self-reliance that come with the sure knowledge that you are the master of any dangerous situation with which you may have to cope.

The methods described in this book I have carefully worked out and developed over a period of many years. They owe something to the famous Japanese judo (jiu-jutso), and something else to Chinese boxing. But, largely, they were developed from my own experience and observation of how most effectively to deal with the ruffians, thugs, bandits, and bullies of one of the toughest waterfront areas in the world.

Although every method described in the following pages is practicable—and so proved by the author and his students by years of experience, it is not essential to master them all. I suggest that at

v

9

first you select about ten which, for reasons of your height, weight, build, etc., seem most suitable, and specialize in mastering these thoroughly.*

Do not consider yourself an expert until you can carry out every movement *instinctively* and *automatically*. Until then, spend at least ten minutes daily in practice with a friend. At first, practice every movement slowly and smoothly. Then gradually increase your speed until every movement can be executed with lightning rapidity.

I should like in conclusion to give a word of warning. Almost every one of these methods, applied vigorously and without restraint, will result, if not in the death, then certainly in the maiming of your opponent. Extreme caution, then, should be exercised in practice, care being taken never to give a blow with full force or a grip with maximum pressure. But, once closed with your enemy, give every ounce of effort you can muster, and victory will be yours.

Captain W. E. Fairbairn

* The author will be glad to answer questions from readers concerning the execution of the methods described in this book. Address the author in care of the publisher, enclosing a self-addressed stamped envelope.

vi

CONTENTS

vii

viii

ix

BLOWS

NO. I—EDGE-OF-THE-HAND

Deliver edge-of-the-hand blows with the inner (i.e., little-finger) edge of the hand, fingers straight and close together, thumb extended; contact is made with the edge only, about half-way between the knuckle of the little finger and the wrist, as shown in Fig. 1.

1. Deliver the blow with a bent arm (never with a straight arm), using a chopping action from the elbow, with the weight of the body behind it. Practise by striking the open palm of your left hand, as in Fig. 2.
2. There are two ways in which this blow can be delivered:
   (*a*) *Downwards*, with either hand;
   (*b*) *Across*, with either hand; the blow always being delivered outwards, with the palm of the hand downwards, never on top (Fig. 3).
3. Attack the following points on your opponent's body, delivering every blow as quickly as possible:
   (*a*) The sides or back of the wrist;
   (*b*) The forearm, half-way between the wrist and elbow;
   (*c*) The biceps;
   (*d*) The sides or back of the neck;
   (*e*) Just below the "Adam's apple";
   (*f*) The kidneys or base of the spine.

Note.—If your opponent catches hold of you, strike his wrist or forearm; a fracture will most likely result. This would be almost impossible with a blow from a clenched fist.

2

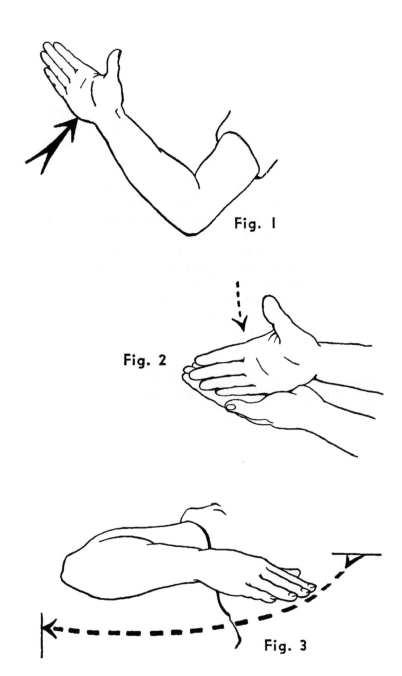

Fig. 1

Fig. 2

Fig. 3

NO. 2—CHIN JAB

Deliver this blow with the heel of your hand, full force, with the weight of your body behind it, and fingers spread so as to reach your opponent's eyes, as in Fig. 4. Always aim at the point of your opponent's chin (Fig. 5).

1. Deliver the blow upwards from a bent arm and only when close to your opponent. The distance the blow will have to travel will depend on the height of your opponent, but will seldom exceed six inches.

2. Never draw your hand back, thus signaling your intention of striking. From start to finish, make every movement as quickly as possible.

3. Remember that an attack, or an attempt to attack, with the knee at your opponent's testicles will always bring his chin forward and down.

Note.—Practise this blow as follows: Hold your left hand at the height of your own chin, palm downwards; jab up quickly with your right, striking your left hand, as in Fig. 6.

4

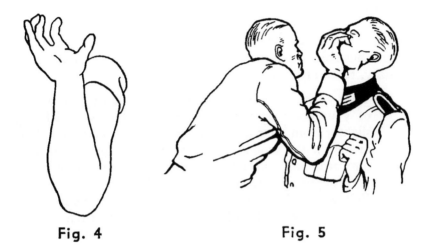

Fig. 4   Fig. 5

Fig. 6

NO. 3—BOOT (SIDE KICK)

With a few exceptions, you should always kick sideways, for you are thus able to put more force behind your blow and can, if necessary, reach farther.

1. Turn your right side to your opponent, putting the weight of your body on your left foot. Bending your left leg slightly from your knee, raise your right foot two to four inches off the ground, as in Fig. 7. Shoot your right foot outwards and upwards to your right, aiming to strike your opponent's leg just below the knee-cap.

2. Follow the blow through, scraping down your opponent's shin with the edge of your boot from the knee to the instep, finishing up with all your weight on your right foot, smashing the small bones of his foot. If necessary, follow up with a chin jab with your left hand (Fig. 8).

Note.—Where the kick is to be made with the left foot, reverse the above.

6

Fig. 7

Fig. 8

NO. 3A—BOOT DEFENSE

Your opponent has seized you around the body from in front, pinning your arms to your sides.

1. Having put your weight on one foot, raise the other and scrape your opponent's shin-bone downwards from about half way from the knee, finishing up with a smashing blow on his foot (Fig. 9).
2. An alternative method to Fig. 9, permitting you to use the inner edge of the boot, is shown in Fig. 10.

Note A.—Whether you should use the outside or inside of your boot will depend upon how the weight of your body is distributed at the time. Provided that you are equally balanced on both feet, you can use either; otherwise, use the one opposite to that on which you have your weight.

Note B.—If seized from behind, stamp on your opponent's foot with the heel of either boot, turning quickly and following up with a chin jab with either hand.

8

Fig. 9

Fig. 10

NO. 3B—BOOT ("BRONCO KICK")

Your opponent is lying on the ground.

1. Take a flying jump at your opponent, drawing your feet up by bending your knees, at the same time keeping your feet close together (Fig. 11).
2. When your feet are approximately eight inches above your opponent's body, shoot your legs out straight, driving both of your boots into his body, and smash him.

Note.—It is almost impossible for your opponent to parry a kick made in this manner, and, in addition, it immediately puts him on the defensive, leaving him only the alternative of rolling away from you in an attempt to escape. Further, although he may attempt to protect his body with his arms, the weight of your body (say 150 pounds), plus the impetus of your flying jump (say another 150 pounds), will drive your heels into your opponent's body with such terrific force that you will almost certainly kill him. Steel heel-plates on your boots will make his attack even more effective.

Practise this kick on a dummy figure or on the grass as in Fig. 12.

10

Fig. 11

Fig. 12

NO. 4—KNEE

This blow can be delivered only when you are very close to your opponent.

1. Putting the weight of your body on one leg, bend the knee of the other by drawing your heel slightly backwards, and drive your knee quickly upwards into your opponent's testicles (Fig. 13).

Note.—This blow is frequently used to bring your opponent into a more favorable position for applying the chin jab (Fig. 14).

12

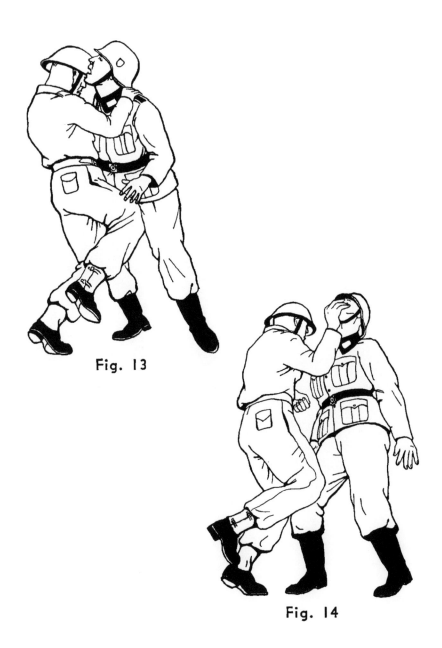

Fig. 13

Fig. 14

RELEASES

NO. 5—FROM A WRIST HOLD (ONE HAND)

1. You are seized by the right wrist, as in Fig. 15. Bend your wrist and arm towards your body, twisting your wrist outwards against your opponent's thumb (Fig. 16).

Note A.—This must be accomplished with one rapid and continuous motion.

Note B.—No matter with which hand your opponent seizes either of your wrists, *the important thing to remember is to twist your wrist against his thumb.*

16

Fig. 15

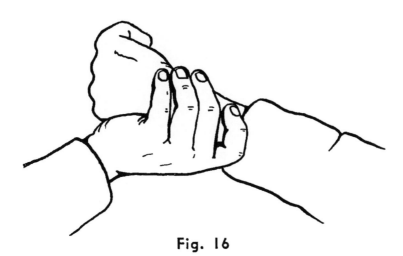

Fig. 16

NO. 5A—FROM A WRIST HOLD (TWO HANDS)

1. You are seized by the left wrist, by two hands, as in Fig. 17, your opponent's thumbs being on top. Reach over and catch hold of your hand with your right. Pull your left hand sharply towards your body, against his thumbs (Fig. 18).

Note A.—The pressure on his thumbs, which is slightly upwards and then downwards, will force him to release his hold immediately.

Note B.—Follow up with chin jab, edge-of-the-hand, or knee kick to the testicles.

Should your opponent seize you as in Fig. 19 (his thumbs underneath), pass your right hand under and catch hold of your left hand as in Fig. 20. Pull down sharply towards you.

18

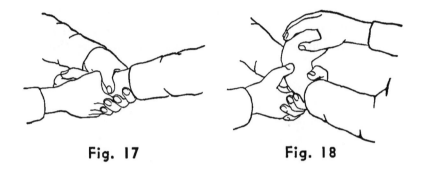

Fig. 17   Fig. 18

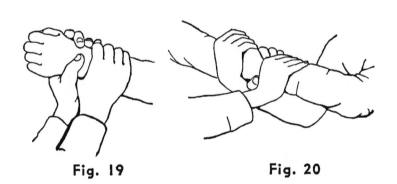

Fig. 19   Fig. 20

NO. 6—FROM A STRANGLE HOLD (ONE HAND)

You are seized by the throat, as in Fig. 21, and forced back against a wall.

1. With a smashing blow with the edge of your right hand, strike your opponent's right wrist towards your left-hand side. Follow up with a knee kick to his testicles (Fig. 22).

20

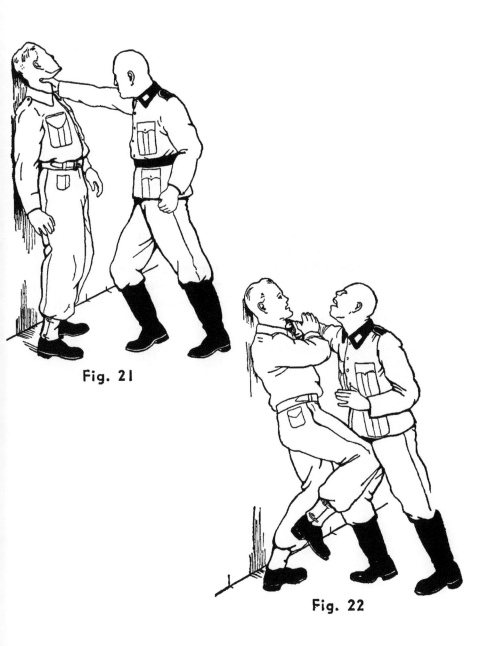

Fig. 21

Fig. 22

NO. 6A—FROM A STRANGLE HOLD (TWO HANDS)

You are seized from in front by the throat, as in Fig. 23.

1. With your left hand seize your opponent's right elbow from underneath, your thumb to the right.
2. With your right hand, reach over his arms and seize his right wrist (Fig. 24).
3. With your right arm apply pressure downwards on his left arm; at the same time, with a circular upward motion of your left hand, force his elbow towards your right side. This will break his hold of your throat and put him off balance (Fig. 25).
4. Keeping a firm grip with both hands, turn rapidly towards your right-hand side by bringing your right leg to your right rear. Follow up with edge-of-the-hand blow on his right elbow (Fig. 26).

Note.—All the above movements must be one rapid and continuous motion.

22

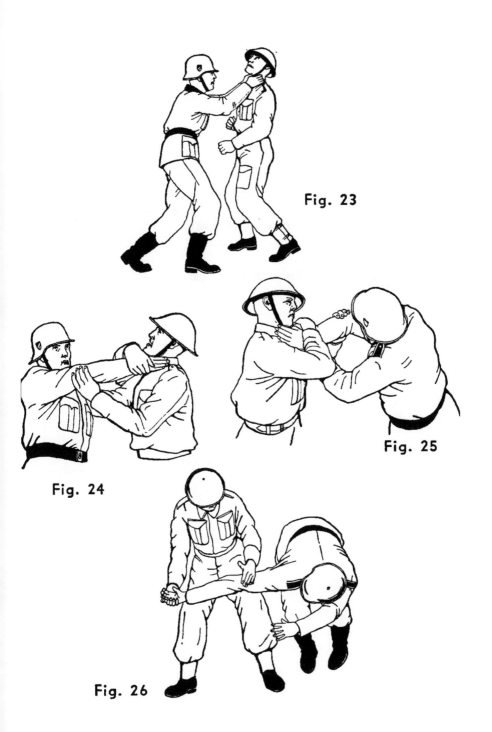

Fig. 23

Fig. 24

Fig. 25

Fig. 26

NO. 7—FROM A BEAR HUG (FRONT, OVER THE ARMS)

You are gripped around the waist (Fig. 27).

1. Knee your opponent in the testicles.
2. With the outer or inner edge of either boot, scrape his shin-bone from about half way from the knee and follow through by stamping on his instep.
3. If, as a soldier, you are wearing a helmet, smash him in the face with it.
4. Seize his testicles with either hand.

24

Fig. 27

NO. 7A—FROM A BEAR HUG (FRONT, OVER THE ARMS) Alternative Release

You are gripped around the waist (Fig. 27).

1. If possible, bite his ear. Even though not successful, the attempt will cause him to bend forward and into a position from which you can seize his testicles with your right hand (Fig. 28).
2. Reach over his arm with your left forearm (Fig. 29).
3. Apply pressure on his right arm with your left (causing him to break his hold), and force his head downwards. Smash him in the face with your right knee (Fig. 30).

If necessary, follow up with edge-of-the-hand blow on back of his neck.

Note.—Should your opponent anticipate your intention when you are in the position shown in Fig. 29 and resist the pressure of your left arm (¶ 3), go after his eyes with your left hand as in Fig. 30A, and follow up with a knee to the testicles.

26

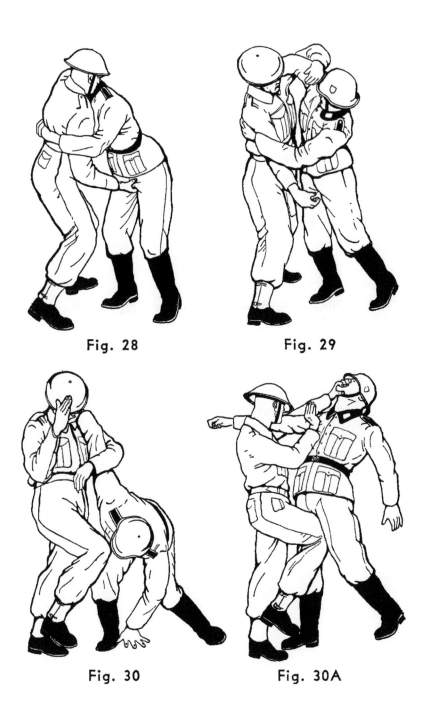

Fig. 28

Fig. 29

Fig. 30

Fig. 30A

NO. 8—FROM A BEAR HUG (FRONT, ARMS FREE)

You are gripped around the waist (Fig. 31).

1. Place your left hand in the small of his back and apply a chin jab, as in Fig. 32.

If necessary, knee him in the testicles.

NO. 9—FROM A BEAR HUG (BACK, OVER THE ARMS)

You are gripped around the chest (Fig. 33).

1. If you are wearing a helmet, smash your opponent in the face with it.
2. Stamp on his feet with either foot.
3. Seize him by the testicles with your right or left hand.

28

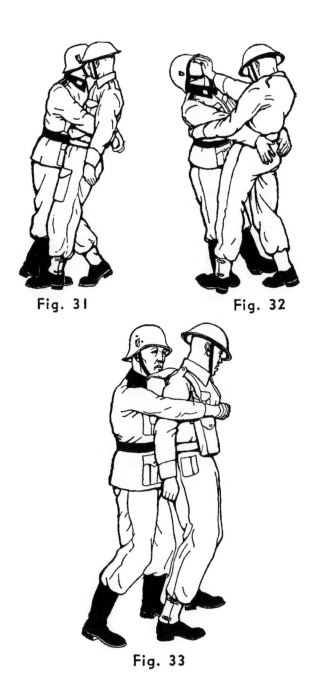

Fig. 31   Fig. 32

Fig. 33

NO. 9A—FROM A BEAR HUG (BACK, OVER THE ARMS) Alternative Release

You are gripped around the chest (Fig. 33).

1. Seize your opponent's testicles with your left hand (causing him to break his hold).
2. Pass your right arm over his right (Fig. 34).
3. Slip out from under his arm by turning to your left and stepping backwards with your right foot, seizing his right wrist with both hands and jerking it downwards. Finish up by kicking him in the face (Fig. 35).

NO. 10—FROM A BEAR HUG (BACK, ARMS FREE)

You are gripped around the chest (Fig. 36).

1. If you are wearing a helmet, smash your opponent's face with it.
2. Stamp on his feet with either foot.
3. Seize his little finger with your right hand, bend it backwards, and walk out of the hold (Fig. 37).

30

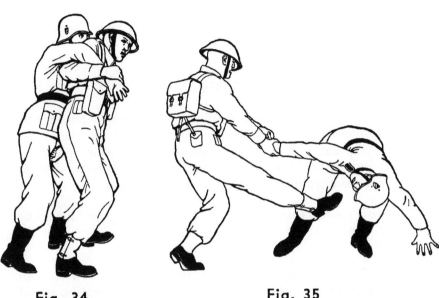

Fig. 34   Fig. 35

Fig. 36

Fig. 37

NO. 11—FROM A HAIR HOLD (BACK)

You are seized by the hair from behind and pulled back, as in Fig. 38.

1. With both hands, seize your opponent's right wrist and arm with a very firm grip, making him keep the hold shown in Fig. 39.
2. Turn to your left (inwards, towards your opponent) by pivoting on your left foot. This will twist his arm.
3. Step backwards as far as possible with your right foot, jerking his hand off your head in a downward and backward direction between your legs (Fig. 40).

Note.—It is possible that this will tear quite a bit of your hair out by the roots, but it is very unlikely that you will notice it at the time.

4. Keep a firm grip on his wrist and arm, and follow up with a smashing kick to your opponent's face with the toe of your right boot.

Note A.—All the above movements must be one rapid and continuous motion.

Note B.—When in the position shown in Fig. 40, you can increase the force of your kick to the face by pulling your opponent's arm slightly upwards and towards you. This movement also enables you to get back on balance.

32

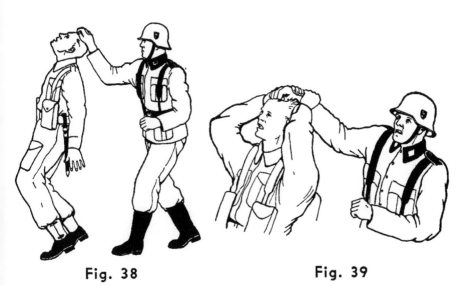

Fig. 38   Fig. 39

Fig. 40

HOLDS

NO. 12—THUMB HOLD

This is the most effective hold known, and very little exertion on your part (three to four pounds' pressure) is required to make even the most powerful prisoner obey you. It is possible also for you to conduct him, even if resisting, as far as he is able to walk. You have such complete control of him that you can, if necessary, use him as cover against attack from others.

The movements you have to make to secure this hold are very complicated, which is mainly the reason why it is almost unknown outside of the Far East. But the advantage one gains in knowing that he can effectively apply this hold more than repays for the time that must be spent in mastering it.

First concentrate on making every move slowly, gradually speeding up until all movements become one continuous motion. When you have thoroughly mastered the hold, then learn to secure it from any position in which you have secured your opponent.

It should be understood that this hold is not a method of attack, but simply a "mastering hold," which is applied only after you have partially disabled or brought your opponent to a submissive frame of mind by one of the "follow up" methods (BLOWS).

Should your opponent not be wearing a helmet or similar protection which covers his ears, the following will be found to be a very simple method of making him submissive:

Cup your hands and strike your opponent simultaneously over both ears (Fig. 41). This will probably burst one or both ear drums and at least give him a mild form of concussion. It can be applied from the front or from behind.

36

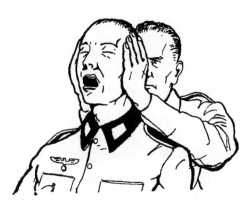

Fig. 41

NO. 12—THUMB HOLD (cont.)

Stand facing your opponent and slightly to his left.

1. Insert your right thumb between the thumb and fore-finger of his left hand, your fingers under the palm of his hand, your thumb to the right (Fig. 42).
2. Seize his left elbow with your left hand, knuckles to the right, and thumb outside and close to your own fore-fingers (Fig. 43).
3. Step in towards your opponent; at the same time, turn your body so that you are facing in the same direction, simultaneously forcing his left forearm up across his chest and towards his left shoulder by pulling his elbow with your left hand over your right forearm and forcing up-wards with your right hand (Fig. 44).

Release the hold with your left hand just as soon as you have pulled his elbow over your right forearm, and hold your oppo-nent's left elbow very close to your body.

4. Keeping a firm grip on the upper part of his left arm with your right arm, immediately seize the fingers of his left hand with your left. This will prevent him from trying to seize one of the fingers of your right hand and also give you an extra leverage for applying pressure as follows:
5. Press down on the back of his hand towards your left-hand side with your right hand. Should your opponent be a very powerful man and try to resist, a little extra pressure ap-plied by pulling his fingers downwards towards your left-hand side with your left hand will be sufficient to bring him up on his toes and convince him that he has met his master (Fig. 45).

38

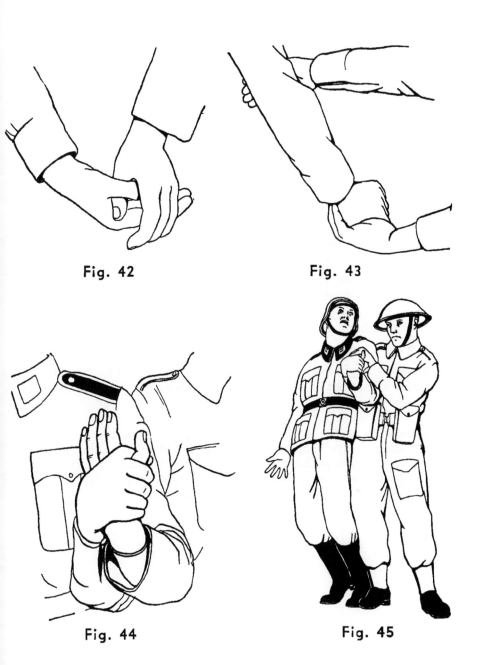

Fig. 42

Fig. 43

Fig. 44

Fig. 45

NO. 13—SENTRY HOLD

The successful execution of this method of attack on a sentry—presupposing thorough mastery of every move—depends entirely on careful preparation. First, the man selected to make the attack should be an *expert at stalking*. The stalk or approach should be made during the hours of dark or semi-dark, and the sentry should be kept under observation long enough for the attacker to familiarize himself with the sentry's movements and equipment.

Now let us assume that conditions are somewhat as follows:

1. The sentry's rifle is slung or carried on his right shoulder.
2. He is wearing a steel helmet covering the back of his neck and his ears.
3. He is wearing a respirator on the small of his back, projecting as much as six inches (see Fig. 46).
4. There are other sentries within shouting distance.

These conditions are not too favorable for the attacker, but are what might have to be met, and training should be carried out under conditions as near as possible to those which would be met in actual war.

Note.—The stalker should not be handicapped with any equipment, other than a knife or a pistol. He should wear rubber or cloth shoes, socks pulled well up over the trousers, cap-comforter well pulled down, with the collar of his blouse turned up and his hands and face camouflaged (See Fig. 47, page 43).

40

Fig. 46

NO. 13—SENTRY HOLD (cont.)

1. Approach the sentry from behind to within three to four feet and take up the position shown in Fig. 47. This will permit you to make a lightning-like attack by springing on him.

2. With the fingers and thumb of your left hand fully extended, *strike* him across the throat with the inner edge of your left forearm (i.e. with the forearm bone), and simultaneously *punch* him with your clenched right hand in the small of his back or on his respirator case (Fig. 48).

The effect of these blows, if applied as above, will render your opponent unconscious or semi-conscious. Further, the blow on the throat will cause your opponent to draw in his breath, making it impossible for him to shout and give the alarm.

3. The blows should be immediately followed with a very fast movement of your right hand from the small of his back, over his right shoulder, clapping it over his mouth and nose (Fig. 49). This will prevent him from breathing or making a noise if the blow on the throat was not effectively applied.

Very likely the blows on his throat and in the small of his back will cause him to drop his rifle or will knock his helmet off his head. Should this happen, do not attempt to prevent their falling on the ground. Just keep still for about ten seconds, after which it is unlikely that anyone having heard the noise will come to investigate. Retaining your hold around his neck with your left arm, drag him away backwards.

Note.—The extraordinary effectiveness of this hold will be readily understood if you have a friend apply it on you as above, being careful to exert no more than one-twentieth of the required force.

42

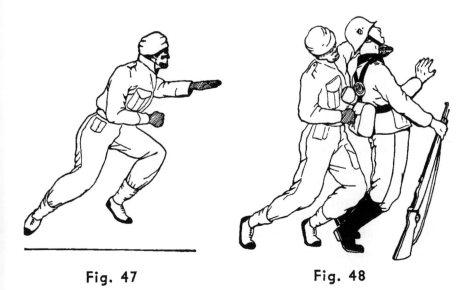

Fig. 47   Fig. 48

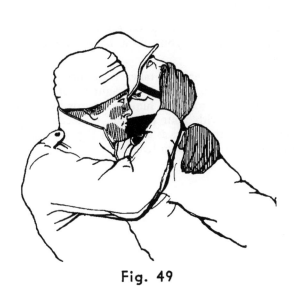

Fig. 49

NO. 14—JAPANESE STRANGLE HOLD

1. Approach your opponent from behind.
2. Place your left arm around his neck, with your forearm bone bearing on his "Adam's apple."
3. Place the back of your right arm (above the elbow) on his right shoulder and clasp your right biceps with your left hand.
4. Place your right hand on the back of his head.
5. Pull him backwards with your left forearm and press his head forward with your right hand, and strangle him (Fig. 50).

Note.—Should your opponent attempt to seize you by the testicles:

(*a*) Keep your grip with both arms, straightening out the fingers and thumbs of both hands. With the edge of your left hand in the bend of your right arm, place the edge of your right hand just below the base of the skull.

(*b*) Step back quickly, at the same time jolting his head forward with the edge of your right hand, and dislocate his neck (Fig. 51).

(*c*) If your opponent is a taller man than yourself, making it difficult for you to reach his right shoulder with your right arm, as in Fig. 50, bend him backwards by applying pressure on his neck with your left arm. If necessary, punch him in the small of the back, as shown in Fig. 48, page 43, and bring him down to your own height.

44

Fig. 50

Fig. 51

NO. 14A—JAPANESE STRANGLE HOLD APPLIED FROM IN FRONT

1. Stand facing your opponent.
2. Seize his right shoulder with your left hand and his left shoulder with your right hand.
3. Simultaneously push with your left hand (retaining the hold) and pull towards you with your right hand, turning your opponent around (Fig. 52). Your left arm will now be around his neck and most likely you will have caused your opponent to cross his legs, making it almost impossible for him to defend himself.
4. Place the back of your right arm (above the elbow) on his right shoulder and clasp your right biceps with your left hand.
5. Grasp the back of his head with your right hand, and apply pressure by pulling him backwards with your left forearm and pressing his head forward with your right arm (Fig. 52A).

Note.—Although the final position and the method of applying pressure are identical with that shown in No. 14 on the previous page, there is a difference in the amount of pressure necessary to strangle your opponent. If his legs are crossed (and they almost always will be when he is suddenly twisted round in this manner), approximately only half the amount of pressure will be required.

46

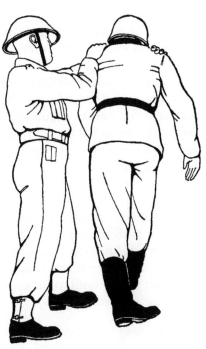

Fig. 52

Fig. 52A

NO. 15—HANDCUFF HOLD

1. You are facing your opponent. Make a dive at his right wrist, seizing it with both hands, right above left, and jerk it violently downwards, as in Fig. 53. This will produce a considerable shock, amounting almost to a knock-out blow on the left side of his head.

2. Swing his arm up to the height of your shoulder, at the same time twisting his arm towards you so as to force him off-balance on to his left leg (Fig. 54).

3. Keeping his arm at the height of your shoulder, pass quickly underneath it by taking a pace forward with your right foot. (It may be necessary for you to reduce your height to permit your doing this; do so by bending your legs at the knees.) Turn inwards towards your opponent, jerking his arm downwards, as in Fig. 55.

4. Step to his back with your left foot, and, with a circular upward motion, force his wrist well up his back. Retain the grip with your left hand and seize his right elbow with your right hand, forcing it well up his back. Then slide your left hand around his wrist, bringing your thumb inside and finger over the back of the hand, and bend his wrist. Apply pressure with both hands until your opponent's right shoulder points to the ground (Fig. 56).

Note A.—This is a very useful hold for marching your prisoner a short distance only. For a longer march, a change to the Thumb Hold (Fig. 45, page 39) is recommended.

Note B.—A method of tying up your prisoner is shown on page 83 (Figs. 98 and 99).

48

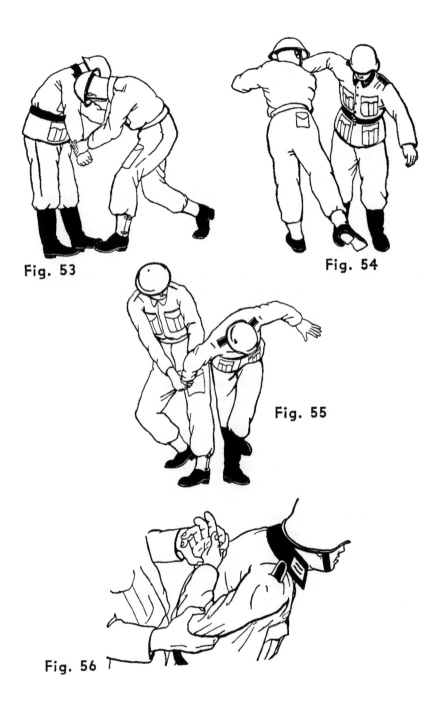

Fig. 53

Fig. 54

Fig. 55

Fig. 56

NO. 16—BENT-ARM HOLD

Note.—Students are strongly recommended to specialize in mastering this hold.

1. Your opponent has taken up a boxing stance, or raised his right arm as if about to deliver a blow.
2. Seize his right wrist with your left hand, bending his arm at the elbow, towards him (Fig. 57). Continue the pressure on his wrist until his arm is in the position shown in Fig. 58.

Note.—These movements must be one rapid and continuous motion. Note that forcing your opponent's right forearm backwards places him off-balance, making it almost impossible for him to attack you with his left fist.

3. Immediately step in with your right foot, placing your right leg and hip close in to your opponent's thigh.
4. Pass your right arm under the upper part of his right arm, seizing his right wrist with your right hand above your left.
5. Keeping a firm grip with both hands, force his right elbow and arm against your chest, applying pressure by jerking his wrist towards the ground. At the same time, force the forearm bone of your right arm up and in to the back muscles of the upper part of his right arm (Fig. 59).
6. Should your opponent, when in this position, attempt to strike you with his left hand: Straighten out the fingers and thumb of your right hand, placing the edge of the hand over your left wrist, and apply pressure by a sudden jerk upwards of your right forearm, taking care to keep his elbow well in to your chest (Fig. 60).

50

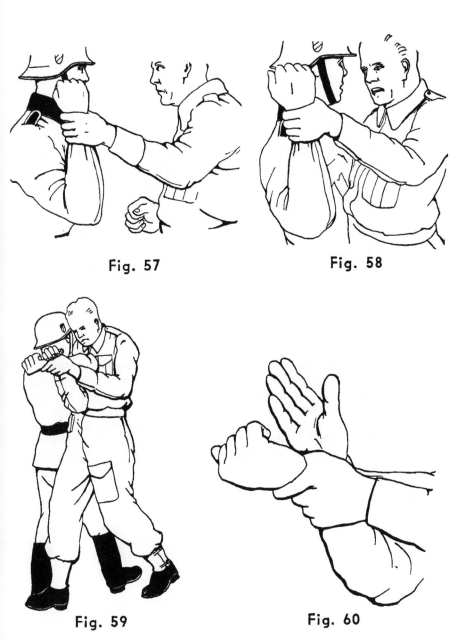

Fig. 57

Fig. 58

Fig. 59

Fig. 60

NO. 17—HEAD HOLD

Approach your opponent from the front.

1. Keeping the fingers of your right hand straight and thumb extended, strike him on the left side of his neck with the inside of your right forearm (Fig. 61). This blow will render your opponent "punch-drunk" or dazed.

2. Immediately after delivering the blow with your right forearm, slide it around your opponent's neck, simultaneously stepping across his front with your right leg, bending him forward from the waist and catching hold of your right wrist with your left hand (Fig. 62).

3. Force your right forearm bone into the right side of his face (anywhere between the temple and the chin will do) by pulling on your right wrist with your left hand and forcing downwards on the left side of his face with your body.

Note.—Observe that the outside of your right forearm is resting on your right thigh and that the weight of your body is being forced on to your right leg by pressure from your left foot. Any attempt of your opponent to seize your testicles should immediately be countered by a slight increase of pressure. If necessary, apply an edge-of-the-hand blow as follows: Release your hold with your left hand, straighten up slightly, and apply the blow on the left side of his neck.

52

Fig. 61

Fig. 62

THROWS

NO. 18—HIP THROW

You are facing your opponent.

1. Seize his equipment, arms, or clothing slightly above the height of his elbows. Pull down with your right hand and lift up with your left hand, pulling him off-balance. Simultaneously shoot your left leg as far as possible behind him, keeping your left leg rigid and close up to his thigh. Take care that your left foot is pointing as in Fig. 63.

2. Continue the downward pull of your right hand and the upward lift of your left hand, at the same time bending forward and downwards from your waist towards your right foot. All the above movements must be one rapid and continuous motion and will throw your opponent as in Fig. 64. Follow-up with a kick on his spine with either boot, somewhere near the small of his back.

Note.—An alternative method of applying the Throw when dealing with an opponent approaching you on your left side is as follows:

1. Seize his equipment or left arm with your right hand and pull downwards, simultaneously striking him up under the chin with your left hand (Chin Jab) and kicking his legs from under him with a backward kick of your rigid left leg, as in Fig. 65. This will throw your opponent backwards with smashing force, after which it will be a simple matter for you to dispose of him in any manner you may wish.

56

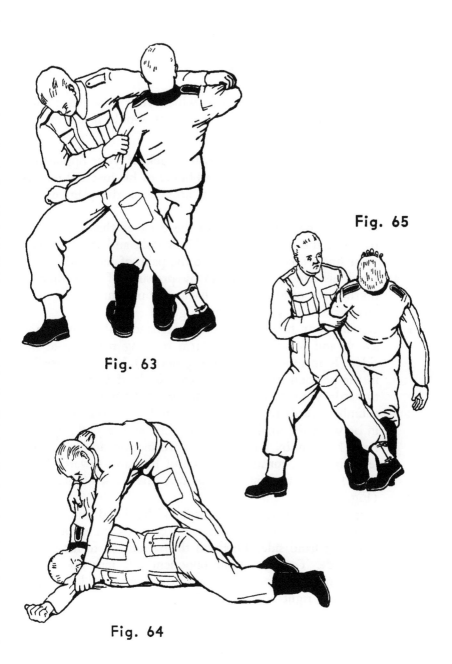

Fig. 65

Fig. 63

Fig. 64

NO. 19—WRIST THROW

Because of the unusual manner in which your opponent's hand is seized at the initial start of this throw, you should first learn the hold as follows:

1. Force your left thumb into the back of your opponent's right hand, between the small bones of his first and middle fingers, your fingers passing around to the palm of his hand.

2. Force your right thumb into the back of this same hand, between the small bones of his middle and third fingers, your fingers passing around to the palm of his hand.

3. Bend his hand towards him by pressure of your thumbs on the back of his hand and backward pressure on the palm and wrist with your fingers (Fig. 66).

4. Retain your hold with your left hand, take your right away, and permit his right arm to hang naturally at his side. (Remember, this is only practice.) You will then be in the position shown in Fig. 67. (Back of your left hand towards your right-hand side, your fingers around his thumb towards the palm of his hand, your thumb forced in between the small bones of his first and second fingers.)

5. Bend his arm, by a circular upward motion, towards your left-hand side, turning the palm of his hand towards him; then force both your thumbs into the back of his hand (Fig. 66).

6. Applying pressure on the back of his hand and on his wrist (as in ¶ 3), force his hand towards the ground on your left-hand side. This will throw him on to his right-hand side. To finish your opponent off, jerk up on his right arm, simultaneously smashing down on his lower ribs with your right boot (Fig. 68).

58

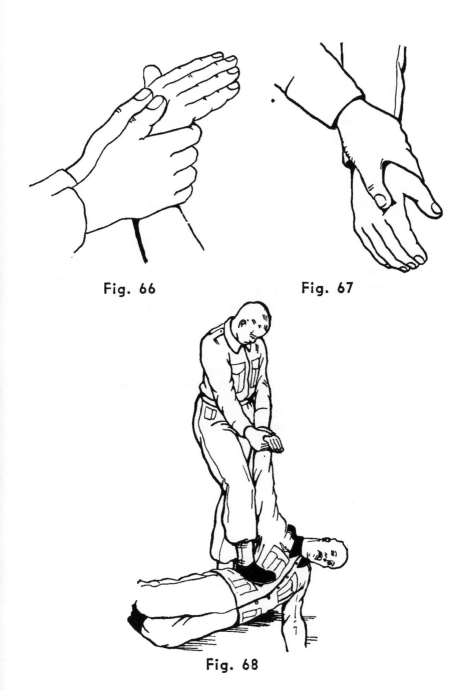

Fig. 66   Fig. 67

Fig. 68

NO. 20—BACK BREAK

1. Approach your opponent from his left-hand side, bend your legs slightly, reach down, and seize him by passing your right arm over his chest and your left arm under his legs, just behind the knee, as in Fig. 69.
2. Lift him up, mainly by straightening your legs, as in weight lifting, to approximately the height of your chest, as in Fig. 70.
3. Take a short pace forward with your right foot, bending your right leg so that the upper part (thigh) is approximately parallel to the ground. With all the strength of your arms, assisted by the forward movement of the upper part of your body, smash him down on your right knee and break his spine (Fig. 71).

Note.—If you carry out these directions correctly, you will be surprised how easily you can lift a man much heavier than yourself. You are partially aided by the fact that your opponent will instinctively try to save himself by clutching hold of you with one or both hands. Provided that you use the weight of your body in your downward smash, he cannot prevent you from breaking his spine.

60

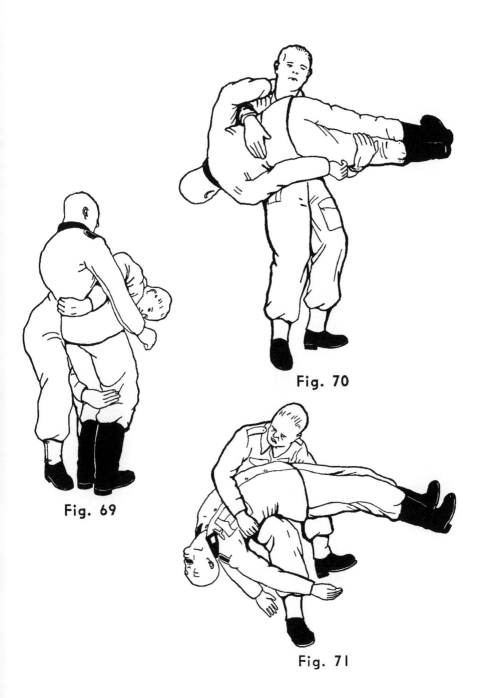

Fig. 69

Fig. 70

Fig. 71

MISCELLANEOUS ADVICE

NO. 21—CHAIR AND KNIFE

Most lion tamers consider a small chair to be sufficient to keep a lion from attacking them. Should you be so fortunate as to have a chair handy when your opponent is attacking you with a knife, seize the chair as in Fig. 72. Rush at him, jabbing one or more of the legs of the chair into his body. The odds in favor of your overpowering your opponent are roughly three to one, and well worth taking (Fig. 73).

64

Fig. 72

Fig. 73

NO. 22—THE MATCH-BOX ATTACK

You are sitting down, say, in a railway coach. Your opponent, who is on your left, sticks a gun in your ribs, holding it in his right hand.

1. Take a match-box and hold it as in Fig. 74, the top of the box being slightly below the finger and thumb.
2. Keeping the upper part of the right arm close to the right side of your body, with a circular upward motion of your right fist, turning your body from the hip, strike your opponent hard on the left side of his face, as near to the jawbone as possible (Fig. 75); parry the gun away from your body with your left forearm.

Note.—The odds of knocking your opponent unconscious by this method are at least two to one. The fact that this can be accomplished with a match-box is not well-known, and for this reason is not likely to raise your opponent's suspicion of your movements. Naturally, all movements, from the start of the blow, must be carried out with the utmost speed.

66

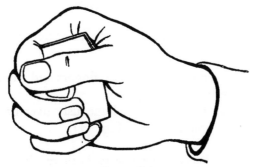

Fig. 74

Fig. 75

NO. 23—SMACKING THE EARS

This method should be applied when your opponent has no protection over his ears.

1. Cup your hands, keeping the fingers and thumbs bent and close together, as in Fig. 76.
2. Strike your opponent simultaneously over both ears, using five to ten pounds force (Fig. 77).

Note.—This will probably burst one or both ear-drums, give him at least a mild form of concussion, and make him what is known in boxing circles as "punch-drunk." You will then have no difficulty in dealing with him in any way you wish.

So that you may realize what the effect of a blow given as above is like, apply it on yourself, as in Fig. 77A. Care must be taken to use *only* half a pound force with each hand.

68

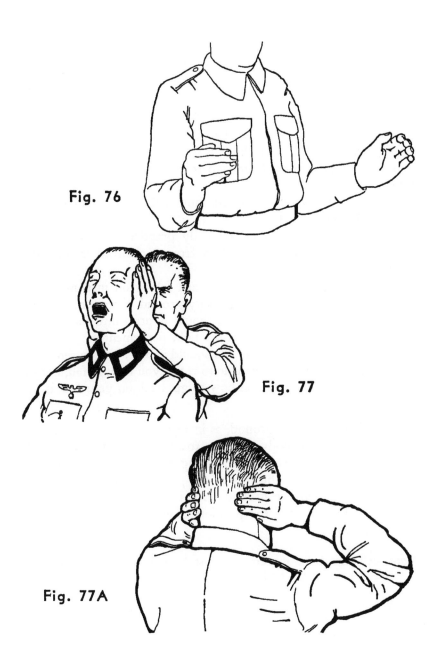

Fig. 76

Fig. 77

Fig. 77A

NO. 24—THE ART OF GETTING UP FROM THE GROUND

You will have noted that no holds or locks on the ground are demonstrated. The reason for this is:

(*a*) *THIS IS WAR:* your object is to kill or dispose of your opponent as quickly as possible and go to the assistance of your comrades.

(*b*) Once on the ground, you are more vulnerable to attack. (See No. 3B, Bronco Kick.)

(*c*) It takes months of constant daily practice to master the art of falling, and personal instruction from a qualified instructor is essential.

(*d*) There is a vast difference between falling on mats in a gymnasium and falling on a road or rocky ground. Even a roll on to a stone or a small stump of a tree, should it press into the kidneys, would certainly put you out of the fight permanently.

It is, therefore, obvious that you should concentrate on remaining on your feet. No attempt is made to teach you how to fall, but the following guides are given on how to get back on your feet if you do fall or are thrown:

1. You are on the ground, as in Fig. 78.
2. Turn your body sharply towards your left-hand side, stomach to the ground, rising by the help of the right forearm and right knee to the position shown in Fig. 79.
3. Pushing on the ground with both hands, force yourself backwards into the position shown in Fig. 80, and then stand up.

Note.—All the above movements must be one rapid and continuous roll or twist of the body.

If, when in the position shown in Fig. 80, your opponent is behind you, place your right foot as near as possible to your left hand (Fig. 81), turn sharply on both feet towards your left-hand side, and you will find yourself facing your opponent.

70

Fig. 78

Fig. 79

Fig. 80

Fig. 81

NO. 24A—GETTING UP FROM THE GROUND (BACKWARDS)

1. You have fallen on to your back on the ground.
2. Lie flat on your back and place your right arm at an angle of 90 degrees from the body, the back of your hand on the ground and your head turned towards your left shoulder (Fig. 82).
3. Raise your legs from the waist and shoot them over your right shoulder (Fig. 83). When in this position, allow your right arm and hand to turn with your body.
4. Bend your right leg and bring it to the ground as close to your right arm as possible. Keeping your left leg straight reach as far back with it as possible (Fig. 84).
5. Your left hand will be on the ground approximately opposite your right knee. Press on the ground with both hands and force yourself up on to your right knee. Continue the pressure until you are on your feet (Fig. 85).

Note.—The reason for keeping your feet apart in the movement shown in ¶ 4 is that you will immediately be on-balance when you come up on your feet. This is a very important point to note and is very seldom taken care of by the average man. A man off-balance can be pushed down again with a few pounds' pressure of either hand. Moreover, he cannot administer an effective blow or even defend himself properly.

72

Fig. 82

Fig. 83

Fig. 84

Fig. 85

NO. 25—ATTACK WITH A SMALL STICK OR CANE

A man without a weapon to defend himself, especially after long exposure, is very likely to give up in despair. It is remarkable what a difference it would make in his morale if he had a small stick or cane in his hand. Now, add to this the knowledge that he could, with ease, kill any opponent with a stick, and you will then see how easy it is to cultivate the offensive spirit which is so essential in present-day warfare.

1. A small stick of 18 to 24 inches in length and about 1 inch in thickness will make an ideal weapon. (If one is not available, it can be broken off a tree.)

Note.—If you are to be successful in the application of this method, it is essential for you to have the element of surprise on your side. This can best be obtained by taking the position shown in Fig. 86.

2. Retaining your hold of the stick with your right hand, swing the other end up and catch it in your left hand about six inches from the end. This should be done without looking down at your hands or stick. Pay particular attention to the position of the hands (Fig. 87).

Note.—The reason for using this unusual hold of the stick should be obvious. It is not at all likely that anyone (not previously aware of this particular method of attack) would have the slightest suspicion that he was in danger of being attacked.

74

Fig. 86

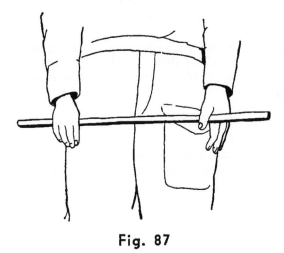

Fig. 87

NO. 25—ATTACK WITH A SMALL STICK OR CANE (cont.)

You are close up and facing your opponent, as in Fig. 88.

1. Strike your opponent *across* the stomach with the left end of the stick by a vicious circular motion towards your right-hand side.

   In delivering this blow, there are four essential points that must be carried out simultaneously:

   (*a*) Your loose grip on the stick, both hands (Fig. 87), must be changed to one as strong as possible.

   (*b*) The movement of your left hand is towards your right-hand side.

   (*c*) The movement of your right hand is inwards to the left, but much shorter than that of the left hand, because of your right hand's coming against your right side.

   (*d*) The movement of your left foot is forward towards the right. This permits you to put the weight of your body behind the blow. See Fig. 89.

Note.—This blow *across* your opponent's stomach would not, if he were wearing thick clothing, put him out, but it would surely make him bring his chin forward, which is exactly the position you want him in.

2. Keeping the firmest possible grip of the stick with both hands, jab upwards with the end of the stick (left-hand end) and drive it into his neck and kill him (Fig. 90). The mark you are after is the soft spot about two inches back from the point of the chin.

76

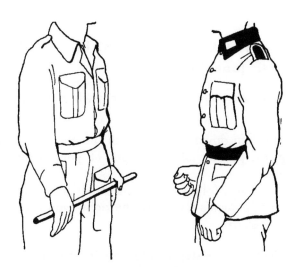

Fig. 88

Fig. 89

Fig. 90

NO. 25—ATTACK WITH A SMALL STICK OR CANE (concl.)

You have missed your opponent's chin when you attacked as in Fig. 90.

3. Smash him down the face with the end of the stick, as in Fig. 91, putting all the weight of your body behind the blow.
4. If necessary, follow-up with a smash across the left side of your opponent's face with the right-hand end of the stick, as in Fig. 92.

Note.—You have taken a step to your left front with your right foot to permit of the weight of the body being behind the blow.

5. If at any time after the initial attack across the stomach your opponent's head is high in the air, exposing the front part of his neck: Aim to strike the "Adam's apple" with the center of the stick, putting every ounce of strength behind the blow. This should kill him, or at least knock him unconscious (Fig. 93).

Note.—Methods No. 2 (the point, up under the chin) and No. 5 (the center, into the "Adam's apple") are finishing-off or killing blows, but you must first bring your opponent into the position that permits you to deal them effectively. Method No. 1 (the point across the stomach) will, on account of its unexpectedness, enable you to accomplish this, and your attack should always start with the stomach attack.

78

Fig. 91

Fig. 92

Fig. 93

NO. 26—VARIOUS METHODS OF SECURING A PRISONER

All raiding parties should have among their equipment a small roll of adhesive tape, preferably of one or more inches in width, and a length of silk rope or cord, about a quarter of an inch in diameter and about five yards in length, for gagging and securing a prisoner whom they wish to leave unguarded.

To Gag a Prisoner.—Force a piece of cloth or a lump of turf into his mouth; then place two or more strips of adhesive tape, approximately four and a half inches in length, firmly over his mouth, taking care not to cover his nostrils.

Tying the Highwayman's Hitch.—This knot should be practised on a pole or the back of a chair, until it can be done in the dark.

1. Holding the cord with a *short* end (about two feet), pass it behind the pole, with the *short* end to the left and the *long* to the right (Fig. 94).
2. Pass the *long* end, in a loop, up and over the pole and through the loop held in the left hand. Then pull down on the *short* end with the right hand (Fig. 95).
3. Pass the *short* end of the cord, in a loop, up and over the pole and through the loop held in the left hand, and form the knot shown in Fig. 96.
4. Holding the loop in the left hand, pull down on the *long* end of the cord, pass the left hand through the loop and then pull on both *ends* of the cord (Fig. 97).

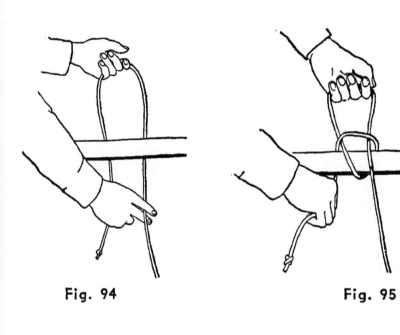

Fig. 94   Fig. 95

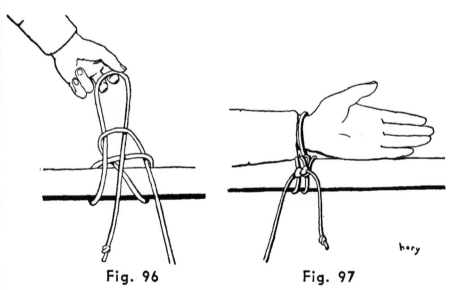

Fig. 96   Fig. 97

hary

NO. 26—VARIOUS METHODS OF SECURING A PRISONER (cont.)

A—From the Handcuff Hold

1. Throw your prisoner to the ground on his stomach, tying his wrists together behind his back by means of the Highwayman's Hitch, as in Fig. 98, and force his arms well up his back.

2. Pass the cord around his neck; then back and around his wrists again; then bend his legs backwards and tie his legs together, as in Fig. 99.

Note.—If your prisoner keeps still, he will not hurt himself, but should he attempt to struggle, he will most likely strangle himself.

82

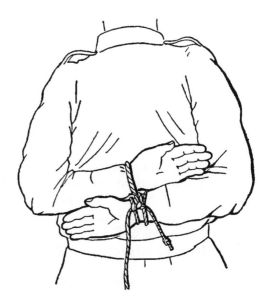

Fig. 98

Fig. 99

NO. 26—VARIOUS METHODS OF SECURING A PRISONER (cont.)

B—"The Grape Vine"

Select a tree, post, or lamp-post of about seven inches in diameter.

1. Make your prisoner climb on the tree as in Fig. 100.
2. Place his right leg around the front of the tree, with his foot to the left. Place his left leg over his right ankle, as in Fig. 101, and take his left foot back behind the tree.
3. Force him well down the pole until the weight of his body locks his left foot around the tree, as in Fig. 102.

Note.—Even though you have left your prisoner's hands free, it will, if he has been forced well down the tree, be almost impossible for him to escape. Normally, the average man placed in this position would get cramp in one or both legs within ten to fifteen minutes, when it is not at all unlikely that he would throw himself backwards. This would kill him.

Caution.—To release your prisoner: Two persons are necessary, one on either side. Take hold of his legs and lift him up the tree; then unlock his legs.

84

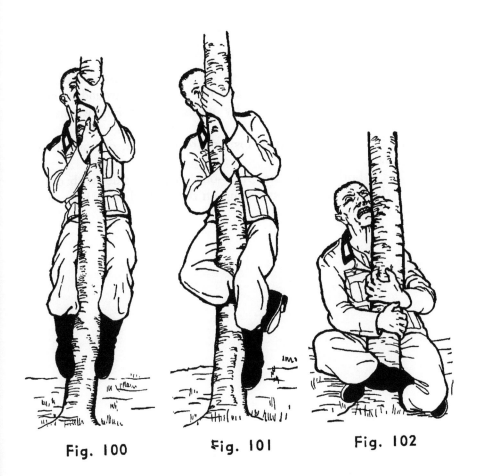

Fig. 100   Fig. 101   Fig. 102

NO. 26.—VARIOUS METHODS OF SECURING
A PRISONER (cont.)

C—The Chair

A chair with an open back is preferable.

1. Force your prisoner to sit on the chair, pass one of his arms through the back and the other arm around it, and tie his wrists together by means of the Highwayman's Hitch (Fig. 103).
2. Tie the upper part of his arms to the chair, one on either side (Fig. 104).
3. Tie both feet to the chair—one on either side—with only the toes of his boots resting on the ground, as in Fig. 105.
4. Gag him, if necessary.

86

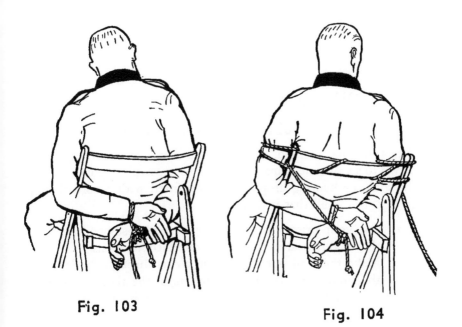

Fig. 103

Fig. 104

Fig. 105

NO. 26—VARIOUS METHODS OF SECURING A PRISONER (cont.)

D—A Substitute for Handcuffs

The following method, whereby one man can effectively control two to six prisoners, may be found very useful. A police baton, night stick, or hunting crop, preferably fitted with a cord thong, as in Fig. 106, is all that is required.

1. Cut your prisoners' trouser-belts and/or suspenders, then thoroughly search them for concealed weapons.
2. Make them all put their right wrists through the loop of the thong, and twist the baton until the thong cuts well into their wrists (Fig. 107). Then march them off.

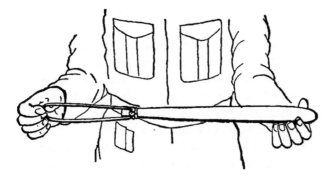

Fig. 106

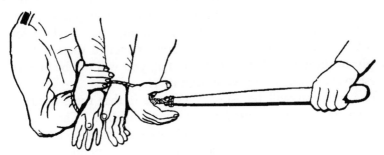

Fig. 107

NO. 27—BREAK-AWAYS FROM "COME-ALONG" GRIPS

A number of so called "come-along" grips are frequently demonstrated and taught as being 100 per cent perfect, and impossible, once secured, for any man to escape. Under certain circumstances it would, indeed, be difficult and painful to escape them; also it might result in a badly strained ligament. Nevertheless, any man of average build and strength can, with at least a 50 per cent chance of success, not only break away from these holds, but he will also be in a position from which he can with ease break his opponent's limbs and, if necessary, kill him.

Two fairly well-known holds that are so regarded are shown on the opposite page: Fig. 108—Police Come-Along Grip, and Fig. 109—Collar and Wrist Hold.

You must face the fact that a man fighting for his life or to prevent capture is a vastly different person from one you may meet in competition. It is an established fact that a man in fear of death will be prepared to undertake the lifting of five times the weight he would in normal times, also that he can, under such circumstances, take about five times the usual amount of punishment.

This is not said with the idea of preparing you to take a lot of punishment should you attempt to break either of these holds, but simply to show you that even if you fail, you will not be in a much worse position than you were originally.

The question will be asked: "Why is it that these holds have been so commonly accepted as being unbreakable?" The answer is: Those of us who have made a study of the art of attack and defense well know that the average student is too inclined to demonstrate his prowess on his friends after only a few lessons, and before he has mastered even the initial movements. This often results in broken bones, etc. Further, the counter-measures used to break holds such as these are drastic in the extreme, and are shown to students only after they have proved beyond doubt that they would not wilfully mis-apply them.

90

Fig. 108

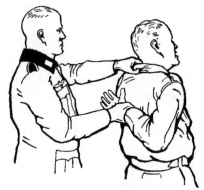

Fig. 109

NO. 27—BREAK-AWAYS FROM "COME-ALONG" GRIPS (cont.)

Note.—It is presumed that your opponent is not acquainted with the counter-methods you intend to apply.

A—Your Opponent Has Hold of You as in Fig. 108

1. Exaggerate the pain you are receiving by shouting or groaning. Try to be out of step with him, which makes it easier to apply your counter. Only resist sufficiently to prevent him from being suspicious.

2. Do not be in a hurry to apply your counter. The opening will be there every time he puts the weight of his body on his left foot.

3. Smartly jab the outside of your right leg against the outside of his left leg, forcing his leg inwards, and break it (Fig. 110), simultaneously pulling your right arm towards you, which, in addition to increasing the force of your leg blow, also permits you to bend your arm and break his hold. If necessary, apply the edge-of-the-hand blow on the back of his neck with your left hand, and kill him.

B—Your Opponent Has Hold of You as in Fig. 109

1. As in the previous method, wait until your opponent is off his guard and only resist slightly.

2. Turn sharply around towards your left-hand side, simultaneously bending your legs at the knees and your head forward to permit your head to go under his left arm. Then straighten up your head. (These movements, in addition to twisting his arm, will lock his left hand in the back of your collar.) Strike the elbow of his left arm a vicious upward jab with the palm of your right hand, as in Fig. 111. If necessary, follow up with a chin jab with your left hand, or knee to the testicles with either knee.

92

Fig. 108

Fig. 110

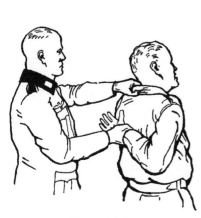

Fig. 109

Fig. 111

USE OF THE KNIFE

NO. 28—USE OF THE KNIFE

In close-quarters fighting there is no more deadly weapon than the knife. An entirely unarmed man has no certain defense against it, and, further, merely the sudden flashing of a knife is frequently enough to strike fear into your opponent, causing him to lose confidence and surrender.

In choosing a knife there are two important factors to bear in mind: balance and keenness. The hilt should fit easily in your hand, and the blade should not be so heavy that it tends to drag the hilt from your fingers in a loose grip. It is essential that the blade have a sharp stabbing point and good cutting edges, because an artery *torn* through (as against a clean cut) tends to contract and stop the bleeding. If a main artery is cleanly severed, the wounded man will quickly lose consciousness and die.

The Fairbairn-Sykes Fighting Knife (shown on the opposite page) developed by the author and a colleague, is highly recommended as possessing the requisite qualities. This knife and similar types have found wide favor among experts.

There are many positions in which the knife can be carried. Selection of this position depends upon individual preference based on length of arm, thickness of body, etc. The following considerations, however, should always be borne in mind. A quick draw (an essential in knife fighting) can not be accomplished unless the sheath is firmly secured to the clothing or equipment. Moreover, speed on the draw can be accomplished only by constant daily practice. The author favors a concealed position, using the left hand, for in close-quarters fighting, the element of surprise is the chief ingredient of success.

96

NO. 28—USE OF THE KNIFE (cont.)

Certain arteries are more vulnerable to attack than others, because of their being nearer the surface of the skin, or not being protected by clothing or equipment. Don't bother about their names so long as you can remember where they are situated.

In the accompanying diagram (Fig. 112), the approximate positions of the arteries are given. They vary in size from the thickness of one's thumb to that of an ordinary pencil. Naturally, the speed at which loss of consciousness or death takes place will depend upon the size of the artery cut.

The heart or stomach, when not protected by equipment, should be attacked. The psychological effect of even a slight wound in the stomach is such that it is likely to throw your opponent into confusion.

No.	Name of Artery	Size	Depth below Surface in inches	Loss of Consciousness in seconds	Death
1....	Brachial	Medium	½	14	1½ Min.
2....	Radial	Small	¼	30	2 "
3....	Carotid	Large	1½	5	12 Sec.
4....	Subclavian	Large	2½	2	3½ "
5....	(Heart)	—	3½	Instantaneous	3 "
6....	(Stomach)	—	5	Depending on depth of cut	

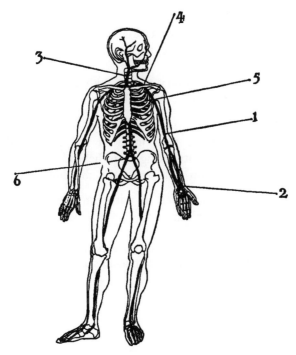

Fig. 112

NO. 28—USE OF THE KNIFE (concl.)

Method of Making the Cut

Artery #1. Knife in the right hand, attack opponent's left arm with a slashing cut outwards, as in Fig. A.

Artery #2. Knife in the right hand, attack opponent's left wrist, cutting downwards and inwards, as in Fig. B.

Artery #3. Knife in right hand, edges parallel to ground, seize opponent around the neck from behind with your left arm, pulling his head to the left. Thrust point well in; then cut sideways. See Fig. C.

Artery #4. Hold knife as in Fig. D; thrust point well in downwards; then cut.

Note.—This is not an easy artery to cut with a knife, but, once cut, your opponent will drop, and no tourniquet or any help of man can save him.

Heart #5. Thrust well in with the point, taking care when attacking from behind not to go too high or you will strike the shoulder blade.

Stomach #6. Thrust well in with the point and cut in any direction.

Note.—If knife is in left hand, when attacking arteries #1 and #2, reverse the above and attack opponent's right arm.

100

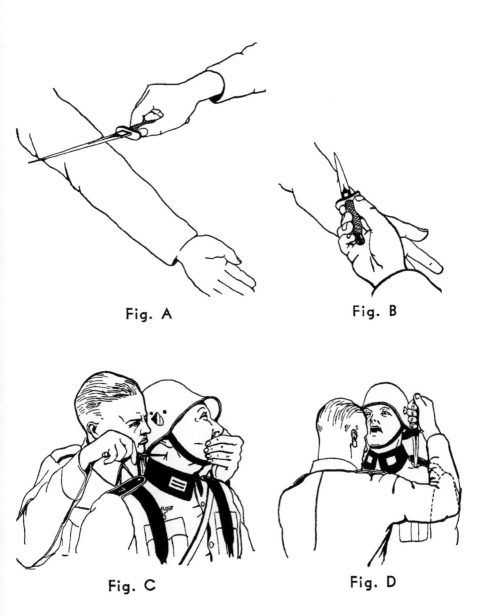

Fig. A

Fig. B

Fig. C

Fig. D

THE SMATCHET

NO. 29—THE SMATCHET

The psychological reaction of any man, when he first takes the smatchet in his hand, is full justification for its recommendation as a fighting weapon. He will immediately register all the essential qualities of a good soldier—confidence, determination, and aggressiveness.

Its balance, weight, and killing power, with the point, edge, or pommel, combined with the extremely simple training necessary to become efficient in its use, make it the ideal personal weapon for all those not armed with a rifle and bayonet.

Note.—The smatchet is now in wide use throughout the British armed forces. It is hoped that it will soon be adopted by the United States Army.

Carrying, Drawing, and Holding

1. The smatchet should be carried in the scabbard on the left side of the belt, as in Fig. 113. This permits one to run, climb, sit, or lie down.

Note.—Any equipment at present carried in this position should be removed to another place.

2. Pass the right hand through the thong and draw upwards with a bent arm (Fig. 114).
3. Grip the handle as near the guard as possible, cutting edge downwards (Fig. 115).

104

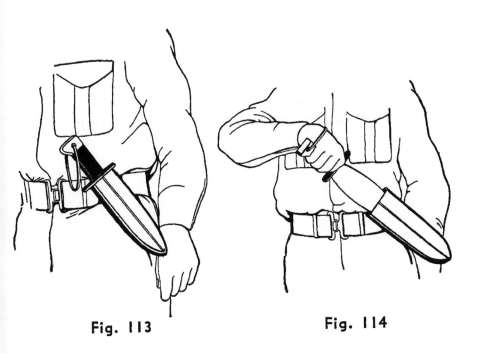

Fig. 113   Fig. 114

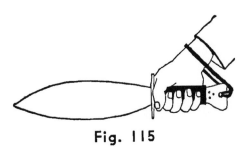

Fig. 115

NO. 29—THE SMATCHET (cont.)

Close-In Blows

1. Drive well into the stomach (Fig. 116).
2. "Sabre Cut" to right-low of neck (Fig. 117).
3. Cut to left-low of neck (Fig. 118).
4. Smash up with pommel, under chin (Fig. 119).

106

Fig. 116

Fig. 117

Fig. 118

Fig. 119

NO. 29—THE SMATCHET (cont.)

Close-In Blows (cont.)

5. Smash down with pommel into the face (Fig. 120).

Attacking Blows

1. "Sabre Cut" to left or right wrist (Fig. 121).
2. "Sabre Cut" to left or right arm (Fig. 122).

108

Fig. 120

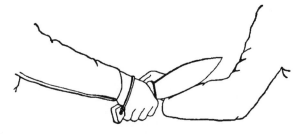

Fig. 121

Fig. 122

DISARMING AN OPPONENT OF HIS PISTOL

NO. 30—DISARMING AN OPPONENT OF HIS PISTOL

You are held up with a pistol and ordered to put your hands up. The fact that you have not been shot on sight clearly shows that your opponent wants to take you as a prisoner or is afraid to fire, knowing that it will raise an alarm.

Lead him to suppose, by your actions, manner, etc., that you are scared to death, and wait until he is close up to you. Provided that all your movements are carried out with speed, it is possible for you to disarm him, with at least a ten to one chance of success.

A—Disarming from in Front

1. Hold your hands and arms as in Fig. 123.
2. With a swinging downward blow of your right hand, seize your opponent's right wrist, simultaneously turning your body sideways towards the left. This will knock the pistol clear of your body (Fig. 124). Note that the thumb of your right hand is on top.
3. Seize the pistol with the left hand as in Fig. 125.
4. Keeping a firm grip with the right hand on his wrist, force the pistol backwards with your left hand, and knee him or kick him in the testicles (Fig. 126).

Note.—All the above movements must be one rapid and continuous motion.

112

Fig. 123   Fig. 124

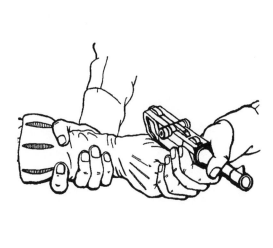

Fig. 125   Fig. 126

NO. 30—DISARMING AN OPPONENT OF HIS PISTOL (cont.)

B—Disarming from in Front (Alternative Method)

It will be noted that in this method the initial attack is made with the left hand instead of the right as was demonstrated in the previous method.

1. Hold your hands and arms as in Fig. 127.
2. With a swinging downward blow of your left hand, thumb on top, seize your opponent's right wrist, simultaneously turning your body sideways, towards your right. This will knock the pistol clear of your body (Fig. 128).
3. Seize the pistol with the right hand, as in Fig. 129.
4. Keeping a firm grip with your left hand on his wrist, bend his wrist and pistol backwards; at the same time, knee him in the testicles (Fig. 130).

114

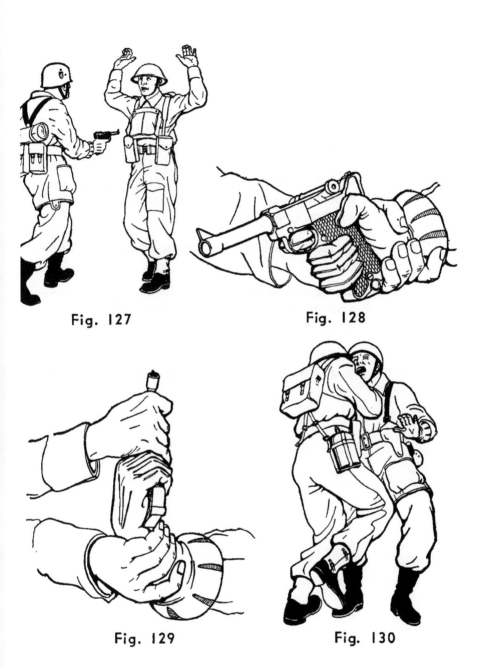

Fig. 127

Fig. 128

Fig. 129

Fig. 130

NO. 30—DISARMING AN OPPONENT OF HIS PISTOL (cont.)

C—Disarming from Behind

1. Hold your arms as in Fig. 131.
2. Turn rapidly inwards towards your left-hand side, passing your left arm over and around your opponent's right forearm, as near the wrist as possible, and bring your left hand up your chest (Fig. 132).

Note.—It is impossible for him to shoot you or release his arm from this grip.

3. Immediately the arm is locked, knee him in the testicles with your right knee and chin-jab him with your right hand, as in Fig. 133.

Note.—If the knee blow and chin jab do not make him release his hold of the pistol, go after his eyes with the fingers of your right hand.

116

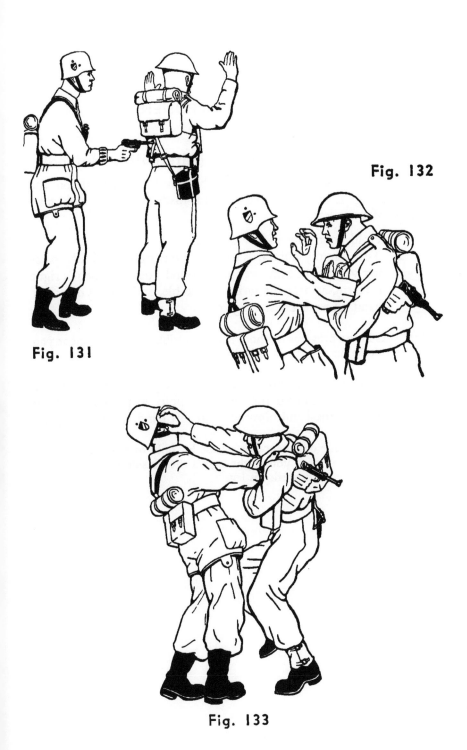

Fig. 131

Fig. 132

Fig. 133

NO. 30—DISARMING AN OPPONENT OF HIS PISTOL (cont.)

D—Disarming from behind (Alternative Method)

The difference between this method and that shown on the previous page is that the initial attack is made with your right arm instead of your left.

1. Hold your arms as in Fig. 134.
2. Turn rapidly outwards towards your right-hand side, passing your right arm over and around your opponent's right forearm, as near the wrist as possible, and bring your right hand up your chest (Fig. 135).

Note.—As in the previous method, it is impossible for him to shoot you or release his arm from this grip.

3. Immediately the arm is locked, strike your opponent across the throat, as near the "Adam's apple" as possible, with an edge-of-the-hand blow of your left hand, as in Fig. 136.

Note.—Should your opponent not release his hold of the pistol, follow up by pressing with your right leg on the outside of his right leg, as in Fig. 137, and break his leg.

118

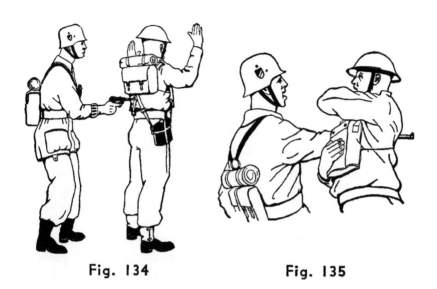

Fig. 134   Fig. 135

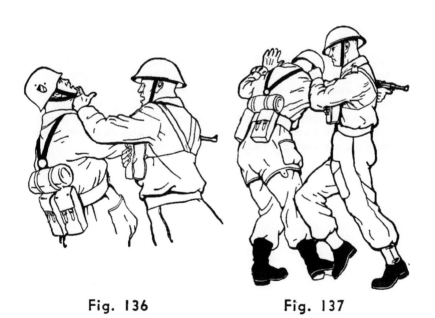

Fig. 136   Fig. 137

NO. 30—DISARMING AN OPPONENT OF HIS PISTOL (concl.)

E—Disarming a Third Party

It is quite possible that, upon coming around a corner, you find one of your own men being held up, as in Fig. 138.

1. Come up on your opponent's pistol arm, seize his pistol and hand from underneath, simultaneously coming down hard with your left hand on his arm, just above the elbow joint (Fig. 139).

2. Jerk his hand upwards and backwards, and force his elbow upwards with your left hand, at the same time pivoting inwards on your left foot. Continue the pressure of your right hand in a downward direction (Fig. 140).

Note A.—This will cause him to release his hold of the pistol; if necessary, knee him in the testicles with your right knee.

Note B.—The initial upward movement of the pistol (¶ 2) is recommended in preference to a downward blow because the pistol is jerked away from the direction of your own man very quickly, and it also permits you to obtain a hold of his pistol hand, from which you can force him to release his hold of the weapon. Further, your own man can, by means of a kick to the opponent's testicles, considerably help you in disarming.

120

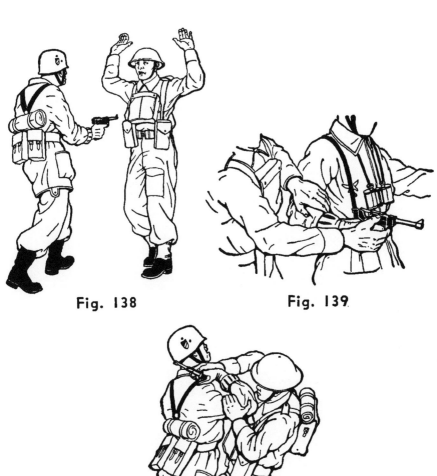

Fig. 138   Fig. 139.

Fig. 140   (8.)

ALL-IN FIGHTING

W.E.FAIRBAIRN

www.naval-military-press.com

Captain W. E. Fairbairn, in addition to having made a study of practically every known method of attack and defence, spent over thirty years in the Shanghai Municipal Police, where he was the founder and, up to 1940, in charge of their famous Riot Squads. He was their Chief Instructor in self-defence, and includes amongst his pupils royalty and several of the highest jiu-jitsu experts of Japan. He is the first foreigner living outside Japan to be awarded the Black Belt Degree by the Kodokan Jiu-Jitsu University, Tokio, and was further honoured in 1931 by being promoted to Black Belt 2nd Degree. He also studied under Tsai Ching Tung, who at one time was employed at the Imperial Palace, Peking, as instructor in Chinese 'boxing' to retainers of the late Dowager Empress.

From July 1940 the author has been Captain Instructor in Close Combat at the Special Training Centre. His methods have been approved and adopted as the standard instructions for the British Army.

In order to make the illustrations as clear and concise as possible, in many cases soldiers have been shown not wearing army packs, pouches, etc., but it should be understood that all the methods shown can be carried out with full equipment.

Captain P. N. Walbridge, Weapon Training Officer at the Special Training Centre, the author of the section in this book on the use of the rifle in close combat, is well known for his prowess with the rifle, both at slow and rapid fire. He was a member of the Army VIII Shooting Team from 1935 to 1939, while, in addition, he has been the winner of the following:

1935—Elkington Grand Aggregate. Shot at Bisley National Meeting at 900 and 1,000 yards.

1937—'The Army 100 Cup'.

1938—'The Army 100 Cup'.

1938—His Majesty the King's Medal and Championship of the Regular Army.

ALL-IN FIGHTING

by Captain W. E. Fairbairn
Late Assistant Commissioner
Shanghai Municipal Police

RIFLE SECTION
by Captain P. N. Walbridge

Diagrams by 'Hary'

The Naval & Military Press Ltd

PREFACE

by Lieut.-Colonel J. P. O'Brien Twohig

There seems little doubt that one of the causes of our failures during this war comes from the cricket (or baseball) mentality. It was the French equivalent of this which, in the case of the French nation when confronted with total war, caused it to close its eyes in horror and give up the struggle.

Unlike the war of 1914–1918 the proportion of *individual* fighting in this struggle is large, and it is not enough for front-line soldiers to be skilled in arms and determined; *every* soldier, sailor, airman, and in many cases every man and woman, may be called on to defend their lives in sudden emergencies. This defence can only be achieved by *killing* or disabling the enemy.

To conquer our ingrained repugnance to *killing* at close quarters is essential, and no better means of doing this has been discovered than by following the training methods given in Captain Fairbairn's book.

To the civilian without a weapon or the soldier surprised without his or deprived of it, it gives the necessary confidence, determination and ruthlessness to gain victory.

It will soon be found that the principal value of the training lies not so much in the actual physical holds or breaks, but in the psychological reaction which engenders and fosters the necessary attitude of mind which refuses to admit defeat and is determined to achieve victory.

5

INTRODUCTION

This book is based upon earlier works issued under the titles of *Défendu*, which was written for the police forces of the Far East, and *Scientific Self-Defence*, published by D. Appleton, of New York. Every method shown in these books has stood the criticism of police from practically every country in the world, including the Far East, which is the recognized home of jiu-jitsu (judo). A more expert community for criticizing works on self-defence it would be impossible to find.

The majority of the methods shown are drastic in the extreme. In contrast to judo, they recognize no accepted rules. They are not intended to provide amusement for all-in wrestling spectators, but for use in these dangerous times as part of the national preparedness against our enemies.

The question may well be asked, 'Why should I trouble to learn this "rough-house" method of fighting?' We wish to make it clear that there is no intention of belittling boxing, wrestling, or rugby football. A knowledge of these is an asset to anyone intending to study all-in fighting, and those who already have it start off with a great advantage over those who have never taken part in these sports. No-one will dispute the effectiveness of a straight left or a right hook to the jaw or body, but unfortunately it takes months of practice to develop a good punch. Quite a number of persons, after long and intensive training, have given it up in despair. The edge of the hand blow and the chin jab, if applied as demonstrated in this manual, will quickly convince the student that in a matter of days he has developed a blow that is not only as effective as a good punch with the fist, but one which permits him to obtain a knock-out under conditions in which it would be almost impossible to punch effectively with the fist. Every method shown in this manual is practicable, and the majority of them have been successfully used in actual combat on many occasions during the past thirty years by the author or his students. They were specially selected to enable the young man of only average strength, and those past middle age, who have not led an active life, to overpower a much stronger opponent. In critical moments the trouble you have taken to master a few of them will more than repay you, and the knowledge that you can deal effectively with one or more opponents has its psychological value at all times.

Some readers may be appalled at the suggestion that it should be necessary for human beings of the twentieth century to revert to the

7

INTRODUCTION

grim brutality of the Stone Age in order to live. But it must be realized that, when dealing with an utterly ruthless enemy who has clearly expressed his intention of wiping this nation out of existence, there is no room for any scruple or compunction about the methods to be employed in preventing him. The reader is requested to imagine that he himself has been wantonly attacked by a thug who has put the heel of his hand under his nose and pushed hard. Let him be quite honest and realize what his feelings would be. His one, violent desire would be to do the thug the utmost damage—regardless of rules. In circumstances such as this he is forced back to quite primitive reactions, and it is the hope of the author that a study of this book will fit the ordinary man with the skill and the ability to deal *automatically* with such a situation.

There are very few men who would not fire back if they were attacked by a man with a gun, and they would have no regrets if their bullet found its mark. But suggest that they retaliate with a knife, or with any of the follow-up methods explained in this manual, and the majority would shrink from using such uncivilized or un-British methods. A gun is an impersonal weapon and kills cleanly and decently at a distance. Killing with the bare hands at close quarters savours too much of pure savagery for most people. They would hesitate to attempt it. But never was the catchword, 'He who hesitates is lost,' more applicable. When it is a matter of life and death, not only of the individual but indeed of the nation, squeamish scruples are out of place. The sooner we realize that fact, the sooner we shall be fitted to face the grim and ruthless realities of total warfare.

In war, your attack can have only two possible objects: either to kill your opponent or to capture him alive. You must realize that he will be fighting for his life or to prevent capture, and that it will be a very difficult matter for you to apply a 'hold', etc., without first having made him receptive by striking him either with your hand, foot, or knee, etc., thus disabling him or rendering him semi-conscious, after which you will have no difficulty in disposing of him by one of the methods shown.

We do not advocate that students should attempt to master all the methods, but that they should select about ten, and specialize in thoroughly mastering them. Although we claim that every method is practicable, it is natural that individuals should find they can master one much more quickly than another. This is mainly on account of

8

INTRODUCTION

one's height, weight, build, or, in some cases, slight deformity, all of which will have to be taken into consideration before making the final selection.

Students are warned not to consider themselves experts until they can carry out every movement *instinctively* and *automatically*. Until then they should spend at least ten minutes daily in practice with a friend. Every movement is made either with the object of putting your opponent off-balance, or to permit of your getting into position to deal an effective blow or to secure a hold. Students should first practise every movement slowly and smoothly. They should then gradually increase the speed. Pressure should be applied on the points indicated, and only when necessary. Where breaks are indicated in practice, the pressure should.be applied gradually and with smoothness—not with a jerk, which will be sure to be painful. Provided that reasonable care is taken, with reasonable consideration for the feelings of your friend, no harm other than a slightly stretched muscle will result.

It will be noted that several methods are demonstrated of breaking away from holds that have been considered unbreakable; and also that ground wrestling and holds on the ground are not shown. The reasons are as follows. The author and his students have had the advantage of trying out these holds in that very hard school of learning—practical experience, where they have not infrequently met their master. Ground wrestling is excluded because it takes years of practice to become proficient, even in dealing with one opponent. To attempt it in time of war, when one is not unlikely to be attacked by two or more opponents, cannot be recommended.

No manual of this nature would be complete without reference to the use of the rifle, and we have been very fortunate in obtaining the services of Captain P. N. Walbridge, who is one of the greatest authorities on the subject.

W.E.F.

1942.

9

CONTENTS

11

CONTENTS

4. THROWS

5. MISCELLANEOUS ADVICE

6. DISARMING (PISTOL)

12

CONTENTS

7. THE RIFLE IN CLOSE COMBAT
by Captain P. N. Walbridge

13

I. BLOWS

No. I. Edge of the Hand

Edge of the hand blows are delivered with the inner (i.e. little finger) edge of the hand, fingers straight and thumb extended; the actual blow being made with the edge only, about half way between the knuckle of the little finger and the wrist, as shown in Fig. 1.

1. The blow is delivered from a bent arm (never with a straight arm), using a chopping action from the elbow, with the weight of the body behind it. Students are advised to practise this blow by striking the open palm of their left hand, as in Fig. 2.

2. There are two ways in which this blow can be delivered:

   (a) **downwards**, with either hand;
   (b) **across**, with either hand; the blow always being delivered outwards, with the palm of the hand downward, never on top (Fig. 3).

The following are the points on your opponent's body that should be attacked, every blow being delivered as quickly as possible

   (a) on the sides or back of the wrist;
   (b) on the forearm, half way between the wrist and elbow;
   (c) on the biceps;
   (d) on the sides or back of the neck;
   (e) just below the 'Adam's apple';
   (f) on the kidney or base of the spine.

Note.—In the event of your opponent having caught hold of you, strike his wrist or forearm; a fracture will most likely result. This would be almost impossible with a blow from a clenched fist.

14

BLOWS

No. I. Edge of the Hand

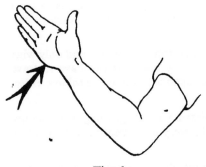

Fig. 1

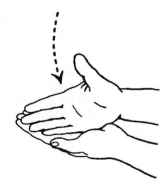

Fig. 2

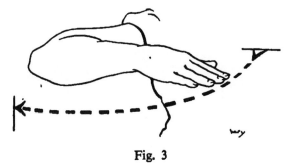

Fig. 3

No. 2. Chin Jab

The chin jab is delivered with the heel of the hand, full force and with the weight of the body behind it, fingers spread so as to reach the eyes, as in Fig. 4: the point aimed at is your opponent's chin (Fig. 5).

1. The blow is delivered upwards from a bent arm and only when close to your opponent. The distance the blow will have to travel will depend on the height of your opponent, but it will seldom exceed six inches.

2. The hand must never be drawn back, 'signalling' the intention of striking. From start to finish, every movement must be made as quickly as possible.

3. It should be noted that an attack or attempt to attack with the knee at your opponent's testicles will always bring his chin forward and down.

Note.—Students should practise this blow as follows: hold your left hand at the height of your own chin, palm downwards; jab up quickly with your right, striking your left hand as in Fig. 6.

16

No. 2. Chin Jab

Fig. 4

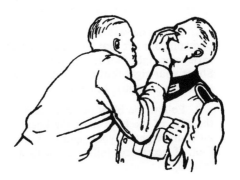

Fig. 5

Fig. 6

No. 3. Boot (Side Kick)

With a few exceptions, the kick with the boot should be made sideways. It will be noted that in this method you are able to put more force behind your blow and can, if necessary, reach farther.

1. Turn sideways to your opponent, taking the weight of your body on your left foot. Bending your left leg slightly from your knee, raise your right foot two to four inches off the ground, as in Fig. 7. Shoot your right foot outwards to your right, aiming to strike your opponent's leg just below the knee-cap.

2. Follow the blow through, scraping your opponent's shin with the edge of the boot from the knee to the instep, finishing up with all your weight on your right foot, and smash the small bones of the foot. If necessary, follow up with a chin jab with your left hand (Fig. 8).

Note.—Where the kick is to be made with the left foot, reverse the above.

18

No. 3. Boot (Side Kick)

Fig. 7

Fig. 8

No. 3(a). Boot Defence

Your opponent has seized you around the waist from in front, pinning your arms to your sides.

1. Having taken your weight on one foot, raise the other and scrape your opponent's shin bone downwards from about half-way from the knee, finishing up with a smashing blow on his foot (Fig. 9).

2. An alternative method to Fig. 9, permitting you to use the inner edge of the boot, should be applied as in Fig. 10.

Note A.—The question of when you should use the outside or inside of your boot will depend upon how the weight of your body is distributed at the time. Provided that you are equally balanced on both feet, you can use either; otherwise, use the opposite one to that on which you have your weight.

Note B.—If seized from behind, stamp on your opponent's foot with the heel of either boot, turning quickly, and follow up with a chin jab with either hand.

20

No. 3(a). Boot Defence

Fig. 9

Fig. 10

B

BLOWS

No. 3(b). Boot. ' Bronco Kick '

It is not advisable to attempt to kick your opponent with the toe of your boot when he is lying on the ground, unless you have hold of an arm or clothing, etc. Method recommended:

1. Take a flying jump at him, drawing your feet up by bending your knees, at the same time keeping your feet close together (Fig. 11).

2. When your feet are approximately eight inches above your opponent's body, shoot your legs out straight, driving both of your boots into his body, and smash him.

Note.—It is almost impossible for your opponent to parry a kick made in this manner, and in addition it immediately puts him on the defensive, leaving him only one alternative of rolling away from you in an attempt to escape. Further, it should be noted that although he may attempt to protect his body with his arms, he cannot prevent you from killing him. The reason for this is that the sharp edges of the iron heel-plates of your boots, which cover a surface of much less than half an inch, are driven into your opponent's body by the combined strength of your legs, each delivering a blow of approximately 75 lb. = 150 lb., plus the weight of your body, say = 150 lb.: Total 300 lb.

Now try to visualize a peg of approximately half an inch being struck with a 300-lb. force and how far it would be driven into a man's body; or better still practise the kick on a dummy figure or on the grass as in Fig. 12.

22

No. 3(b). Boot. ' Bronco Kick '

Fig. 11

Fig. 12

No. 4. Knee

It will be noted that this blow can only be delivered when you are very close to your opponent.

1. Taking the weight of your body on one leg, bend the knee of the other by drawing your heel slightly backwards, and drive your knee quickly upwards into your opponent's fork, as in Fig. 13.

Note.—In addition to being a method of attack and defence, it is frequently used for the purpose of bringing your opponent in a more favourable position for applying the chin jab (Fig. 14).

24

BLOWS

No. 4. Knee

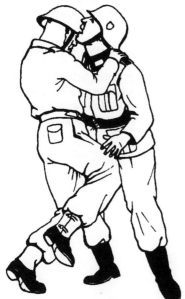

Fig. 13

Fig. 14

2. RELEASES

No. 5. Against a Wrist Hold

1. You are seized by the right wrist as in Fig. 15. Bend your wrist and arm towards your body, twisting your wrist outwards against his thumb (Fig. 16).

Note A.—The above must be one continuous motion, with speed.

Note B.—If your left wrist is seized, your opponent using his right hand, bend your wrist and arm as above and twist your wrist against his thumb. If necessary, 'follow up' with a chin jab or edge of the hand blow to the neck.

26

No. 5. Against a Wrist Hold

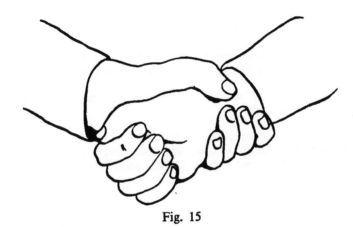

Fig. 15

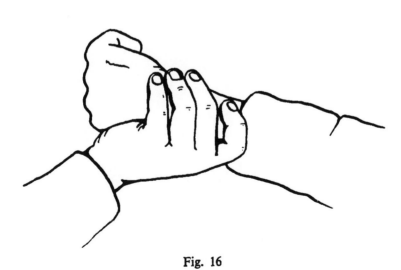

Fig. 16

No. 5(a). Against a Wrist Hold with Two Hands

1. You are seized by the left wrist, by two hands, as in Fig. 17, your opponent's thumbs being on top. Reach over and catch hold of your left hand with your right. Pull your left hand sharply towards your body, against his thumbs (Fig. 18).

Note A.—The pressure, which is slightly upwards and downwards, will force him to release his hold immediately.

Note B.—'Follow up' with chin jab, edge of the hand, or knee kick to the fork.

Should your opponent seize you as in Fig. 19 (his thumb underneath), pass your right hand under and catch hold of your left hand as in Fig. 20. Pull down sharply towards you.

28

No. 5(a). Against a Wrist Hold with Two Hands

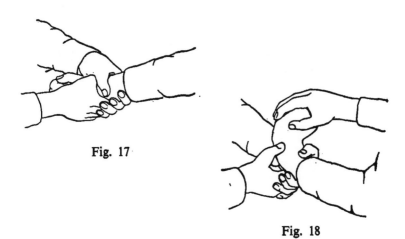

Fig. 17

Fig. 18

Fig. 19

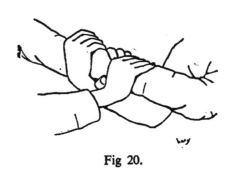

Fig 20.

No. 6. Strangle (One Hand)

You are seized by the throat as in Fig. 21 and forced back against a wall.

1. With a smashing blow of your right hand, strike your opponent's right wrist towards your left-hand side. Follow up with a knee kick to his testicles (Fig. 22).

30

No. 6. Strangle (One Hand)

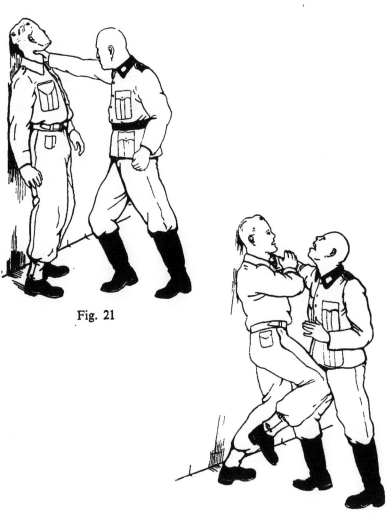

Fig. 21

Fig. 22

No. 6(a). Strangle (Two Hands)

You are seized by the throat as in Fig. 23.

1. Seize your opponent's right elbow with your left hand from underneath, your thumb to the right.

2. Reach over his arms and seize his right wrist with your right hand (Fig. 24).

3. Apply pressure on his left arm with your right, at the same time with a circular upward motion of your left hand, force his elbow towards your right side. This will break his hold of your throat and put him off balance (Fig. 25).

4. Keeping a firm grip with both hands, turn rapidly towards your right-hand side by bringing your right leg to your right rear. Follow up with edge of hand blow on his elbow (Fig. 26).

Note.—All the above movements must be continuous.

32

No. 6(a). Strangle (Two Hands)

Fig. 24

Fig. 23

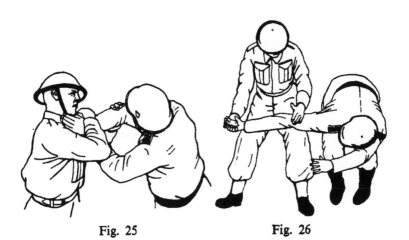

Fig. 25   Fig. 26

No. 7. Bear Hug (Front, over the Arms)

You are gripped around the waist (Fig. 27).

1. Knee him in the testicles.

2. With the outer or inner edge of either boot, scrape his shin bone from about half way from the knee and follow through by stamping on his instep.

3. Smash him in the face with your tin hat.

4. Seize his testicles with either hand.

34

No. 7. Bear Hug (Front, over the Arms)

Fig. 27

No. 7(a). Bear Hug (Front, over the Arms)

(An alternative method to No. 7.)
You are gripped around the waist, Fig. 27.

1. If possible, bite his ear. Even although not successful, this will cause him to bend forward and into a position from which you can seize his testicles with your right hand (Fig. 28).

2. Reach over his arm with your left forearm (Fig. 29).

3. Apply pressure on his right arm with your left (causing him to break his hold) and force his head downwards. Smash him in the face with your right knee (Fig. 30).
If necessary, follow up with edge of hand blow on back of his neck.

Note.—Should your opponent anticipate your intention when you are in the position shown in Fig. 29 and resist the pressure of your left arm (para. 3), go after his eyes with your left hand as in Fig. 30A, and follow up with a knee to the testicles.

36

No. 7(a). Bear Hug (Front, over the Arms)

Fig. 28

Fig. 29

Fig. 30

Fig. 30A

c

No. 8. Bear Hug (Front, Arms Free)

You are gripped around the waist (Fig. 31).

1. Place your left hand in the small of his back and apply a chin jab as in Fig. 32.
If necessary, knee him in the testicles.

No. 9. Bear Hug (Back, over the Arms)

You are gripped around the waist (Fig. 33).

1. Smash him in the face with your tin hat.

2. Stamp on his feet with either foot.

3. Seize him by the testicles with your right or left hand.

38

No. 8. Bear Hug (Front, Arms Free)

No. 9. Bear Hug
(Back, over the Arms)

Fig. 31

Fig. 32

Fig. 33

No. 9(a). Bear Hug (Back, over the Arms)

(An alternative method to No. 9.)
You are gripped around the waist (Fig. 33).

1. Seize his testicles with your left hand (causing him to break his hold).

2. Pass your right arm over his right, as in Fig. 34.

3. Slip out from under his arm by turning to your left and stepping backwards with your right foot, seizing his right wrist with both hands and jerking it downwards. Finish up by kicking him in the face, as in Fig. 35.

No. 10. Bear Hug (Back, Arms Free)

You are gripped around the waist as in Fig. 36.

1. Smash him in the face with your tin hat.

2. Stamp on his feet with either foot.

3. Seize his little finger with your right hand, bend it backwards, and walk out of the hold, as in Fig. 37.

No. 9(a). Bear Hug (Back, over the Arms)

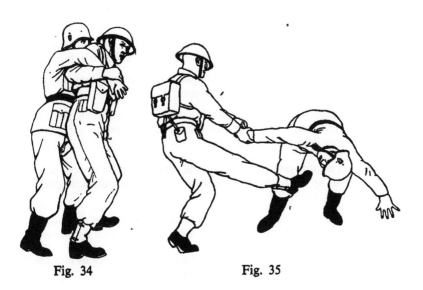

Fig. 34   Fig. 35

No. 10. Bear Hug (Back, Arms Free)

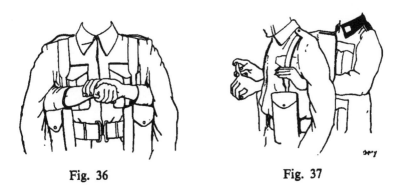

Fig. 36   Fig. 37

No. II. Hair Hold (from Behind)

You are seized by the hair from behind and pulled back, as in Fig. 38.

1. Seize (with both your hands) your opponent's right wrist and arm with a very firm grip, making him keep the hold shown in Fig. 39.

2. Turn to your left (inwards, towards your opponent) by pivoting on your left foot. This will twist his arm.

3. Step backwards as far as possible with your right foot, jerking his hand off your head in a downward and backward direction between your legs (Fig. 40).

Note.—It is quite possible that this will tear quite a bit of your hair out by the roots, but it is very unlikely that you will notice it at the time.

4. Keep a firm grip on his wrist and arm, and follow up with a smashing kick to your opponent's face with the toe of your right boot.

Note A.—All the above movements must be one continuous motion and must be carried out with speed.

Note B.—When in the position shown in Fig. 40, you can increase the force of your kick to the face by pulling your opponent's arm slightly upwards and towards you. This movement also enables you to get back on balance.

42

No. II. Hair Hold (from Behind)

Fig. 38   Fig. 39

Fig. 40

3. HOLDS

No. 12. Thumb Hold

This is the most effective hold known, and very little exertion on your part (three to four pounds' pressure) is required to make even the most powerful prisoner obey you. It is possible also for you to conduct him, even if resisting, as far as he is able to walk. You have such complete control of him that you can, if necessary, use him as cover against attack from others.

The movements you have to make to secure this hold are very complicated, which is mainly the reason why it is almost unknown outside of the Far East. But the advantage one gains in knowing that one can effectively apply this hold more than repays for the time that must be spent in mastering it.

Students should first concentrate on making every move slowly, gradually speeding up, until all movements become one continuous motion. When they have thoroughly mastered it, as demonstrated, they should then learn to obtain it from any position in which they have secured their opponent.

Students must also understand that the hold is not a method of attack, but simply a 'mastering hold', which is only applied after they have partially disabled or brought their opponent to a submissive frame of mind by one of the 'follow up' methods (Blows).

Should your opponent not be wearing a tin hat or similar protection which covers his ears, the following will be found to be a very simple method of making him submissive:

Cup your hands and strike your opponent simultaneously over both ears, as in Fig. 41. This will probably burst one or both ear drums and at least give him a mild form of concussion. It can be applied from the front or from behind.

44

No. 12. Thumb Hold

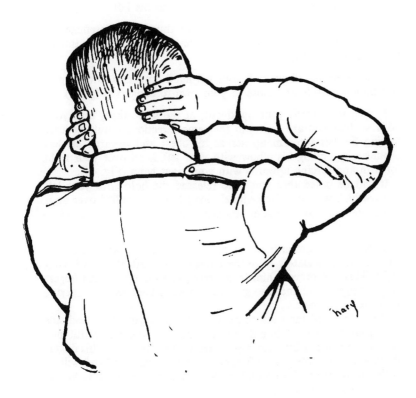

Fig. 41

No. 12. Thumb Hold (contd.)

Stand facing your opponent and slightly to his left.

1. Insert your right thumb between the thumb and forefinger of his left hand, your fingers under the palm of his hand, your thumb to the right (Fig. 42).

2. Seize his left elbow with your left hand, knuckles to the right, and thumb outside and close to your own forefingers (Fig. 43).

3. Step in towards your opponent; at the same time, turn your body so that you are facing in the same direction, simultaneously forcing his left forearm up across his chest and towards his left shoulder by pulling his elbow with your left hand over your right forearm and forcing upwards with your right hand (Fig. 44).

It will be noted that you have released the hold with your left hand, which was done immediately his elbow was pulled over your right forearm. Also that your opponent's left elbow is held very close to your body.

4. Keeping a firm grip on the upper part of his left arm with your right arm, immediately seize the fingers of his left hand with your right. This will prevent him from trying to seize one of the fingers of your right hand and also give you an extra leverage for applying pressure as follows:

Press down on the back of his hand towards your left-hand side with your right hand. Should your opponent be a very powerful man and try to resist, a little extra pressure applied by pulling his fingers downwards towards your left-hand side with your left hand will be sufficient to bring him up on his toes and convince him that he has met his master (Fig. 45).

46

No. 12. Thumb Hold (*contd.*)

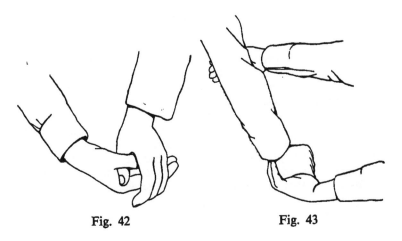

Fig. 42   Fig. 43

Fig. 44   Fig. 45

No. 13. Sentry Hold

The success or otherwise of any attempt to carry out this method of attack on a sentry will, apart from the fact that you have thoroughly mastered every movement, depend entirely on every possible condition having been taken into account. It would, to say the least, be very inadvisable to take it for granted that the sentry would be standing in a certain manner or that he would be wearing his equipment (gas mask, pouches, or rifle, etc.) in the orthodox manner.

It is taken for granted that the attack will be applied from behind; the stalk or approach to the sentry will be during the hours of dark or semi-dark; the sentry has been under observation for a sufficient length of time to permit of his habits (length of his post, position of his rifle, if carried, and his normal halting or resting position) being known; and that the man selected for the attack is an *expert at stalking*.

Now let us assume that conditions are somewhat on the following lines:

1. Rifle slung or carried on the right shoulder.

2. Wearing a steel helmet covering the back of the neck and the ears.

3. Wearing a respirator on the small of his back, projecting as much as six inches (See Fig. 46).

4. There are other sentries within shouting distance.

It will be admitted that these conditions are not too favourable for the attacker, but are what might have to be met, and students are advised to carry out their training under conditions as near as possible to those they will have to contend with in actual war.

Note.—The stalker should not be handicapped with any equipment, other than a knife or a pistol. He should wear rubber or cloth shoes, socks pulled well up over the trousers, capcomforter, well pulled down with the collar of his blouse turned up and his hands and face camouflaged (See Fig. 47, page 51).

48

No. 13. Sentry Hold

Fig. 46

No. 13. Sentry Hold (*contd.*)

1. Having approached the sentry from behind to within three to four feet, take up position shown in Fig. 47. This will permit you to make a lightning-like attack by springing on him.

2. With the fingers and thumb of your left hand fully extended, *strike* him across the throat with the inner edge of your left forearm (i.e. with the forearm bone), and simultaneously *punch* him with your clenched right hand in the small of his back or on his respirator case (Fig. 48).

The effect of these blows, if applied as above, will be that you have rendered your opponent unconscious or semi-conscious. Further, it should be noticed that the blow on the throat will cause your opponent to draw his breath, making it impossible for him to shout and give the alarm.

3. The blows should be immediately followed with a very fast movement of your right hand from the small of his back, over his right shoulder, clapping it over his mouth and nose (Fig. 49). This will prevent him from breathing or making a noise in the event of the blow on the throat not having been effectively applied.

It is not unlikely that the blows on the throat and in the small of the back may cause him to drop his rifle or knock his helmet off his head. Should this happen, no attempt should be made to prevent them falling on the ground. Just simply keep still for a matter of ten seconds, after which it is unlikely that anyone having heard the noise will come to investigate. Retaining your hold around the neck with your left arm, drag him away backwards.

Note.—To enable students to form some idea of how effective this method is when applied as above, and so that they will also have confidence that it can be successfully used by a man of normal strength, we advise them to have it applied on themselves by a friend, care being taken that no more than one-twentieth of the normal force is used.

50

No. 13. Sentry Hold (*contd.*)

Fig. 47   Fig. 48

Fig. 49

No. 14. Japanese Strangle

1. Approach your opponent from behind.

2. Place your left arm round his neck, with your forearm bone bearing on his Adam's apple.

3. Place the back of your right arm (above the elbow) on his right shoulder and clasp your right biceps with your left hand.

4. Place your right hand on the back of his head.

5. Pull him backwards with your left forearm and press his head forward with your right hand, and strangle him (Fig. 50).

Note.—Should your opponent attempt to seize you by the testicles:

(a) Keep your grip with both arms, straightening out the fingers and thumbs of both hands. With the edge of your left hand in the bend of your right arm, place the edge of your right hand just below the base of the skull.

(b) Step back quickly, at the same time jolting his head forward with the edge of your right hand, and dislocate his neck (Fig. 51).

(c) In the event of your opponent being a taller man than yourself, making it difficult for you to reach his right shoulder with your right arm, as in Fig. 50, bend him backwards by applying pressure on his neck with your left arm. If necessary, punch him in the small of the back, as shown in Fig. 48, page 51, Sentry Hold, and bring him down to your own height.

52

No. 14. Japanese Strangle

Fig. 50

Fig. 51

D

No. 14(a). Japanese Strangle Applied from in Front

1. Stand facing your opponent.

2. Seize his right shoulder with your left hand and his left shoulder with your right hand.

3. Simultaneously push with your left hand (retaining the hold) and pull towards you with your right hand, turning your opponent completely round (Fig. 52). It should be noted that your left arm will be in a position around his neck and most likely you will have caused your opponent to have crossed his legs, making it almost impossible for him to defend himself.

4. Place the back of your right arm (above the elbow) on his right shoulder and clasp your right biceps with your left hand.

5. Grasp the back of his head with your right hand, and apply pressure by pulling him backwards with your left forearm and pressing his head forward with your right arm (Fig. 50).

Note.—Although the final position and the method of applying pressure are identical with that shown in No. 14 on the previous page, there is a difference in the amount of pressure necessary to strangle your opponent. If his legs are crossed (and they nearly always will be, when he is suddenly twisted round in this manner), approximately only half the amount of pressure is required.

54

No. 14(a). Japanese Strangle Applied from in Front

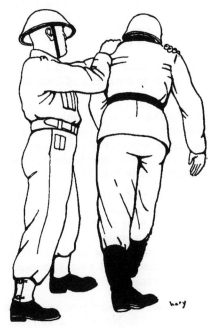

Fig. 52

Fig 50

No. 15. Handcuff Hold

1. You are facing your opponent. Make a dive at his right wrist, seizing it with both hands, right above left, jerking it violently downwards, as in Fig. 53. This will produce a considerable shock, amounting almost to a knockout blow on the left side of his head.

2. Swing his arm up to the height of your shoulder, at the same time twisting his arm towards you so as to force him off-balance on to his left leg (Fig. 54).

3. Keeping his arm the height of his shoulder, pass quickly underneath by taking a pace forward with your right foot. (It may be necessary for you to reduce your height to permit of your doing this; do so by bending your legs at the knees). Turn inwards towards your opponent, jerking his arm downwards, as in Fig. 55.

4. Step to his back with your left foot, and with a circular upward motion, force his wrist well up his back. Retain the grip with your left hand and seize his right elbow with your right hand, forcing it well up his back. Then slide your left hand around his wrist, bringing your thumb inside and finger over the back of the hand, and bend his wrist. Apply pressure with both hands until your opponent's right shoulder points to the ground (Fig. 56).

Note A.—This is a very useful hold for marching your prisoner a short distance only. A change to No. 12 Thumb Hold, Fig. 45, page 47, is recommended.

Note B.—A method of tying up your prisoner is shown on page 86, method A.

56

No. 15. Handcuff Hold

Fig. 53

Fig. 54

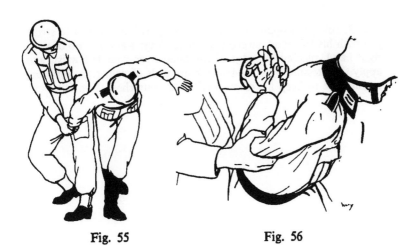

Fig. 55   Fig. 56

No. 16. Bent Arm Hold

Note.—Students are strongly recommended to specialize in mastering this hold.

1. Your opponent has taken up a boxing stance or raised his right arm, as if about to deliver a blow.

2. Seize his right wrist with your left hand, bending his arm at the elbow, towards him (Fig. 57). Continue the pressure on his wrist until his arm is in the position shown in Fig. 58.
These movements must be continuous, and carried out as quickly as possible. It will be noted that forcing your opponent's right forearm backwards places him off-balance, making it almost impossible for him to attack you with his left fist.

3. Immediately step in with your right foot, placing your right leg and hip close in to your opponent's thigh.

4. Pass your right arm under the upper part of his right arm, seizing his right wrist with your right hand above your left.

5. Keeping a firm grip with both hands, force his right elbow and arm against your chest, applying pressure by jerking his wrist towards the ground. At the same time, force the forearm bone of your right arm up and in to the back muscles of the upper part of his right arm (Fig. 59).

6. Should your opponent, when in this position, attempt to strike you with his left hand, straighten out the fingers and thumb of your right hand, placing the edge of the hand over your left wrist, and apply the pressure by a sudden jerk upwards of your right forearm, taking care to keep his elbow well in to your chest (Fig. 60).

58

HOLDS

No. 16. Bent Arm Hold

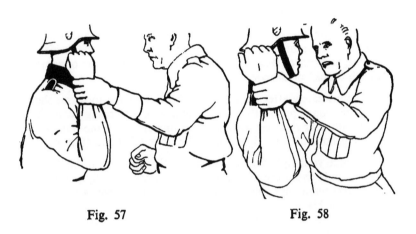

Fig. 57   Fig. 58

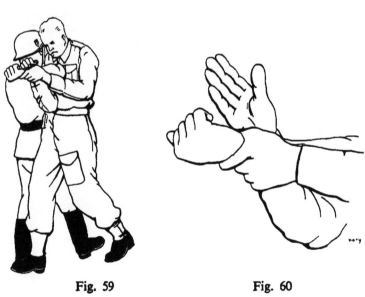

Fig. 59   Fig. 60

No. 17. Head Hold

Approach your opponent from the front.

1. Keeping the finger of your right hand straight and thumb extended, strike him on the left side of his neck with the inside of your right forearm (Fig. 61). This blow will render your opponent 'punch-drunk' or dazed.

2. Immediately after delivering the blow with the forearm, slide it around your opponent's neck, simultaneously stepping across his front with your right leg, bending him forward from the waist and catching hold of your right wrist with your left hand (Fig. 62).

3. Force your right forearm bone into the right side of his face— (anywhere between the temple and the chin will do)—by pulling on your right wrist with your left hand and forcing downwards on the left side of his face with your body.

It should be noted that the outside of your right forearm is resting on your right thigh and that the weight of your body is being forced on to your right leg by pressure from the left foot. Any attempt of your opponent to seize your testicles should immediately be countered by a slight increase of pressure. If necessary, apply an edge of hand blow—release your hold with the left hand, straighten up slightly, and apply the blow on the left side of his neck.

60

No. 17. Head Hold

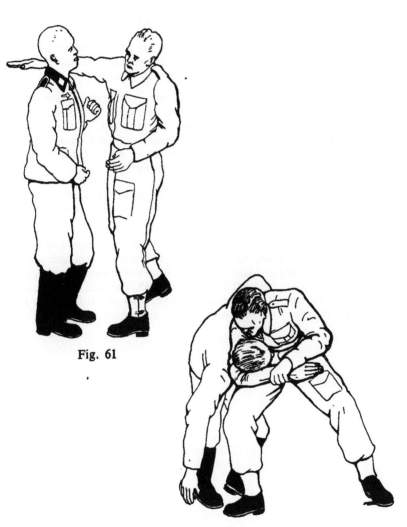

Fig. 61

Fig. 62

4. THROWS

No. 18. Hip Throw

You are facing your opponent:

1. Seize his equipment or arms slightly above the height of his elbows. Pull down with your right hand and lift up with your left hand, pulling him off-balance; simultaneously shoot your left leg as far as possible behind him, your left leg rigid and close up to his thigh. Take care that your left foot is pointing as in Fig. 63.

2. Continue the downward pull of your right hand and the upward lift of your left hand, at the same time bending forward and downwards from your waist towards your right foot. All the above movements must be one continuous motion and will throw your opponent as in Fig. 64. Follow-up with a kick on his spine, somewhere near the small of the back, with either boot.

Note.—An alternative method of applying the throw when dealing with an opponent approaching you on your left side is as follows:

3. Seize his equipment or left arm with your right hand and pull downwards, simultaneously striking him up under the chin with your left hand (chin jab) and kicking his legs from under him with a backward kick of your rigid left leg, as in Fig. 65. This will throw your opponent backwards with smashing force, after which it will be a simple matter for you to dispose of him in any manner you may wish.

62

No. 18. Hip Throw

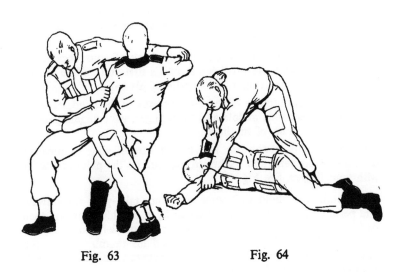

Fig. 63   Fig. 64

Fig. 65

No. 19. Wrist Throw

Owing to the unorthodox manner in which the opponent's hand is seized at the initial start of this throw, students are advised first to learn the hold as follows:

A. Your left thumb is forced into the back of your opponent's right hand, between the small bones of his first and middle finger, your fingers passing around to the palm of his hand.

B. Your right thumb is forced into the back of the hand, between the small bones of his middle and third finger, your fingers passing around to the palm of his hand.

C. Bend his hand towards him by pressure of your thumbs on the back of his hand and backward pressure on the palm and wrist with your fingers. See Fig. 66.

1. Retain your hold with your left hand, take your right away, and permit his right arm to hang naturally at his side. You will then be in the position shown in Fig. 67 (back of your left hand towards your right-hand side, your fingers around his thumb towards the palm of his hand, your thumb forced in between the small bones of his first and second fingers).

2. Bend his arm, by a circular upward motion, towards your left-hand side, turn the palm of his hand towards him; then force your thumbs into the back of his hand (Fig. 66).

3. Applying pressure on the back of his hand and the wrist (as in para. C), force his hand towards the ground on your left-hand side. This will throw him on to his right-hand side. To finish your opponent off, jerk up on his right arm, simultaneously smashing down on his lower ribs with your right boot (Fig. 68).

64

No. 19. Wrist Throw

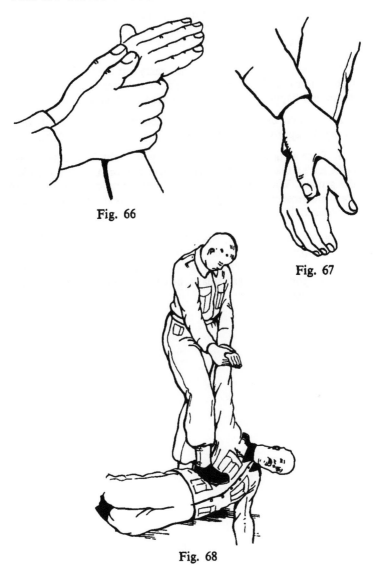

Fig. 66

Fig. 67

Fig. 68

No. 20. The Back Break

1. Approach your opponent from his left-hand side, bend your legs slightly, reach down, and seize him by passing your right arm over his chest and your left arm under his legs, just behind the knee, as in Fig. 69.

Students will be surprised, if they carry out the method as demontrated, how easy it is for them to lift their opponent, even although he should happen to be much heavier than themselves.

2. Lift him up, mainly by straightening your legs, as in weight lifting, to approximately the height of your chest, as in Fig. 70.

3. Take a short pace forward with your right foot, bending your right leg so that the upper part (thigh) is approximately parallel to the ground. With all the strength of your arms, assisted by the forward movement of the upper part of your body, smash him down on your right knee and break his spine (Fig. 71).

Note.—Your opponent, when held as in Fig. 70, will instinctively try to save himself by clutching hold of you with one or both hands. Providing you use the weight of your body in your downward smash, he cannot prevent you from breaking his spine.

66

No. 20. The Back Break

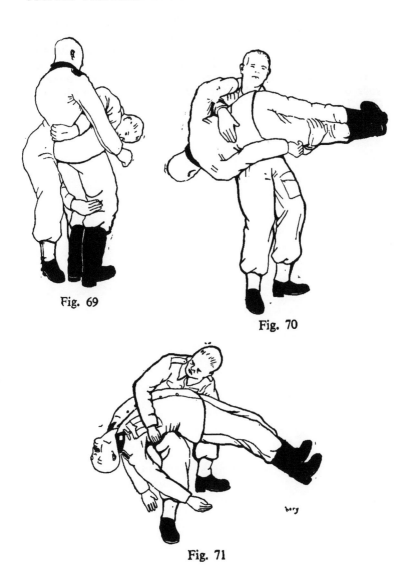

Fig. 69

Fig. 70

Fig. 71

5. MISCELLANEOUS ADVICE

No. 21. Chair and Knife

Most lion-tamers consider a small chair to be sufficient to keep a lion from attacking them. Should you be so fortunate as to have a chair handy when your opponent is attacking you with a knife, seize the chair as in Fig. 72. Rush at him, jabbing one or more of the legs of the chair into his body. The odds in favour of your overpowering your opponent are roughly three to one, and well worth taking (Fig. 73).

68

＼No. 21. Chair and Knife

Fig. 72

Fig. 73

E

No. 22. The Match-Box Attack

You are sitting down, say, in a railway carriage, or have picked up a hitch-hiker. Your opponent, who is on your left, sticks a gun in your ribs, holding it in his right hand.

1. Take a match-box and hold it as in Fig. 74, the top of the box being slightly below the finger and thumb.

2. Keeping the upper part of the right arm close to the right side of your body, with a circular upward motion of your right fist, turning your body from the hip, strike your opponent hard on the left side of his face, as near to the jaw-bone as possible (Fig. 75); parry the gun away from your body with your left forearm.

Note.—The odds of knocking your opponent unconscious by this method are at least two to one. The fact that this can be accomplished with a match-box is not well-known, and for this reason is not likely to raise your opponent's suspicion of your movements. Naturally, all movements, from the initial start of the blow, must be carried out with the quickest possible speed.

70

No. 22. The Match-Box Attack

Fig. 74

Fig. 75

No. 23. Smacking the Ears

This method should be applied when your opponent has no protection over his ears:

1. Cup your hands, keeping the fingers and thumb bent, and close together, as in Fig. 76.

2. Strike your opponent simultaneously over both ears, using five to ten pounds force with both hands, Fig. 77.

Note.—This will probably burst one or both ear-drums and at least give him a mild form of concussion, and make him what is known in boxing circles as punch-drunk. You will then have no difficulty in dealing with him in any way you may wish.

So that students may realize what the effect of a blow given as above is like, we recommend that they should apply it on themselves, as in Fig. 41 opposite. Care must be taken to use *only* half a pound force with each hand.

72

No. 23. Smacking the Ears

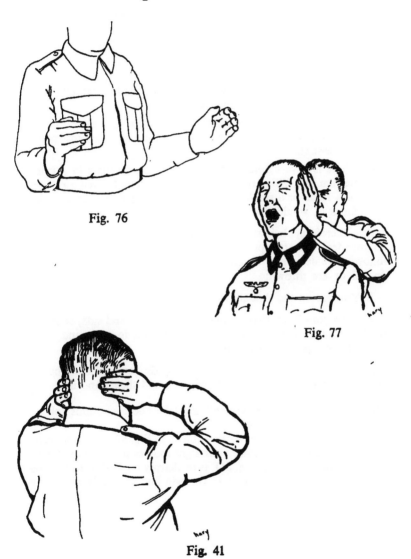

Fig. 76

Fig. 77

Fig. 41

No. 24. The Art of Getting Up from the Ground

Students will have noted that no holds or locks on the ground are demonstrated. The reason for this is:

(a) *This is war:* your object is to kill or dispose of your opponent as quickly as possible and go to the assistance of your comrades.

(b) Once on the ground, you are more vulnerable to attack. (See Method No. 3(b)—'Bronco Kick'.)

(c) It takes months of constant daily practice to master the art of falling, and personal instruction from a qualified instructor is essential.

(d) There is a vast difference between falling on mats in a gymnasium and falling on a road or rocky ground. Even a roll on to a stone or a small stump of a tree, should it press into the kidneys, would, for sure, put you out of the fight for good.

It is, therefore, obvious that you should concentrate on remaining on your feet. No attempt is made to teach you how to fall, but the following guides are given on how to get back on your feet, if you do fall or are thrown:

1. You are on the ground, as in Fig. 78.

2. Turn your body sharply towards your left-hand side, stomach to the ground, raising by the help of the right forearm and right knee to the position shown in Fig. 79.

3. Pushing on the ground with both hands, force yourself backwards into the position shown in Fig. 80, and then stand up.

Note.—All the above movements must be one continuous roll or twist of the body.

If, when in the position shown in Fig. 80, your opponent is behind you, place your right foot as near as possible to your left hand (Fig. 81), turn sharply on both feet towards your left-hand side, and you will find yourself facing your opponent.

74

No. 24. The Art of Getting Up from the Ground

78 Fig.

Fig. 79

Fig. 80

Fig. 81

No. 24(a). Getting Up from the Ground (Backwards)

1. You have fallen on to your back on the ground:

2. Lie flat on your back and place your right arm at an angle of 90 degrees from the body, back of your hand on the ground and your head turned towards your left shoulder (Fig. 82).

3. Raise your legs from the waist and shoot them over your right shoulder (Fig. 83).

When in this position, allow your right arm and hand to turn with your body.

4. Bend your right leg and bring it to the ground as close to your right arm as possible. Keeping your left leg straight, reach as far back with it as possible, as in Fig. 84.

5. Your left hand will be on the ground approximately opposite your right knee: Press on the ground with both hands and force yourself up to your right knee. Continue the pressure until you are on your feet (Fig. 85).

Note.—The reason for keeping your feet apart in the movement shown in para. 4 is that you will immediately be on-balance when you come up on your feet. This is a very important point to note and is very seldom taken care of by the average man. A man off-balance can be pushed down again with a few pounds' pressure of either hand. Moreover, he cannot administer an effective blow or even defend himself properly.

76

No. 24(a). Getting Up from the Ground (Backwards)

Fig. 82

Fig. 83

Fig. 84

Fig. 85

No. 25. Attack with a Small Stick or Cane

A man without a weapon to defend himself, especially after long exposure, is very liable to give up in despair. It is remarkable what a difference it would make in his morale if he had a small stick or cane in his hand. Now, add to this the knowledge that he could, with ease, kill any opponent with a stick and you will then see how easy it is to cultivate the offensive spirit which is so essential in present-day warfare.

1. A small stick of 18 to 24 inches in length and about 1 inch in thickness will make an ideal weapon. (If one is not available, it can be broken off a tree.)

Note.—If you are to be successful in the application of this method, it is essential you must have the element of surprise on your side, and this can best be obtained by adopting the position shown in Fig. 86.

2. Retaining your hold of the stick with your right hand, swing the other end up and catch it in your left hand about 6 inches from the end. This should be done without looking down at your hands or stick. Pay particular attention to the position of the hands (Fig. 87).

Note.—The reason for adopting this unorthodox hold of the stick should be obvious. It is not at all likely that anyone (not previously aware of this particular method of attack) would have the slightest suspicion that they were in danger of being attacked.

78

No. 25. Attack with a Small Stick or Cane

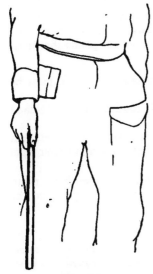

Fig. 86

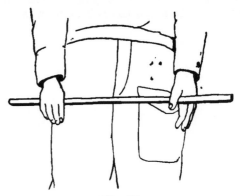

Fig. 87

No. 25. Attack with a Small Stick or Cane (contd.)

You are close up and facing your opponent, as in Fig. 88.

1. Strike your opponent *across* the stomach with the left end of the stick by a vicious circular motion towards your right-hand side. In delivering this blow, there are four essential points that must be carried out simultaneously:

(a) Your loose grip on the stick, both hands (Fig. 87), must be changed to as strong as possible.

(b) The movement of your left hand is towards your right-hand side.

(c) The movement of your right hand is inwards to the left, but much shorter than that of the left hand, owing to your right hand coming against your right side.

(d) The movement of your left foot is forward towards the right. This permits you to put the weight of your body behind the blow. See Fig. 89.

Note.—This blow *across* your opponent's stomach would not, if he was wearing thick clothing, put him 'out', but it will surely make him bring his chin forward, which is exactly the position you want him in:

2. Keeping the firmest possible grip of the stick with both hands, jab upwards with the end of the stick (left-hand end) and drive it into his neck and kill him (Fig. 90). The mark you are after is that soft spot about two inches back from the point of the chin.

80

No. 25. Attack with a Small Stick or Cane (*contd.*)

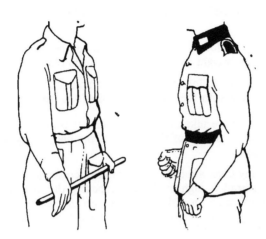

Fig. 88

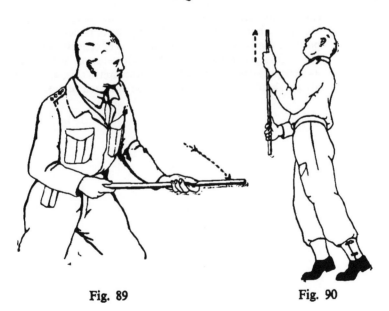

Fig. 89   Fig. 90

No. 25. Attack with a Small Stick or Cane (*contd.*)

You have missed your opponent's chin when you attacked as in Fig. 90:

3. Smash him down the face with the end of the stick, as in Fig. 91, putting all the weight of the body behind the blow.

4. If necessary, follow-up with a smash across the left side of your opponent's face with the right-hand end of the stick, as in Fig. 92.

Note.—You have taken a step to your left front with your right foot to permit of the weight of the body being behind the blow.

5. If at any time, after the initial attack across the stomach, your opponent's head is high in the air, exposing the front part of his neck, aim to strike the Adam's apple with the centre of the stick, putting every ounce of strength behind the blow. This should kill him, or at least knock him unconscious (Fig. 93).

Note.—Methods No. 2 (the point, up under the chin) and No. 5 (the centre, into the Adam's apple) are finishing-off or killing blows, but you must first bring your opponent into the position that permits you to deal them effectively. Method No. 1 (the point across the stomach) will, on account of its unexpectedness, enable you to accomplish this, and your attack should always start with the stomach attack.

No. 25. Attack with a Small Stick or Cane (*contd.*)

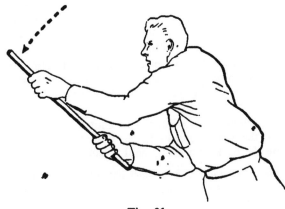

Fig. 91

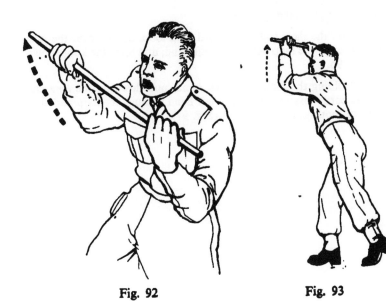

Fig. 92   Fig. 93

No. 26. Various Methods of Securing a Prisoner

All raiding parties should have a small roll of adhesive tape, preferably of one or more inches in width, and a length of silk rope or cord, about a quarter of an inch in diameter and about five yards in length, amongst their equipment for gagging and securing a prisoner whom they wish to leave unguarded.

To Gag a Prisoner. Force a piece of cloth or a lump of turf into his mouth; then place two or more strips of adhesive tape, approximately four and a half inches in length, firmly over his mouth, taking care not to cover his nostrils.

Tying the Highwayman's Hitch. This knot has very appropriately been called the Highwayman's Hitch. It should be practised on a pole or on the back of a chair, until it can be done in the dark.

1. Holding the cord with a *short* end (about two feet), pass it behind the pole, with the *short* end to the left and the *long* to the right (Fig. 94).

2. Pass the *long* end, in a loop, up and over the pole and through the loop held in the left hand. Then pull down on the *short* end with the right hand (Fig. 95).

3. Pass the *short* end of the cord, in a loop, up and over the pole and through the loop held in the left hand, and form the knot shown in Fig. 96.

4. Holding the loop in the left hand, pull down on the *long* end of the cord, pass the prisoner's left hand through the loop and then pull on both *ends* of the cord (Fig. 97).

84

No. 26. Various Methods of Securing a Prisoner

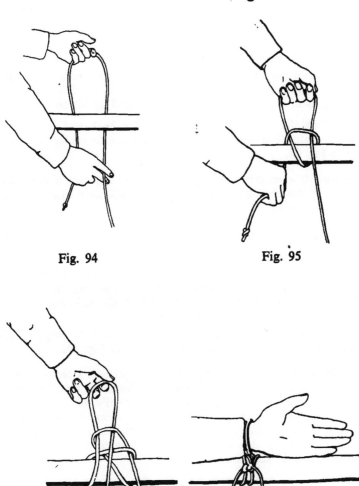

Fig. 94

Fig. 95

Fig. 96

Fig. 97

F

No. 26. Various Methods of Securing a Prisoner. (contd.)
To Secure a Prisoner

A. From the Handcuff Hold.

1. Throw your prisoner to the ground on his stomach, tying his wrists together behind his back by means of the Highwayman's Hitch, as in Fig. 98, and force his arms well up his back.

2. Pass the cord around his neck; then back and around his wrists again; then bend his legs backwards and tie his legs together, as in Fig. 99.

Note.—If your prisoner keeps still, he will not hurt himself, but should he attempt to struggle, he will most likely strangle himself.

B. 'Grape Vine'. On a tree, post, or lamp-post of about seven inches in diameter:

1. Make your prisoner climb on the tree, etc., as in Fig. 100.

2. Place his right leg around the front of the tree, with the foot to the left. Place the left leg over his right ankle, as in Fig. 101, and take his left foot back behind the tree.

3. Force your prisoner well down the pole until the weight of his body locks his left foot around the tree, as in Fig. 102.

Note.—Even though you have left your prisoner's hands free, it will, if he has been forced well down the tree, be almost impossible for him to escape. Normally, the average man placed in this position would get cramp in one or both legs within ten to fifteen minutes, when it is not at all unlikely that he would throw himself backwards. This would kill him.

Caution.—To release your prisoner, two persons are necessary, one on either side. Take hold of his legs and lift him up the tree; then unlock his legs.

86

No. 26. Various Methods of Securing a Prisoner
(contd.)

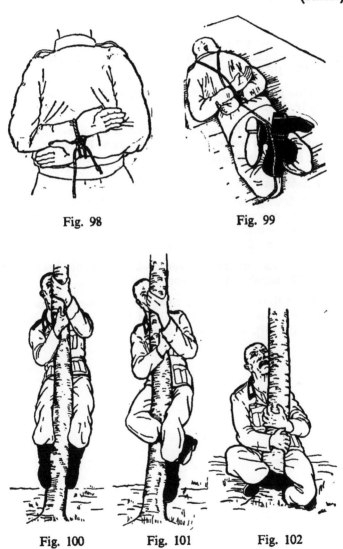

Fig. 98   Fig. 99

Fig. 100   Fig. 101   Fig. 102

MISCELLANEOUS ADVICE

No. 26. Various Methods of Securing a Prisoner
(contd.)

C. The Chair.

A chair with an open back is preferable.

1. Force your prisoner to sit on the chair, pass one of his arms through the back and the other around it, and secure his wrist with cord (Fig. 103).

2. Then tie the upper part of his arms to the chair, one on either side (Fig. 104).

3. Tie both feet to the chair—one on either side—with only the toes of his boots resting on the ground, as in Fig. 105.

Gag him, if necessary.

D. A Substitute for Handcuffs.

The following method, whereby one man can effectively control two to six prisoners, may be found very useful. A police baton, night stick, or hunting crop, preferably fitted with a cord thong, as in Fig. 106, is all that is required.

1. Cut your prisoners' trousers-belts and/or braces; then thoroughly search them for concealed weapons.

2. Make them all put their right wrists through the loop of the thong, and twist the baton until the thong cuts well into their wrists (Fig. 107). Then march them off.

No. 26. Various Methods of Securing a Prisoner
(contd.)

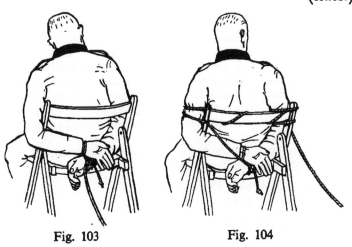

Fig. 103   Fig. 104

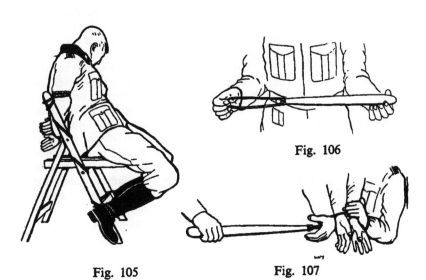

Fig. 106

Fig. 105   Fig. 107

MISCELLANEOUS ADVICE

No. 27. Break-Aways from ' Come-Along ' Grips

A number of so-called 'come-along' grips are frequently demonstrated and taught as being 100 per cent perfect, and it is claimed
that it is impossible, once secured in one of them, for any man to
escape. We admit that under certain circumstances it would be difficult and painful, also that it might result in a badly strained
ligament. But we are well aware that any man of average build and
strength can, with at least a 50 per cent chance of success, not only
break away from these holds, but that he will also be in a position
from which he can with ease break his opponent's limbs and if necessary kill him.

Two fairly well known holds that are so accepted are these
shown on the opposite page:

    Fig. 108—'Police Come-Along Grip'.
    Fig. 109—'Collar and Wrist Hold'.

Students must face the fact that a man fighting for his life or to
prevent capture is a vastly different person to one they may have
met in competition, etc. It is an established fact that a man in fear
of death will be prepared to undertake the lifting of five times the
weight he would in normal times, also that he can, under such circumstances, take approximately the same amount of extra punishment.

The above is not quoted with the idea of preparing the reader to
take a lot of punishment, should he attempt to break either of these
holds, but simply to show him that even if he failed it would be well
worth while making an attempt. One thing is certain; in the event of
failing, he will not be in a much worse position than he was originally.

We rather anticipate that the reader will ask, Why is it that these
holds have been so commonly accepted as being unbreakable? Our
answer would be: Those of us who have made a study of the art of
attack and defence well know that the average student is too inclined
to demonstrate his prowess on his friends, after only a few lessons,
and before he has mastered even the initial movements. This often
results in broken bones, etc. Further, the counter measures used to
break holds such as these are drastic in the extreme and are only
shown to students after they have proved beyond doubt that they
would not wilfully mis-apply them.

90

No. 27. Break-Aways from ' Come-Along ' Grips

Fig. 108

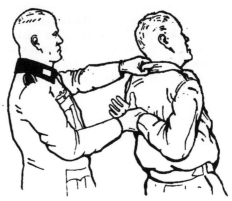

Fig. 109

No. 27. Break-Aways from ' Come-Along ' Grips
(contd.)

Note.—It is presumed that your opponent is not acquainted with the counter methods you intend to apply.

A. Your opponent has hold of you as in Fig. 108.

1. Exaggerate the pain you are receiving by shouting or groaning. Try to be out of step with him, which makes it easier to apply your counter. Only resist sufficiently to prevent him from being suspicious.

2. Do not be in a hurry to apply your counter. The opening will be there every time he takes the weight of his body on his left foot:
    Smartly jab the outside of your right leg against the outside of his left leg, forcing his leg inwards, and break it (Fig. 110), simultaneously pulling your right arm towards you, which, in addition to increasing the force of your leg blow, also permits you to bend your arm and break his hold. If necessary, apply the edge of hand blow on the back of his neck with your left hand and kill him.

B. Your opponent has hold of you as in Fig. 109.

1. As in the previous method, wait until your opponent is off his guard and only resist slightly.

2. Turn sharply and completely around towards your left-hand side, simultaneously bending your legs at the knees and your head forward to permit of your head going under his left arm. Then straighten up your head. (These movements, in addition to twisting his arm, lock his left hand in the back of your collar.) Strike the elbow of his left arm, with a vicious upward jab, with the palm of your right hand as in Fig. 111. If necessary, follow up with a 'chin-jab' with your left hand, or knee to the testicles with either knee.

92

No. 27. Break-Aways from ' Come-Along ' Grips
(contd.)

Fig. 108   Fig. 110

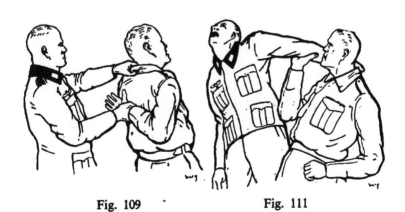

Fig. 109   Fig. 111

No. 28. Use of the Knife

The knife in close-quarter fighting is the most deadly weapon to have to contend with. It is admitted by recognized authorities that for an entirely unarmed man there is no certain defence against a knife. With this we are in entire agreement. We are also aware of the psychological effect that the sudden flashing of a knife will have on the majority of persons.

It has been proved that the British bayonet is still feared, and it is not very difficult to visualize the many occasions, such as on a night raid, house-to-house fighting, or even a boarding party, when a knife or short broad-sword would have been a far more effective weapon.

There are many positions in which the knife can be carried, but what might suit one man and lead him to think that it is the *only* position, will not, owing to the length of arm or thickness of the body, etc., suit another. This is a matter that must be decided by each individual for himself; but before making the final selection, students should note that no matter how good the position or the manner in which the knife is carried, a really quick draw cannot be accomplished unless the sheath is firmly secured to the clothing or equipment. Moreover, speed on the draw can only be acquired by constant daily practice. We, personally, favour a concealed position, using the left hand, well knowing that, in close-quarter fighting, the element of surprise is the main factor of success.

94

No. 28. Use of the Knife (contd.)

It is essential that your knife should have a sharp stabbing point, with good cutting edges, because an artery torn through (as against a clean cut) tends to contract and stop the bleeding. This frequently happens in an explosion. A person may have an arm or a leg blown off and still live, yet if a main artery had been cut they would quickly have lost consciousness and almost immediately have died.

Certain arteries are more vulnerable to attack than others, on account of their being nearer the surface of the skin, or not being protected by clothing or equipment. Don't bother about their names as long as you remember where they are situated.

In the accompanying diagram, the approximate positions of the arteries are given. They vary in size from the thickness of one's thumb to an ordinary pencil. Naturally, the speed at which loss of consciousness or death takes place will depend upon the size of the artery cut.

The heart or stomach, when not protected by equipment, should be attacked. The psychological effect of even a slight wound in the stomach is a point worthy of note.

95

No. 28. Use of the Knife (contd.)

EXPLANATION OF CHART

No.	Name of Artery	Size	Depth below Surface	Loss of Consciousness	Death
1.	Brachial	M	$\frac{1}{2}''$	14 secs.	$1\frac{1}{2}$ mins.
2.	Radial	S	$\frac{1}{4}''$	30	2
3.	Carotid	L	$1\frac{1}{2}''$	5	12 secs.
4.	Subclavian	L	$2\frac{1}{2}''$	2	$3\frac{1}{2}$
5.	(Heart)	—	$3\frac{1}{2}''$	I	3
6.	(Stomach)	—	$5''$	Depending on depth of cut.	

M=Medium   S=Small   L=Large   I=Instantaneous

Fig. A

The F-S Fighting Knife

96

234

No. 28. Use of the Knife (*contd.*)

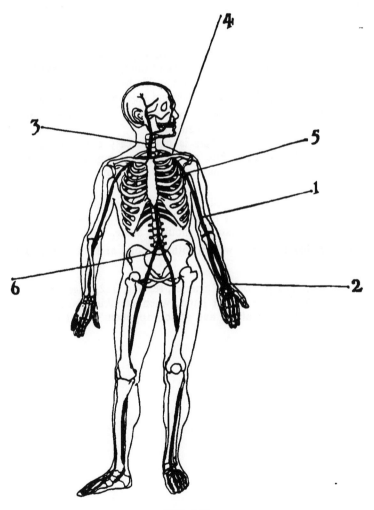

Fig. 112

No. 28. Use of the Knife (*contd.*)

Artery No. 1. Knife in the right hand, attack opponent's left arm with a slashing cut outwards, as in Fig. 113

Artery No. 2. Knife in the right hand, attack opponent's left wrist, cutting downwards and inwards, as in Fig. 114.

Artery No. 3. Knife in right hand, edges parallel to ground, seize opponent around the neck from behind with your left arm, pulling his head to the left. Thrust point well in; then cut sideways. See Fig. 115.

Artery No. 4. Hold knife as in Fig. 116; thrust point well in downwards; then cut.

Note—This is not an easy artery to cut with a knife, but, once cut, your opponent will drop. and no tourniquet or any help of man can save him.

Heart, No. 5. Thrust well in with the point, taking care when attacking from behind not to go too high or you will strike the shoulder blade.

Stomach, No. 6. Thrust well in with the point and cut in any direction.

Note.—(*a*) For position of arteries, see Fig. 112, page 97.

(*b*) If knife in left hand, when attacking No. 1 and 2, reverse the above and attack opponent's right arm.

98

No. 28. Use of the Knife (*contd.*)

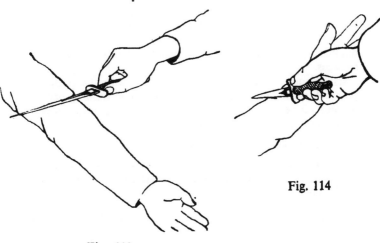

Fig. 114

Fig. 113

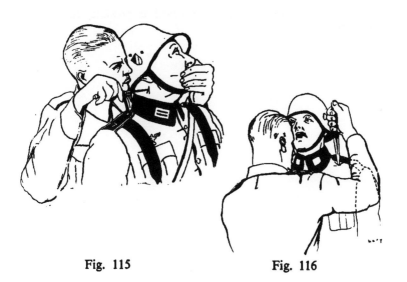

Fig. 115   Fig. 116

No. 29. The Smatchet

The psychological reaction of any man, when he first takes the smatchet in his hand, is full justification for its recommendation as a fighting weapon. He will immediately register all the essential qualities of a good soldier—confidence, determination, and aggressiveness.

Its balance, weight, and killing power, with the point, edge or pommel, combined with the extremely simple training necessary to become efficient in its use, make it the ideal personal weapon for all those not armed with a rifle and bayonet.

Carrying, Drawing, and Holding.

1. The smatchet should be carried in the scabbard on the left side of the belt, as in Fig. 117. This permits one to run, climb, sit, or lie down.

Note.—Any equipment at present carried in this position should be removed to another place.

2. Pass the right hand through the thong and draw upwards with a bent arm (Fig. 118).

3. Grip the handle as near the guard as possible, cutting edge downwards (Fig. 119).

100

No. 29. The Smatchet

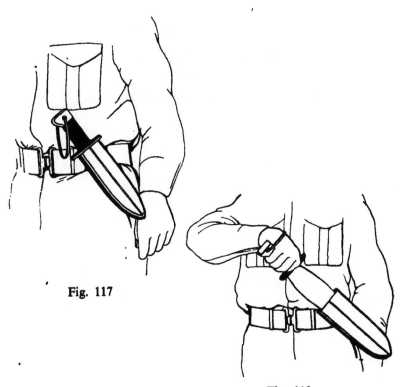

Fig. 117

Fig. 118

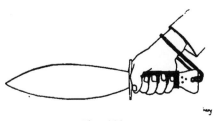

Fig. 119

G

No. 29 The Smatchet (contd).

Close-In Blows.

1. Drive well into the stomach (Fig. 120).
2. 'Sabre Cut' to right-low of neck (Fig. 121).
3. Cut to left-low of neck (Fig. 122).
4. Smash up with pommel, under chin (Fig. 123).

102

No. 29. The Smatchet (*contd.*)

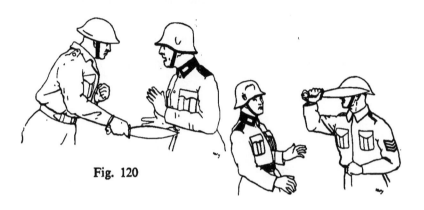

Fig. 120

Fig. 121

Fig. 122

Fig. 123

No. 29 The Smatchet (contd.)

5. Smash down with pommel into the face (Fig. 124).

Attacking Blows.

1. 'Sabre Cut' to left or right wrist (Fig. 125).

2. 'Sabre Cut' to left or right arm (Fig. 126).

104

No. 29. The Smatchet (*contd.*)

Fig. 124

Fig. 125

Fig. 126

6. DISARMING (PISTOL)

No. 30. Disarm, from in Front

You are held-up with a pistol and ordered to put your hands up. The fact that you have not been shot on sight clearly shows that your opponent wants to take you as a prisoner or is afraid to fire, knowing that it will raise an alarm.

Lead him to suppose, by your actions, etc., that you are scared to death, and wait until such time as he is close up to you. Providing all your movements are carried out with speed, it is possible for you to disarm him, with at least a ten to one chance of success.

1. Hold your hands and arms as in Fig. 127.

2. With a swinging downward blow of your right hand, seize your opponent's right wrist, simultaneously turning your body sideway towards the left. This will knock the pistol clear of your body (Fig. 128). Note that the thumb of your right hand is on top.

3. Seize the pistol with the left hand as in Fig. 129.

4. Keeping a firm grip with the right hand on his wrist, force the pistol backwards with your left hand, and knee him or kick him in the testicles (Fig. 130).

Note.—All the above movements must be continuous.

106

DISARMING (PISTOL)

No. 30. Disarm, from in Front

Fig. 127   Fig. 128

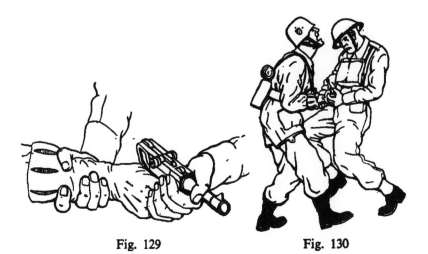

Fig. 129   Fig. 130

No. 30(a). Disarm, from in Front (Alternative Method)

It will be noted that in this method the initial attack is made with the left hand instead of the right, as was demonstrated in the previous method.

1. Hold your hands and arms as in Fig. 127.

2. With a swinging downward blow of your left hand, thumb on top, seize your opponent's right wrist, simultaneously turning your body sideways, towards your right. This will knock the pistol clear of your body (Fig. 131).

3. Seize the pistol with the right hand, as in Fig. 132.

4. Keeping a firm grip with your left hand on his wrist, bend his wrist and pistol backwards; at the same time, knee him in the testicles (Fig. 133).

108

DISARMING (PISTOL)

No. 30(a). Disarm, from in Front (Alternative Method)

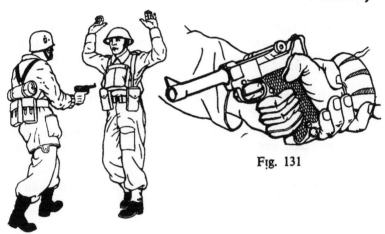

Fig. 131

Fig. 127

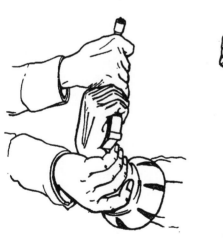

Fig. 132

Fig. 133

No. 30(b). Disarm, from Behind

1. Hold your arms as in Fig. 134.

2. Turning rapidly inwards towards your left-hand side, pass your left arm over and around your opponent's right forearm, as near the wrist as possible, bringing your left hand up your chest (Fig. 135).

Note.—It is impossible for him to shoot you or release his arm from this grip.

3. Immediately the arm is locked, knee him in the testicles with your right knee, and 'chin-jab' him with your right hand, as in Fig. 136.

Note.—In the event of the knee blow and 'chin-jab' not making him release his hold of the pistol, go after his eyes with the fingers of your right hand.

110

No. 30(b). Disarm, from Behind

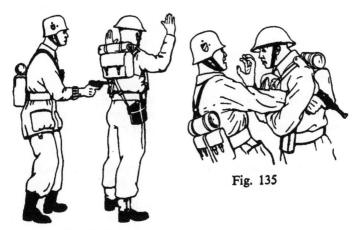

Fig. 135

Fig. 134

Fig. 136

No. 30(c). Disarm, from Behind (Alternative Method)

The difference between this method and that shown on the previous page is that the initial attack is made with your right arm instead of the left.

1. Hold your arms as in Fig. 134.

2. Turning rapidly outwards towards your right-hand side, pass your right arm over and around your opponent's right forearm, as near the wrist as possible, bringing your right hand up your chest (Fig. 137).

Note.—As in the previous method, it is impossible for him to shoot you or release his arm from this grip.

3. Immediately the arm is locked, strike your opponent across the throat, as near the Adam's apple as possible, with an edge-of-the-hand blow, with your left hand, as in Fig. 138.

Note.—Should your opponent not release his hold of the pistol, follow-up by pressing with your right leg on the outside of his right leg, as in Fig. 139, and break his leg.

112

No. 30(c). Disarm, from Behind (Alternative Method)

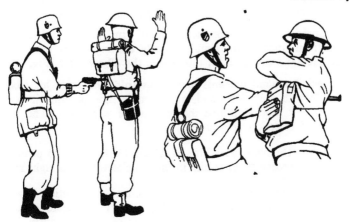

Fig. 134   Fig. 137

Fig. 138   Fig. 139

No. 30(d). Disarming a Third Party

It is not at all unlikely you might, upon coming round a corner, find one of your own men being held up, as in Fig. 140.

1. Come up on the opponent's pistol arm, seize his pistol and hand from underneath, simultaneously coming down hard with your left hand on his arm, just above the elbow joint (Fig. 141).

2. Jerk his hand upwards and backwards, and force his elbow upwards with your left hand, at the same time pivoting inwards on your left foot. Continue the pressure of your right hand in a downward direction (Fig. 142).

Note A.—This will cause him to release his hold of the pistol; if necessary, knee him in the testicles with your right knee.

Note B.—The reason why we recommend the initial upward movement of the pistol (para. 2) in preference to a downward blow is that the pistol is jerked away from the direction of your own man very quickly, and it also permits you to obtain a hold of his pistol hand, from which you can force him to release his hold of the weapon. Further, your own man can, by means of a kick to the opponent's testicles, considerably help you in disarming.

If you are inclined to think these methods are 'not cricket', remember that Hitler does not play this game.

W.E.F.

114

No. 30(d). Disarming a Third Party

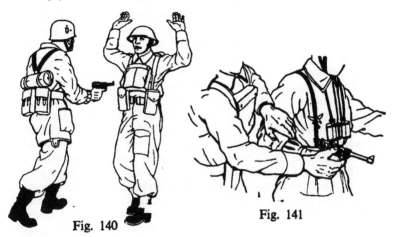

Fig. 140

Fig. 141

Fig. 142

7. THE RIFLE IN CLOSE COMBAT

by Captain P. N. Walbridge

From the work of Captain W. E. Fairbairn you will have obtained some wonderful methods of attack and defence. He will have instilled into you a real fighting spirit and a willingness for close combat. I write only of the use of the rifle and bayonet—a weapon regarded by far too many people as almost obsolete.

Many manuals have been written on the methods of firing, most of them suited only to peace-time conditions and to slow shooting. It is, therefore, the intention of these pages (in as few words and as few lessons as possible) to help to bring back the rifle to its rightful position and real use, and to enable any man to reach a standard of efficiency in handling that will surprise even the expert.

The reader will appreciate that it is necessary to explain a few points about elementary work before advancing to rapid firing.

The rifle is a far more efficient weapon than is generally recognized, and can be used with deadly effect at short ranges in the manner of a sub-machine gun, besides being the best friend at longer distances.

The use of the Short Magazine Lee Enfield (S.M.L.E.) will be assumed, but the same methods may be applied to the Pattern 14 (P. 14) or the .300 American rifle.

It must be borne in mind that the rifle must shoot 'straight'. Errors in elevation can be corrected by backsight adjustment or by aiming up or down. The rifle must never have a lateral error. Test it at a short range, either 25 or 100 yards, and if it is shooting to the left or right, the foresight must be moved. This adjustment is very easily carried out provided you remember that the foresight must be moved in the same direction as the error, i.e. if the shots are to the right, the foresight must be moved to the right; and vice versa.

116

Preparation of the Rifle

Remove the bolt, magazine, and magazine platform. With the aid of a pull-through and flannelette, dry-clean the barrel until all trace of oil is removed. With a stick of suitable size (Fig. 143) and a piece of flannelette, clean out the chamber. This is a most important part in preparation, as the presence of dirt or oil in the chamber will prevent the cartridge from being easily withdrawn, and cause unnecessary delay in re-loading. Remove all trace of oil and dirt from the body of the rifle and the inside of the magazine. Clean the outside, ensuring that the foresight and backsight are free from oil. Thoroughly dry-clean the bolt. Lightly oil the bolt and along the inside of the body of the rifle. Keep the face of the bolt dry. The rifle is now ready for use.

Note.—Care should be taken in the cleaning of 'browned' metal parts. Rub lightly to avoid the browning being removed.

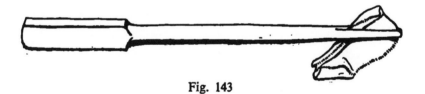

Fig. 143

R 117

Aiming

With the S.M.L.E., aim should always be taken by having the foresight in the centre of the "U" of the backsight and in line with the top of the shoulders (Fig. 144). With the aperture backsight, the foresight must be seen in the centre of the aperture (Fig. 145). With this type of sight, ignore the backsight and *concentrate on the foresight*. The eye will automatically tend to centre it in the aperture, which is generally so small that it permits of few errors. With both sights, aim will always be taken at the centre of the target.

118

Aiming

Fig. 144

Fig. 145

THE RIFLE IN CLOSE COMBAT

Aiming

To enable you to practise aiming on your own, fix your rifle in any convenient way (such as between two sandbags, or on a folded coat) and aim at a prepared target with a hole made at the point of aim (Fig. 146). You are then able to go behind the target and glance back at your sights through the small hole, thus obtaining the view from the 'bullet end'. Errors in aiming will be easy to detect. Fig. 147 shows a correct aim. Fig. 148 shows a low left aim. As a result of this error, the shot would go low and to the left. Fig. 149 shows a high right aim, and in this case the shot would go high and to the right. Constant practice in aiming is necessary to eliminate faults. Occasionally practise aiming with both eyes open, as the left eye is seldom closed in quick firing.

120

Aiming

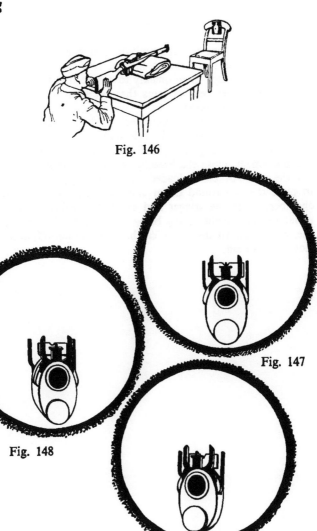

Fig. 146

Fig. 147

Fig. 148

Fig. 149

THE RIFLE IN CLOSE COMBAT

Loading

For quick, clean loading, careful preparation of the charger is essential.

First, ensure that the ammunition and charger are clean; then place the rounds in as shown in Fig. 150, 'one up', 'one down'. Remove and replace them quickly to ensure that the charger works freely. Ninety per cent of jams that occur in loading are due to bad filling of the chargers.

To load, push forward the safety catch, pull out the cut-off (if any), place the charger in the rifle and the right hand and thumb in position, as in Fig. 151. Push the rounds into the magazine in one movement, close the breech, and apply the safety catch.

If the rifle is to remain loaded for a very long period, it is advisable to push the top round down and close the breech on an empty chamber; press the trigger and apply the safety catch. This will avoid the bolt main spring being compressed. When required for use, push forward the safety catch, open the cut-off, and open and close the breech.

122

Loading

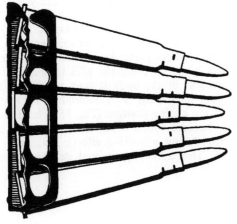

Fig. 150

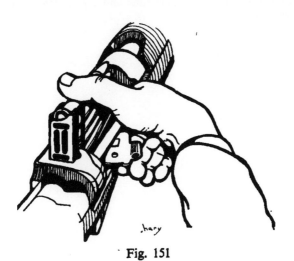

Fig. 151

THE RIFLE IN CLOSE COMBAT

Firing Positions

The basic firing position from which to teach yourself quick and clean manipulation of the rifle is the lying position. This should be adopted as shown in Fig. 152. Notice especially (1) the relative closeness of the elbows, and (2) the forward position of the rifle. Careful attention to these particular points will enable you to use the elbows as a pivot to bring the rifle to the aiming position. No other movement of the body is then necessary. The position of the legs (open or crossed) is immaterial so long as the firer is comfortable. In the aiming position (Fig. 153), hold the rifle firmly back into the shoulder with the left hand, press the cheek firmly on the butt (producing a locking effect), and hold lightly with the right hand. This allows quick and delicate handling of the trigger.

Trigger Pressing

After the rifle has been brought to the shoulder, without undue delay take the first pressure, breathing naturally until you are ready to fire. Then lightly restrain the breathing, and fire. Keep your right eye open the whole time and try to observe the strike of your shot.

124

Firing Positions

Fig. 152

Fig. 153

THE RIFLE IN CLOSE COMBAT

Quick Handling

Let me stress at once that, in rapid firing, each shot is fired in exactly the same manner as a slow shot. The number of rounds you are able to fire in one minute will depend on the length of time it takes you to open and close the breech. When re-loading, only the slightest movement of the right hand and wrist is necessary. Hold the knob of the bolt firmly between the thumb and forefinger; raise it, at the same time tilting the rifle slightly to the right; draw the bolt fully to the rear, and at once close the breech with a sharp forward and downward movement. All these actions should be continuous, and carried out as quickly as possible after the shot has been fired. The action of tilting the rifle will assist the opening of the breech and the ejection of the empty case. The head must be kept still throughout. To enable you to get correct bolt manipulation, practise in the following way. Tie the trigger to the rear (Fig. 154). Then, in the lying position, practise the correct movement of the right hand and wrist in opening and closing the breech. Place the right hand in its correct position and the finger on the trigger each time.

Note.—Tying back the trigger will make practice in manipulation easier, and will prevent unnecessary wear to the face of the cocking piece, and avoid weakening the bolt main spring. On the P.14 and .300 American rifle, it will also be necessary to remove the magazine platform and spring.

When you have mastered the wrist and hand movement so essential to good manipulation, remove the string and practise firing. Each day will see a great change in your ability to fire a large number of accurately aimed shots. Quick inaccurate shooting is of no use. Each shot must be fired by taking the first and second pressures correctly. Only in this way can you hope to become an expert in rapid firing. Try and keep to the suggested programme.

1st day—1 hour: manipulation, with trigger tied.
2nd day—1 hour: manipulation and slow shooting.
3rd day—1 hour: practise firing 15 accurate shots in one minute.
4th day—1 hour: increase to 20 rounds in one minute.
5th day—1 hour: increase to 25 rounds in one minute.
6th day—1 hour: increase to 30 rounds in one minute.

126

Quick Handling (*contd.*)

The above standards are set assuming you will not be able to obtain dummy cartridges. If you train to fire thirty aimed shots in one minute in this manner, you should be capable of firing twenty to twenty-five rounds of ball ammunition in one minute and maintain reasonable accuracy. Get a friend to assist you. He can correct your aims either by (1) glancing through the small hole of a prepared target as described in 'Aiming', or (2) by letting you aim at his eye, previously making sure that the rifle is unloaded. It will be observed that the above programme allows you only six hours to become an expert in rapid fire. This is not impossible. Provided reasonable efficiency has been attained in slow firing, you should now be ready to quicken up.

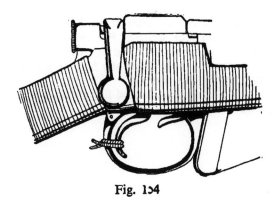

Fig. 134

127

THE RIFLE IN CLOSE COMBAT

Close-Quarter Fighting

In close fighting, such as in streets, clearing woods, etc., speed is essential. You will seldom be given the opportunity to adopt a comfortable firing position, but will have to fire either from the hip (Fig. 155) or from the shoulder whilst in the standing position. In firing from the hip, you must be very close to your target if you are to obtain a hit, whereas from the shoulder, firing is much quicker and accuracy is not so much sacrificed. When approaching an area where your target is likely to appear suddenly, e.g. stalking a mortar post or machine-gun nest, etc., carry the rifle as shown in Fig. 156. This will enable you instantly to bring the rifle to the shoulder and open fire. To increase your speed of firing to a rate previously imagined unattainable, you will have to press the trigger with the first or second finger while retaining your hold on the bolt (Fig. 157) and ignore the fact that the trigger has two pressures.

In this way, you should, after a few hours' practice, be able to fire five shots in four seconds. For close work or crossing a gap, you will find it invaluable to be able to fire at this speed with reasonable accuracy. I have frequently fired at a much faster rate when demonstrating this method.

Fifteen minutes' manipulation and firing daily will increase your handling ability and speed by 100 per cent.

128

THE RIFLE IN CLOSE COMBAT

Close-Quarter Fighting

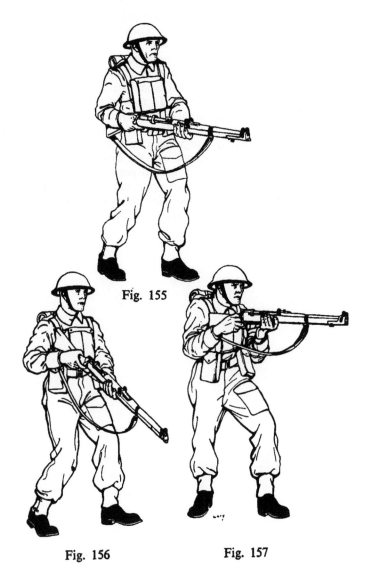

Fig. 155

Fig. 156

Fig. 157

THE RIFLE IN CLOSE COMBAT

The Bayonet

The bayonet will be used in close hand-to-hand fighting where you have no time to reload, or more probably when your magazine is empty. Otherwise you would shoot from the hip or shoulder. Except when in close formation among comrades, *keep the bayonet point low*. Carry the rifle as shown in Fig. 158. In this position there is less chance of your thrust being parried and you are able to deliver a point in any direction. To make a point, lunge forward on either foot and drive the point of the bayonet into the pit of your opponent's stomach (Fig. 159). Most of the upper part of the body will be covered by equipment. To withdraw, take a short pace to the rear as you wrench out the bayonet. You are then in a good position to deliver a second point, should this become necessary. If you are close to your opponent and unable to deliver a point, smash him on the side of his head with the butt (Fig. 160) and follow up with the bayonet or any method previously described.

130

The Bayonet

Fig. 158   Fig. 159

Fig. 160

Cleaning the Rifle after Use

Strip the rifle as already explained in the lesson on Preparation of the Rifle. Clean the barrel with dry flannelette until most of the fouling has been removed. By means of a funnel or a kettle with a thin spout pour either cold or hot water through the barrel. Boiling water should be used whenever possible (about two pints is sufficient). Dry-clean the barrel until all trace of fouling has been removed, and when the barrel is cool, it must be oiled. Clean and lightly oil the outside of the rifle. Special care and attention should be given to the rifle for a period of five days after firing, as during this period the barrel will 'sweat' and will be liable to turn rusty. The barrel must be dry-cleaned and again re-oiled each day. If water is not available, immediately firing has ceased the rifle-barrel must be well oiled, and the first opportunity taken to clean it as already described. When putting the rifle away after cleaning, it is advisable to stand it upside down. This will prevent the oil from the barrel entering the bolt, and avoid the possibility of a splash of oil from the cocking piece getting into the firer's eyes. If linseed oil is obtainable it should be lightly applied to the woodwork.

Note.—Care must be taken to ensure that water does not enter between the woodwork and the barrel.

132

SHOOTING TO LIVE

With the One-Hand Gun

Captain W. E. Fairbairn & Captain E. A. Sykes

www.naval-military-press.com

SHOOTING TO LIVE

WITH THE ONE-HAND GUN

BY

CAPTAIN WILLIAM EWART FAIRBAIRN
LATE ASSISTANT COMMISSIONER, SHANGHAI MUNICIPAL POLICE

AND

CAPTAIN ERIC ANTHONY SYKES
LATE OFFICER IN CHARGE SNIPERS UNIT, SHANGHAI
MUNICIPAL POLICE

ILLUSTRATED BY
RANDOLPH SCHWABE, SLADE PROFESSOR OF FINE ART
IN THE UNIVERSITY OF LONDON, MAINLY FROM
PHOTOGRAPHS BY MAJOR F. A. R. LEITAO, SHANGHAI

The Naval & Military Press Ltd

PREFACE

IT may be said that there is already a sufficiency of books on the one-hand gun and its uses. Some justification for an addition to the list might be considered to exist if the subject could be presented from a different angle, and that is what is now attempted.

Shooting to Live describes methods developed and practised during an eventful quarter of a century and adopted, in spite of their unorthodoxy, by one police organisation after another in the Far East and elsewhere. It is the authors' hope that their relation of these methods may contribute to the efficiency, and therefore safety, of those whose lot it is to use the one-hand gun in the course of duty.

W. E. F.
E. A. S.

1942

CONTENTS

ix

ILLUSTRATIONS

xi

CHAPTER I

PURPOSES OF THE PISTOL

By "Pistol" is meant any one-hand gun. This book is concerned with two types only: (1) pistols with revolving cylinders carrying several cartridges, and (2) self-loading magazine pistols. For convenience, the former will be referred to henceforth as "revolvers" and the latter as "automatics." The word "revolver" has long been accepted by dictionaries in almost every language. If "automatic" has not yet been quite so widely accepted, it is, we think, well on the way to being so, and we shall not be anticipating matters unduly if we continue to use it in the sense indicated.

Excluding duelling (since it is forbidden in most countries and appears to be declining in favour even in those countries in which it is permitted tacitly or otherwise), there seem to remain two primary and quite distinct uses for the pistol. The first of those uses is for target shooting (i.e. *deliberate* shooting with a view to getting all shots in the ten-ring on a stationary target). Its second use is as a weapon of combat.

1   A

This book is concerned solely with the latter aspect, but it must not be inferred on that account that we in any way decry the sport of target shooting. On the contrary, we admire the high degree of skill for which it calls and which we personally cannot emulate. We recognise the great amount of patient practice necessary to attain such skill, and we can see that in suitable circumstances the inclusion of a target pistol in the camper's equipment would not only be a source of pleasure but might be useful as well. Target shooting has its place and we have no quarrel with it.

There probably will be a quarrel, however, when we go on to say that beyond helping to teach care in the handling of fire-arms, target shooting is of no value whatever in learning the use of the pistol as a weapon of combat. The two things are as different from each other as chalk from cheese, and what has been learned from target shooting is best unlearned if proficiency is desired in the use of the pistol under actual fighting conditions.

These views are the outcome of many years of carefully recorded experience with the Police Force of a semi-Oriental city in which, by reason of local conditions that are unusual and in some respects unique, armed crime flourishes to a degree that we think must be unequalled anywhere else in the world. That experience includes not only armed encounters but the responsibility for instructing large numbers of police in those methods of pistol shooting which have been thought best calculated to bring results in the many shooting affrays in which they are called upon to take part.

There are many who will regard our views as rank heresy, or worse. We shall be content for the present, however, if in the light of the preceding paragraph we may be conceded at least a title to those views, and we shall hope to fortify the title subsequently by statistics of actual results of shooting affrays over a number of years.

· At this point it would be advisable to examine very carefully the conditions under which we may expect the pistol to be used, regarding it only as a combat weapon. Personal experience will tend perhaps to make us regard these conditions primarily from the policeman's point of view, but a great many of them must apply equally, we think, to military and other requirements in circumstances which preclude the use of a better weapon than the pistol—that is to say, when it is impracticable to use a shot-gun, rifle or sub-machine gun.

In the great majority of shooting affrays the distance at which firing takes place is not more than four yards. Very frequently it is considerably less. Often the only warning of what is about to take place is a suspicious movement of an opponent's hand. Again, your opponent is quite likely to be on the move. It may happen, too, that you have been running in order to overtake him. If you have had reason to believe that shooting is likely, you will be

keyed-up to the highest pitch and will be grasping
your pistol with almost convulsive force. If you
have to fire, your instinct will be to do so as quickly
as possible, and you will probably do it with a bent
arm, possibly even from the level of the hip. The
whole affair may take place in a bad light or none
at all, and that is precisely the moment when the
policeman, at any rate, is most likely to meet trouble,
since darkness favours the activities of the criminal.
It may be that a bullet whizzes past you and that
you will experience the momentary stupefaction
which is due to the shock of the explosion at very
short range of the shot just fired by your opponent—
a very different feeling, we can assure you, from
that experienced when you are standing behind or
alongside a pistol that is being fired. Finally, you
may find that you have to shoot from some
awkward position, not necessarily even while on
your feet.

There is no exaggeration in this analysis of fighting
conditions. Here we have a set of circumstances
which in every respect are absolutely different
from those encountered in target shooting. Do
they not call for absolutely different methods of
training ?

To answer this question, we must consider the
essential points which emerge from our analysis.
They appear to be three in number, and we should
set them out in the following order :—

1. Extreme speed, both in drawing and firing.

2. Instinctive, as opposed to deliberate aim.
3. Practice under circumstances which approximate as nearly as possible to actual fighting conditions.

In commenting on the first essential, let us say that the necessity for speed is vital and can never be sufficiently emphasised. The average shooting affray is a matter of split seconds. . If you take much longer than a third of a second to fire your first shot, you will not be the one to tell the newspapers about it. It is literally a matter of the quick and the dead. Take your choice.

Instinctive aiming, the second essential, is an entirely logical consequence of the extreme speed to which we attach so much importance. That is so for the simple reason that there is no time for any of the customary aids to accuracy. If reliance on those aids has become habitual, so much the worse for you if you are shooting to live. There is no time, for instance, to put your self into some special stance or to align the sights of the pistol, and any attempt to do so places you at the mercy of a quicker opponent. In any case, the sights would be of little use if the light were bad, and none at all if it were dark, as might easily happen. Would it not be wiser, therefore, to face facts squarely and set to work to find out how best to develop instinctive aiming to the point of getting results under combat conditions ?

It *can* be done and it is not so very difficult.

Everyone is familiar with the fact that he can

point his forefinger accurately at an object at which he happens to be looking. It is just as easy, moreover, to do so without raising the hand so high as the level of the eyes. That he can do so may be co-ordination of eye and hand or just plain instinct, call it what you will.

Please try this little experiment while sitting at your desk. Imagine that you are holding a pistol in your right hand. Sitting squarely and keeping both eyes open, raise your hand from the level of the desk, but not so high as the level of your eyes, and with a straight arm point your extended forefinger at a mark directly in front of you on the opposite wall. Observe carefully now what has taken place. Your forefinger, as intended, will be pointing to the mark which you are facing squarely, and the back of your hand will be vertical, as it would be if it actually held a pistol. You will observe also that you have brought your arm across you until your hand is approximately in alignment with the vertical centre-line of your body and that, under the directing impulse of the master-eye, your hand will be bent from the wrist towards the right.

The elements of that little experiment form the basis of the training system which is elaborated in succeeding chapters. We cannot claim that the system produces nail-driving marksmanship, but that is not what we look for. We want the ability to hit with extreme speed man-sized targets at very short ranges under the difficult circumstances which

have been outlined already. Nail-driving marksmanship will not cope with such conditions.

In this training system nothing is permitted to
interfere with the development of speed. For that
reason we have steadily set our faces against competitions or rewards of any kind. The instant that
competitions, with the accompanying medals, badges,
etc., are introduced, men will try to shoot deliberately,
whether consciously or not, and we find our object
is being defeated.

For long shots, and they are necessary occasionally,
different methods must be employed ; but even for
long shots speed must still be regarded as essential,
and any tendency to deliberate shooting should be
discouraged by such means as the exposure of the
targets for very brief periods only.

The theories involved in the square stance, the
position of the pistol in line with the vertical centre
of the body, and the hand bent over to the right
have proved in practice to be of immense assistance
in the development of the desired standard of
accuracy when shooting at speed. Though still very
willing to learn, the authors doubt now whether any
other methods would answer the particular purposes
in view. In general, the training system given in this
book may fairly be said to have achieved its object,
but perhaps it is time now for the promised statistics
to play their part in the discussion.

The records of the particular police force of the
semi-Oriental city referred to earlier show that the

force, consistently trained in the methods of this book, has to its credit in twelve and a half years no less than 666 armed encounters with criminals. The following table, referring only to encounters in which *pistols* were used by the police, gives the results :—

	Police.	Criminals.
Killed	42	260
Wounded . . .	100	193

CHAPTER II

CHOOSING A PISTOL

WE open this chapter with a warning.

Without an adequate knowledge of its use, there can be few things so purposeless and dangerous as a pistol. Adequate knowledge comes only from competent instruction. If you have never received such instruction and are not prepared to do so, do not buy a pistol, or if you own one already, surrender it to the police. That will help to lighten the burden of their cares.

We shall assume, however, that our readers are sufficiently interested to recognise that the possession of a pistol and efficiency in its use should go hand-in-hand. For them, the starting point in choosing a pistol should be to buy the best they can afford for the particular purpose in view. If a pistol is needed at all it may be needed very badly indeed, and poor quality contributes nothing to either safety or peace of mind.

The type of pistol to be chosen depends on the use to which it is to be put. A pistol that meets the needs of the detective or plain-clothes man, for instance, is not necessarily suitable for individual self-defence or for the uniformed service man.

9

Let us consider first the case of the detective or plain-clothes man. Here the weapon must be carried concealed and the wearer must be prepared for the quickest of quick draws and an instantaneous first shot, most probably at very close quarters. For that purpose, our own choice would be a cut-down revolver of heavy calibre. Fig. 22 (b) on p. 89 will show you better than any description what we mean.

The weapon shown in the illustration started life as a ·45 Colt New Service double-action revolver with a 5-inch barrel. The hammer spur has been cut off, the barrel length reduced to 2 inches, the front part of the trigger-guard has been removed, and grooves have been cut on the left side of the butt for the middle, third and little fingers.

Now for the reasons for this drastic treatment. The big New Service revolver was chosen, primarily, because the butt is of adequate size for the average man's hand to grasp in a hurry without any fumbling. Secondly, 'it is one of the most powerful weapons possible to obtain.

The removal of the hammer spur and the smoothing over of what remains prevent the weapon from catching in the clothing when drawn in a violent hurry. As the hammer cannot be cocked by the thumb, the weapon has to be fired by a continuous pull on the trigger. With a sufficiency of practice, very fast shooting is rendered possible by this method.

The shortening of the barrel is for speed in drawing.

Obviously, it takes less time for 2 inches of barrel to emerge from the holster than 5 inches. Contrary to what might be expected, there is no loss of accuracy, at any rate at the ranges at which the weapon is customarily used.

The front part of the trigger-guard is removed in order to eliminate yet another possible cause of fumbling when speed is the order of the day. The index-finger, no matter of what length or thickness, wraps itself in the proper position round the trigger without any impediment whatever. The grooves on the butt are there to ensure that the fingers grip the weapon in exactly the same way every time.

Lest it be thought that we are the originators of this fearsome but eminently practical weapon, let us say at once that we are not. We owe the idea to a book by Mr J. H. Fitzgerald of the Colt's Patent Fire Arms Manufacturing Company, and we gladly acknowledge our indebtedness.

For a weapon to be carried openly by uniformed police and officers and men of the fighting services, we unhesitatingly avow our preference for the automatic pistol. We shall treat it as a matter of personal preference and shall not abuse the supporters of the revolver for having other views. They are quite welcome to those views and we trust we may be allowed to retain ours. We shall do so, in any case, until we have good reason to alter them.

We are familiar with the criticisms so often made

of the automatic pistol. It is said that it is un-
reliable, will often jamb without provocation and
certainly will do so if mud, sand or water gets into
the mechanism, and above all, it is not safe.

There have been and possibly still are automatics
like that, but one is not obliged to use them.

We think it is only in Great Britain that the
reliability of the automatic is still questioned. In
the United States, while many people adhere to
their preference for the revolver, we have never
heard any doubts expressed in the matter, and it is
worthy of note that both there and in Germany the
automatic has long been in use as a standard weapon
of the fighting services.

There are in existence types of automatic pistols
which are perfectly reliable. We base this statement
on our actual experience of them over a period of
twenty years. That experience includes an intimate
knowledge of a service consisting of over six thousand
men, most of them armed with automatics and having
a surprising record of shooting affrays to their credit.
If their weapons had been in any way unsatisfactory,
twenty years should have sufficed to reveal the
defects. But in all that time nothing has occurred,
either in the training of the service referred to or
in the affrays in which the service has taken part,
to cast the slightest doubt on the reliability of the
automatic, nor has there been a single instance of
injury or death due to accident.

Apart from the question of reliability, we have

found that in comparison with the revolver, the automatic offers the following advantages :—

It is easier and quicker to recharge.
It can be fired at far greater speed.
It is easier to shoot with.

The first point will be readily conceded but the other two may meet with opposition.

It is probably the case that, *for the first shot*, the cut-down revolver which has been described is fractionally quicker, but for subsequent shots the rate of fire of the automatic is much higher. A great deal of the recoil is absorbed in the operation of the mechanism and the trigger pull is much shorter and easier than that of the revolver. We refer, of course, to the use of the double-action revolver. If the hammer were to be cocked for each shot, the rate of fire would be funereal by comparison. A skilled shot can do excellent work with the automatic even while making it sound like a machine-gun.

It seems to follow logically that the absorption of so much of the recoil, combined with the shorter trigger-pull, furnish theoretical proof of our contention that the automatic is easier to shoot with. Practical proof of our contention is found in the training results. Critical observation has demonstrated that a beginner can be trained in the use of the automatic in a third of the time and with the expenditure of less than half the ammunition required for the revolver. Furthermore, once trained in the use of the automatic, men appear definitely to need less subsequent practice to maintain the standard of shooting which has been attained in the course of training.

We shall endeavour to throw more light on this subject in the chapters on training methods, and by way of preface to those chapters we must introduce and describe one more point in connection with the automatic, and this time we shall certainly be accused of heresy.

We have an inveterate dislike of the profusion of safety devices with which all automatic pistols are regularly equipped. We believe them to be the cause of more accidents than anything else. There are too many instances on record of men being shot by accident either because the safety-catch was in the firing position when it ought not to have been or because it was in the safe position when that was the last thing to be desired. It is better, we think, to make the pistol permanently " unsafe " and then to devise such methods of handling it that there will be no accidents. One of the essentials of the instruction courses which follow is that the pistols used shall have their side safety-catches permanently pinned down in the firing or " unsafe " position. How this matter is taken care of is described at length in Chapter III. Suffice it to say here that our unorthodox methods have been subjected to the acid test of many years of particularly exacting conditions and have not been found wanting.

Having dealt with weapons suited to the detective or plain-clothes man and the uniformed services respectively, there remains the case of the private individual who wishes to carry a gun. In most countries it is illegal to do so and we have no wish to encourage law-breaking. Nevertheless, there are still some countries and circumstances in which it may be necessary and advisable for the private individual to go armed.

Our recommendation to the private individual who can justifiably claim the right to carry a pistol is to buy an automatic and carry it in a shoulder holster such as is described in a succeeding chapter. We are not greatly in favour of small weapons. No small weapon can possess the strength and reliability of a large one. The material and work- manship may be as good but the margins of tolerance are too small to provide the absolute reliability which is so desirable. We recommend the automatic of good size and calibre partly because we are assured of its reliability and partly because of its shape. It does not " bulge " like the revolver and therefore is less noticeable (we are presuming that the private individual will carry his pistol concealed). Do not forget the obligation which you are under to make yourself thoroughly safe and efficient with the weapon of your choice.

We are often asked what is the best weapon to

have in the house for purely protective purposes. Most of the people who make this enquiry know little of fire-arms and say so quite frankly. It usually happens, too, that they have neither the intention nor the opportunity to make themselves efficient with any kind of one-hand gun. If they are of this type, we are convinced that they would be better off with a good watch-dog, or even a police-whistle. There are, however, many men whose knowledge of fire-arms is limited to the shot-gun, in the use of which they are both proficient and reliable. If this type of man insists on possessing some kind of weapon " to keep in the house " we would recommend him to acquire a " sawn-off " shot gun, with external hammers of the re-bounding type and barrels of about 18 inches in length. The ease with which it can be manipulated, the accuracy with which it can be aimed, either from the shoulder or the hip, and the spread of the shot charge combine to make it a much safer and more efficient weapon than any kind of one-hand gun in the use of which he is not proficient.

CHAPTER III

TRAINING : PRELIMINARY COURSE
FOR RECRUITS

THE course of instruction which follows relates primarily to the Colt automatic. The elimination by us of any use of the side safety catch necessitates the introduction of special features, and the system consequently differs considerably from that in use by the American forces, who are armed with this particular weapon.

It might be thought that it would have been better to have devised separate courses of instruction for revolver and automatic respectively, but in actual fact that would have entailed going over the same ground twice. The methods of instruction given in this chapter apply equally to any pistol, revolver or automatic, if the reader will regard them from two aspects, making a careful distinction between the two. The first of those aspects is merely that of the mechanics of the Colt automatic and, with suitable modifications due to differences of design, applies equally to any other automatic. The second relates solely to *the method of shooting* and that, without any modification whatever, applies equally to any form of one-hand gun from the flint-lock onwards. The revolver user who wishes to make use of this

17   B

301

chapter has only to disregard, therefore, anything
which obviously relates to the mechanics of the Colt
automatic. He will have uo difficulty in doing
that.

The mechanics of the revolver are so simple and
so familiar by now to everyone that it is unnecessary,
we think, to include any description of them. We
would emphasise, however, our preferences for the
very firm grip, with the fully extended thumb, the
exclusive use of the double-action, firing in bursts,
for all short range shooting and for the single-action
at longer ranges, in circumstances which afford the
necessary time for its use. Speed with the double-
action is attainable more easily than is generally
thought, but only by training the trigger-finger by
means of continual snapping practice.

The instructor should commence by taking up a
pistol and " proving " it. This is done by removing
the magazine, working the slide back and forth
several times, and finally pulling the trigger. The
insertion of a magazine and the loading and unloading of the pistol should then be demonstrated
and explained. Each operation is described in detail
and illustrated in the following pages. This is the
moment for the instructor to point out and give the
reason for the pinning-down, out of action, of the
safety-catch on the left-hand side of the pistol. He
should make it perfectly clear that the pistol, when
carried on service, should have a charged magazine
inserted but that *it should never be carried with a*

round in the breech. He should show that when it is desired to fire all that has to be done is to load in the manner described in para. 2 (*c*). He should then proceed to demonstrate the extreme speed with which it is possible to draw, load and fire by this method, which compares more than favourably with the alternative of drawing, pulling down the safety-catch and firing a round already in the breech. It should be shown, too, that the first method (with the breech empty) eliminates the fumbling and uncertainty inherent in the use of the safety-catch.

With this preface, all is now ready for the course to commence.

1. ONE HOUR'S " DRY " PRACTICE

(*a*) On taking the pistol in the hand, we recommend, as an aid to accurate pointing, that the thumb be fully extended and pointing forward in the same plane as the pistol barrel (Fig. 1).

FIG. 1.—The Correct Grip.

(*b*) Stand square with the target, gripping the pistol now as if it weighed twenty or thirty pounds, pistol arm straight, rigid and across the body (Fig. 2). Bend the hand slightly to the right, to bring the pistol exactly in line with the vertical centre-line of the body (Fig. 3).

(c) Raise the pistol (pistol arm still rigidly straight and pivoting from the shoulder), keeping it exactly in line with the vertical centre-line of the body until it covers the aiming mark on the target (Fig. 4). Both eyes are to be kept open and the recruit simply sees the target surrounding his pistol, making no attempt to look at or line up the sights, or to let the master-eye control the aim.

(d) Immediately the aiming mark is covered, pull the trigger and lower the pistol to the position shown in Fig. 3 (the " ready " position).

Notes

Paragraphs (b) and (c) in conjunction with Fig. 4 reveal a deliberate attempt to eliminate *conscious* control by the master-eye. Instead, the aim is controlled by the combination of the square stance and the manner of holding the pistol, *i.e.* in the centre of the body, with the hand bent over to the right, elements which were employed unconsciously in the experiment on page 6. The mastery of this combination is all that is required for effective aiming at short range; a point which will emerge more clearly,

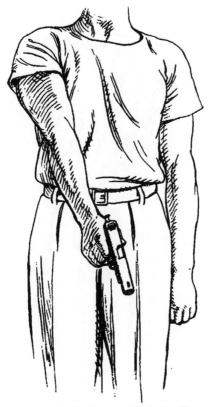

FIG. 2.—Preliminary to Ready Position.

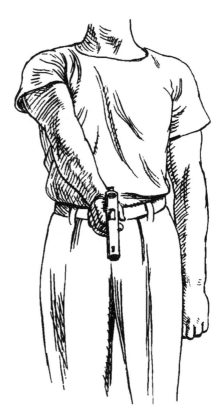

FIG. 3.—Ready Position.

FIG. 4.—Firing, Arm Fully Extended.

perhaps, in the next chapter in discussing shooting with the pistol held well below the line of sight.

Trembling due to the firm grip will *not* cause a wild shot.

The trigger must be released, not by violent pressure of the forefinger alone but by increasing pressure of the whole hand. The combination of the very firm grip and the pressure of the fully-extended thumb are of great assistance in the proper release of the trigger.

The firm grip helps also in two other ways. It ensures smoother action in raising the pistol from the " ready " (Fig. 3) to the firing position (Fig. 4) and it counteracts the tendency to raise the pistol higher than the point of aim.

2. ONE HOUR'S PRACTICE IN SAFETY PRECAUTIONS LOADING AND UNLOADING

(a) Demonstrate the proper ways of charging and uncharging magazines. To charge, press cartridges downwards against the forward end of either the magazine platform or the topmost cartridge, as the case may be, sliding the cartridge rearwards *under* the inwardly curving lips of the magazine. If cartridges are forced vertically downwards past these lips, the magazine cannot escape deformation. To uncharge, hold the magazine in the right hand and eject the cartridges one by one by pressure of the right thumb on their bases. The cartridges should be caught in the left hand and on no account should they be allowed to drop on the ground.

(b) Hold the pistol as in Fig. 5. Insert the charged magazine. To make sure that it is locked in place, push up, with the left thumb, on the base plate of the magazine. Relax the pressure, and it will be obvious by touch whether the magazine is locked.

(c) *To load the pistol* turn it over, as in Fig. 6, grasping the slide firmly with the thumb and forefinger of the left hand. Push forward with the right hand until the slide is felt to be open to its fullest extent (Fig. 7). Immediately that point is reached, release the hold with the left hand. The slide flies forward, taking with it and forcing into the breech the topmost cartridge of the magazine, the pistol pointing to the ground meanwhile (Fig. 8). Turn the hand to the " ready " position (Fig. 3), the pistol being now cocked and ready for action.

(d) *To remove the magazine,* hold the pistol as in Fig. 9 and release the magazine by pressing the magazine catch with the left thumb. The magazine must be caught in the palm of the left hand and should then be restored to pouch or pocket, as the case may be, or handed to the instructor if the latter so directs. The pistol meanwhile *must* be kept pointing to the ground, since it is still cocked

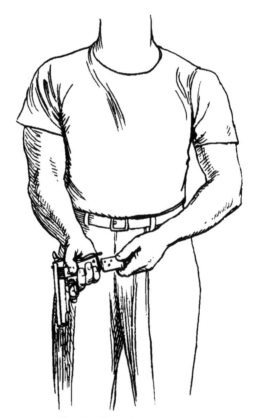

FIG. 5.—Inserting Magazine.

FIG. 6.—First Position of Loading.

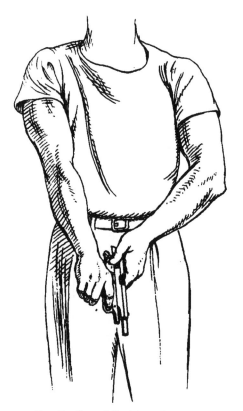

FIG. 7.—Second Position of Loading.

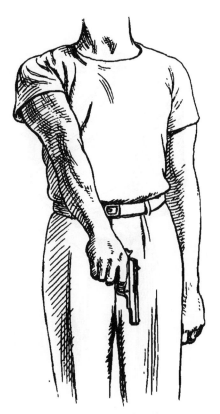

FIG. 8.—Third Position of Loading.

Fɪɢ. 9.—Removing Magazine.

and has a live round in the breech. The magazine being disposed of, turn the pistol with the wrist into the position of Fig. 10, and eject the live round by pulling back the slide with the finger and thumb of the left hand (with a little practice the live round can be saved from damage by catching it in the left hand as it is ejected). Work the slide back and forth a few times, as an added measure of safety, and pull the trigger, the pistol pointing all the while to the ground.

(e) *Dismounting the pistol for cleaning.* A knowledge of how to dismount the pistol, as far as is necessary for cleaning and of assembling it subsequently, is essential, and this is a convenient stage in the proceedings at which to teach it. It provides also a good opportunity to impress on the recruit the necessity for *always* treating a pistol as loaded until proved otherwise. Before he is allowed to place his pistol on the bench on which it is to be dismounted, the weapon is to be " proved " by removing the magazine, working the slide back and forth several times and pulling the trigger, the pistol being held as shown in Figs. 9 and 10.

Note

" Dummy " ammunition should be used throughout this practice.

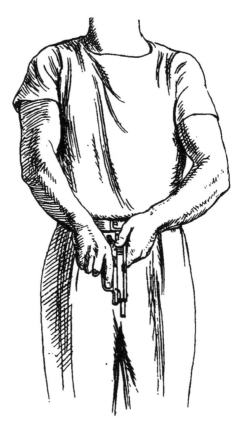

FIG. 10.—Working the Slide.

3. INITIAL FIRING PRACTICE

(a) The target should be white, not less than 8 feet square and should have in the middle a life-size outline of a man, full view (Fig. 11). The recruit is to stand not more than 2 yards away from this target. The size of the target and the distance at which the recruit is to fire need explanation. The combination of these two factors renders it almost impossible for even the most awkward beginner to score a clean miss. With every shot registered, the instructor sees plainly what fault has been committed and is at once able to correct it. The recruit experiences pleasurable surprise that even he is able to hit the target, and that is a much better beginning to his training than the mortification of missing a small target altogether, without knowing in the least where his shot has gone. In short, by the use of these methods the instructor has far less trouble, the recruit gains confidence, and whoever has to pay for it is saved a whole lot of ammunition.

(b) Target and distance as above, the recruit is given six cartridges. After charging his magazine, inserting it in the pistol and putting one round in the breech, all as described in para. 2 (sections (a), (b) and (c)), the recruit stands at the "ready" position.

C

317

He should then be told to keep both eyes open,
concentrate his gaze on the centre of the figure

FIG. 11.—Recruits' Target.

target, bring the pistol up quickly and, as described
in para. 1 (sections (c) and (d)), fire immediately it
covers that point on the target on which his eyes
are focussed, returning subsequently to the " ready "

position without delay. Repeat until the recruit has fired four out of his six shots. The last two shots should be fired as a " burst," *i.e.* in succession and as rapidly as the recruit can manage. He should remain afterwards in the firing position until told by the instructor to lower his arm to the " ready."

Notes

This practice should not be hurried. The first four shots, as each is fired, should be pointed out on the target, the recruit standing at the " ready " while the instructor explains the causes of any which are badly placed. The causes are normally simple enough—hand insufficiently bent to the right, " dipping " the hand downwards, or not gripping firmly enough to prevent the trigger from being " yanked off." If the two rapid-fire shots are widely apart it is conclusive evidence of a loose grip.

The instructor should not be content unless his explanations produce an immediate improvement in the recruit's shooting. These recruits who are not firing should be " fallen in " eight to ten yards in rear of the firing point. From there they can watch the shooting and its results. They should be permitted to talk but not loudly enough to prevent the man who is shooting from hearing what the instructor is saying.

4. SECOND FIRING PRACTICE

(a) Same target and distance.

(b) Hand the recruit a magazine containing one "dummy" and five live rounds. The "dummy" is to be included without the recruit's knowledge and its position in the magazine should be different for each man who takes his turn at the firing point. Men waiting to fire should not be allowed to watch the practice described below.

(c) The recruit is to fire as previously but this time in three "bursts" of two shots each. Errors of aiming should be corrected between "bursts."

(d) When the "dummy" round is arrived at, treat it as a misfire. Have the recruit eject it *immediately* and carry on firing his next burst *without any delay.*

(e) At the conclusion of this practice, explain to the recruit that it is useless, wasteful of time and extremely dangerous to look down the muzzle of his pistol when he has a misfire. Some of them *will* do it. Explain also that a bad jamb can be caused by covering the ejector cut with the left hand when retracting the slide in order to eject a cartridge. This is a fault which is frequently found and should be corrected as soon as possible in the training course. See Fig. 10, p. 32, for how it ought to be done.

5. THIRD FIRING PRACTICE

Repetition of practice given under para. 4 but this time at 4 yards. If the recruit's shooting has been satisfactory so far, he may be allowed to fire this practice in two " bursts " of three rounds each.

Notes

The instructor will be well advised to give his pupils short " rest " periods at fairly frequent intervals and to utilise such intervals to impress upon them the conditions under which they may be called upon to use their pistols eventually. Reference to Chapter I (pp. 3-4) will indicate the general line to take, the points requiring special emphasis being the short range at which most encounters take place, the likelihood of unfavourable light and terrain, the advisability of firing in " bursts " and the paramount importance of speed. If prominence is given to points of that nature, recruits will be assisted to comprehend more readily the reasons underlying the instruction they are receiving. It will be plain to them, for instance, that they must not look at their sights because they will never have time to do so, that they must grip their pistols hard because that is what they will do infallibly in the stress of actual combat, and that, when obliged to shoot, they will have to do so with all the aggressiveness of which they are capable.

CHAPTER IV

TRAINING : ADVANCED METHODS

CHAPTER III has taken care of all the stages of the recruit's preliminary training, but before he is turned loose on the world as qualified to use a pistol there is one more thing for him to learn. This is shooting from what, for want of a better term, we call the " three-quarter hip " position illustrated in Fig. 12.

This position is designed to meet a condition referred to in the first chapter when describing the circumstances under which shooting affrays are likely to take place. We indicate there that in moments of stress and haste men are apt to fire with a bent arm.

Examination of the illustration shows exactly this position. Closer examination shows also that the firer is facing his adversary squarely, has one foot forward (it does not matter which), and that he is crouching slightly.

From this position, pistol hand in the vertical centre-line of the body and hand bent to the right. as before, the recruit fires a burst of two or three shots, but *quickly*, at a distance of 3 yards. If he succeeds in making nothing worse than a 6-inch group, he should repeat the practice at 4 yards.

The instructor should make a special point of

38

explaining all the elements of this practice. The bent arm position is used because that would be instinctive at close quarters in a hurry. The square stance, with one foot forward, is precisely the attitude in which the recruit is most likely to be if he had to fire

Fig. 12.—" Three-quarter Hip " Position.

suddenly while he was on the move. The " crouch," besides being instinctive when expecting to be fired at, merits a little further explanation.

Its introduction into this training system originates from an incident which took place in 1927. A raiding party of fifteen men, operating before daybreak, had to force an entrance to a house occupied by a gang of criminals. The only approach to the house was through a particularly narrow alley, and it was expected momentarily that the criminals would open fire. On returning down the alley in daylight after the raid was over, the men encountered, much to their surprise, a series of stout wires stretched at intervals across the alley at about face height. The entire party had to duck to get under the wires, but no one had any recollection of either stooping under or running into them when approaching the house in the darkness. Enquiries were made at once, only to reveal that the wires had been there over a week and that they were used for the wholly innocent purpose of hanging up newly dyed skeins of wool to dry. The enquiries did not, therefore, confirm the suspicions that had been aroused, but they did serve to demonstrate conclusively and usefully that every single man of the raiding party, when momentarily expecting to be fired at, must have crouched considerably in the first swift traverse of the alley. Since that time, men trained in the methods of this book have not only been permitted to crouch but have been encouraged to do so.

The qualification we require before the recruit's course can be successfully passed is 50 per cent. of hits anywhere on the man-sized targets employed. Time has shown this to be adequate for the purpose in view.

We indicate elsewhere our aversion to trophies,

badges, etc. No "expert's" or "marksman's" badges are issued to men who pass our recruit or other courses, no matter how much in excess of 50 per cent. their scores may have been. If a man makes "possibles" throughout, his only reward is the resultant confidence in himself and the satisfaction of knowing that if he has to "shoot it out" with a pistol he will be a better man than his opponent.

Similarly, we have a dislike of "team shoots." We feel that the ammunition would be much more usefully employed in giving additional practice under instruction.

From now on, in proceeding to more advanced training, the use of stationary targets should be abandoned in favour of surprise targets of all kinds and in frequently varied positions. Such targets would include charging, retreating, bobbing, and traversing figures of man-size. Traversing targets can be either at right or oblique angles. Musketry officers will have no difficulty in devising for themselves endless variations on this theme, and current incidents, more especially in the nature of actual happenings to men of their particular service, often provide valuable suggestions.

We will give one example of a practice which has been frequently carried out with good results. It is designed not only as a test of skill with the pistol under difficult conditions, but also a test of bodily fitness and agility, qualities which to the policeman

at any rate are every bit as necessary in the circumstances which are so often encountered in shooting
affrays.

In this practice, which we have called the " Pursuit," the shooter is started off at the run, outside
the range, on an obstacle course consisting of jumping a ditch, running across a plank over water,
crawling through a suspended barrel, climbing a
rope, a ladder, and over a wall, finishing up with a
100 yards dash ending at 4 yards from the targets.
Without warning or waiting, two surprise targets are
pulled, one after the other, and at each he fires a
" burst " of three shots. The targets are exposed for
no longer than it takes to fire three shots at the
highest possible speed.

Yet another practice, a "mystery shoot," is
described in the chapter entitled " A Practical Pistol
Range."

In all practices at surprise targets, opportunity
must be found for the performance of two very
essential operations. In order of importance, these
are :—

1. Making safe after firing only a portion of the
   contents of the magazine.
2. Inserting a second magazine after totally
   expending the contents of the first and
   continuing to fire without delay.

In the first instance, after firing one or two shots
from a fully charged magazine, the instructor should

give the order to cease fire. The shooter should then come to the "ready," remove the magazine, eject the live round from the breech, work the slide back and forth several times and finally pull the trigger, all as described on pp. 25 and 31 (Figs. 9 and 10).

In the second instance, immediately the last shot has been fired, the shooter comes to the "ready," removes the empty magazine, inserts a fresh one and reloads, either by pressing down the slide release stop with the thumb of the left hand or by slightly retracting and then releasing the slide. The slide flies forward, taking a cartridge into the breech, and the shooter resumes the "ready" position by bending his hand to the right and awaits the appearance of the next target.

Practice at surprise targets can be carried out first with the arm fully extended and later from the "three-quarter" hip position. There are still two other methods of close-quarter shooting to be described, but before doing so this will be perhaps an opportune moment to call the attention of instructors to several points which will be of assistance in getting results.

When firing at surprise targets, never let men anticipate matters by standing in the firing position. They must be standing at the "ready" before the first target appears. If the succeeding targets are pulled with no perceptible interval, the men may continue to stand in the firing position. Otherwise they should come down to the "ready" again after each shot or " burst " while awaiting the appearance of the next target.

Attention has been drawn already to the necessity for the square stance. When turning from one target to another the square stance must be preserved by turning the body. This can be effected by scraping the feet round or even jumping round if the extent of the turn warrants it. It does not matter how it is done so long as the firer faces each fresh target squarely and is thus enabled to retain the pistol in its original position, *i.e.* in alignment with the vertical centre-line of the body.

In firing at a crossing target (" running man "), it will soon be observed that 90 per cent. of all the misses are traceable to firing ahead of it or, as a man accustomed to the shot-gun would say, to " leading it." This holds good even when the range is only 4 yards and the target only travels at about 3 miles an hour. This is not the place for a controversy over the rival merits of " leading " a moving target or " swinging " with it. Our purpose is merely to assist instructors in correcting their pupils' mistakes, and we content ourselves with pointing out that, distance and speed of target being as stated, a bullet travelling at eight hundred feet a second would strike only about three-quarters of an inch behind the point of aim.

We now turn to the two other methods of close-quarters shooting previously referred to. These are, respectively :—

The " half-hip " (Fig. 13).

The " quarter " or " close-hip " (Fig. 14).

Apart from shortening the arm by bringing the elbow to the side, the " half-hip " is no different from the " three-quarter," and should be practised at not more than 3 yards. Above that distance it would be more natural to shoot from the " three-quarter " position.

The " quarter " or " close-hip " position is for purely defensive purposes and would be used only when the requirements are a very quick draw, followed by an equally quick shot at extremely close quarters, such as would be the case if a dangerous adversary were threatening to strike or grapple with you. Practise this at 1 yard. This is the only position in which the hand is not in the centre of the body.

Before we close the subject of shooting at short ranges, we would ask the reader to keep in mind that if he gets his shot off first, no matter whether it is a hit or a miss by a narrow margin, he will have an advantage of sometimes as much as two seconds over his opponent. The opponent will want time to recover his wits, and his shooting will not be as accurate as it might be.

It will be appropriate now to turn our attention to training ourselves for shooting at longer ranges, for in spite of having said that the great majority of shooting affrays take place within a distance of 4 yards, the need does arise occasionally for a long shot.

Fig. 13.—" Half-Hip " Position.

FIG. 14.—" Quarter " or " Close-Hip " Position.

For a long shot in the standing position, we think the two-handed methods shown in Figs. 15 and 15ᴀ

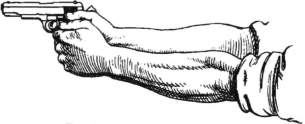

FIG. 15.—Two-Handed, Standing.

are best calculated to produce results. The right arm is rigid and is supported by the left. Practise at any reasonable distance from 10 yards upwards.

FIG. 15ᴀ.—Two-Handed, Standing.

Fig. 15 shows the proper method to employ if you have to shoot from the prone position (Fig. 16). Incidentally, do not be afraid to adopt this position immediately if circumstances demand it, as might be the case if you had to deal with several adversaries simultaneously. Practise yourself in getting quickly into the prone position, remembering that it gives you the dual advantage of being able to do your shooting from a steady position at a mark which is against the sky-line, as it were, while you yourself

FIG. 16.—Two-Handed, Prone.

offer a less conspicuous target for your opponents than if you were standing up.

Kind providence has endowed us all with a lively sense of self-preservation and some of us with a sense of strategy as well. If our readers are in the latter class we need not remind them of the advantages of taking cover whenever possible. It is possible, however, that some of you have not thought of a telephone pole or electric light standard in that connection. Fig. 17 will show you a side view of how to do it most conveniently, and Fig. 18 shows how an adversary will view the matter. Note in the former illustration the position of the feet, knees and left forearm. The left knee and forearm are pressed against the pole, left hand is grasping the right wrist, thumb of

D

FIG. 17.—Side View.

the right hand resting against the pole. Fig. 18 also demonstrates the almost perfect cover provided.

If the long shot gives you enough time to be deliberate, so much the better, because the two-handed position and that of Fig. 17 permit of almost rifle-like accuracy. But do not take it for granted that you will have time to be deliberate. It is wiser to assume that you will not, and it will be to your advantage, therefore, to practise all three of the two-handed methods at the same surprise targets as are used for short-range work.

We have condemned the use of sights for all forms of short-range shooting, but for long shots, such as we have been describing, sights offer a distinct advantage. We have little faith, however, in those usually furnished. Good as some of them are for use against a white target and a black bull's eye, there are very few that can

FIG. 18.—Front View.

be picked up instantly against a dark background, and this difficulty is increased to the point of being insuperable if the light is bad. To overcome this, the authors' personal pistols are fitted with foresights of silver, of exactly the shape of the ordinary shot-gun bead and about the same size. If kept bright, these sights collect any light there is from any angle and can be seen instantly in all circumstances except pitch-darkness. They stand up very well to rough work and can be easily replaced if damaged. We see no reason against the adoption of this type for service issue if some suitable white-metal alloy were used instead of silver. Though not claimed as suitable for target work, these sights answer their purpose admirably where speed is the prime consideration.

The best rear-sight for use in conjunction with the silver bead is a wide and shallow " V." The rear-sight should be affixed with a distinct slope to the rear, and once the gun is sighted-in, should be kept in place with a small set-screw. It will not shoot loose then and will be less liable to displacement or loss by accident or ill-usage.

CHAPTER V

PISTOL AND CARTRIDGE

Mechanical defects. Cartridge defects. Care of ammunition. Supplies, current requirements and reserve stocks of ammunition.

THIS chapter relates only to the products of manufacturing concerns of good standing and with well-deserved reputations which they are not likely to hazard. There are plenty of the other kind of manufacturer but with them we have nothing to do beyond remarking that it is due to their existence that many criminals have been brought to justice and the lives of many policemen have been saved.

The modern one-hand gun and its ammunition have been brought to such a state of perfection that, assuming reasonable care in their use, malfunctions of the former and defects in the latter are of rare occurrence.

The great majority of malfunctions of the modern pistol are due, not to faults in design or manufacture, but to ignorance, neglect or rough handling, accidental or otherwise, on the part of the user.

Generally speaking, the private individual owning a good pistol is too much of a " gun-crank " to be guilty of wilful neglect or rough handling and to him it is superfluous to recommend that, in case of accident, his pistol should be promptly overhauled by a competent armourer.

In the Services, however, matters are rather different. Of necessity, very often, weapons are subjected to rough treatment, and it may happen that the most careful man may drop his pistol by accident. If it is made clear to the men that such accidents are not regarded as punishable offences, they will be far more apt to report them quickly and so ensure that their weapons, on which their lives may depend, are put as soon as possible into serviceable condition once more. We are not legislating for the man who commits wilful damage or the genius in whose hands everything comes to pieces quite naturally. Men of that kind do not, or should not, go very far without being recognised for what they are, and there are suitable and well-established methods of dealing with them.

As far as our experience goes, a comparison between the automatic and the double-action revolver, in respect of their liability to damage, results in favour of the former.

Accident and ill-usage can have deplorable effects on revolvers in the way of broken firing pins, damaged pawls or cylinder ratchets and bent cranes, the last mentioned giving rise to much more trouble than is commonly supposed. Dropping the gun on to a hard surface is often sufficient to put the crane out of alignment, even though there is no visible damage done, and no overhaul of a revolver is complete unless the alignment of the crane is verified by the application of the requisite armourer's gauge. Then, too, there is the fact that barrel catch-springs, if of the flat or leaf variety, break far more frequently than they should, and it is surprising that manufacturers continue to fit them when it is a perfectly simple matter to substitute coil springs, which would be much more reliable.

An automatic of good make is much less liable than a revolver to damage from being dropped on a hard surface. The few instances of cracked slides are due, not to the weapon being dropped, but to long use in rapid fire, such as might be the case with a pistol used by an instructor. Nevertheless, a fall may damage the hammer and sights or may loosen pins and screws.

The extractors and ejectors occasionally give trouble, but this is usually due to wear after very long use.

Otherwise, there is little about the pistol itself that is liable to damage. We must look, rather, to its magazine for the cause of 90 per cent. of the troubles which we used to encounter, and in this connection we shall relate our own experiences in the care and maintenance of large numbers of automatic pistols having magazines of the detachable type.

We have to admit that in the beginning we paid little attention to the magazines or their condition. We soon noticed, however, that some of the magazines in our charge were getting rusty and that others, if not rusty, were clogged up with tobacco dust, fluff and bits of matches, the sort of stuff that is found in most men's pockets. We took the hint and, as opportunity served, had every one of some 9000 magazines stripped and cleaned. The rust was removed, together with astonishing quantities of the stuff referred to above, and, more important still, the overhaul served to reveal a certain amount of damage due to hard knocks and wear and tear. The only sensible thing to do was to recognise at once the wear and tear that existed, and would continue to exist, in an arduous service, the conditions of which could not be modified, and then to apply the remedy of periodic overhauls. It has long been our custom, therefore, to have every pistol, with its two magazines, sent to the armoury for inspection at intervals of six months, regardless of whether or not any defects are apparent. On these occasions, not only do the pistols receive whatever attention is necessary, but, as part of the routine, the magazines are stripped and cleaned (reblued if they need it), the springs are greased and, if found necessary, dents are removed from the shells, base plates are straightened out and splayed sides replaced in position, the completed job having to measure up to gauges specially constructed for each essential dimension. The results of these periodic overhauls have been entirely satisfactory and jambs are now of rare occurrence.

Enough has been said to show that the condition of the magazine is of the utmost importance to the reliable functioning of the pistol and at least ordinary care, therefore, should be exercised in its regard. Those individuals who use their magazines as screwdrivers, or to open beer bottles, have no one to blame but themselves when their pistols refuse to function. If any doubt exists as to its condition, a magazine should be regarded as defective until competent inspection is available. If the doubt is confirmed, competent inspection will include a rapid-fire test with the magazine charged to full capacity. A worthwhile precaution, to keep the spring efficient, is to remove one or two cartridges whenever circumstances permit. This applies, of course, to conditions which necessitate the magazine being kept charged more or less permanently. Properly treated, there is no reason why a well-made magazine should not last twenty years.

No ammunition can be expected to withstand indefinitely the wear and tear of daily use, which implies not only carrying it in all weathers but the frequent loading and unloading of weapons. It becomes necessary, therefore, first to ascertain the period for which ammunition may safely remain in daily use and then to withdraw it from circulation immediately the limit of that period has been reached.

Our conclusions in the matter are based upon the

exigencies of the police service of a great city, a service that functions ceaselessly for twenty-four hours a day and is maintained by large numbers of men whom circumstances compel to go armed with pistols. For a portion of the force, economy demands a ratio of approximately two weapons to three men. It is plain that the same men cannot be on duty all the time and it follows that in the course of twenty-four hours weapons and ammunition must be returned at intervals to police stations for subsequent issue to other men going out on duty. Such "change-overs," as they are known technically, occur not less than three times in twenty-four hours. At each "change-over" safety demands that the weapons be unloaded, only to be reloaded on issue to the next men. Apart from the "change-overs," which are due to motives of economy, it will be recognised, too, that even in those cases where weapons are provided for each individual, a certain amount of loading and unloading is likely to take place in the interests of safety. Add now the fact, mentioned already, that the ammunition is carried in all weathers and we have a set of circumstances definitely indicative of hard usage.

Careful records of over fifteen years show that under these circumstances the extreme length of time for which automatic pistol ammunition can be expected to be reliable is four months. Subsequently, defects begin to be apparent and work out very steadily at about two rounds per ten thousand. But for every week thereafter the number of defective rounds increases with surprising rapidity.

The records referred to show that revolver ammunition does not measure up to this standard. In point of fact, the ratio of defects is approximately double that of automatic pistol ammunition. The reasons are not far to seek.

The loading and unloading of revolvers imply much more handling of the ammunition than is the case with automatic pistols, which carry their ammunition in box magazines. Here the magazines receive most of the rough treatment. With all the care in the world we must expect, too, that occasionally ammunition will be dropped on the ground, possibly on the unsympathetic cement floor of a police station. Such treatment has less effect on automatic pistol ammunition, with its tightly crimped jacketed bullets, than on revolver cartridges, particularly those of large calibre carrying soft lead bullets. While there may be no noticeable deformation of the latter, they are more liable to be jarred loose from the crimping and that is the prelude to other troubles.

Apart from what may be regarded as inherent disadvantages in revolver ammunition, careful comparisons of respective measurements incline us to the belief that very often somewhat less care is exercised in its manufacture than is the case with automatic pistol ammunition. Of sheer necessity, the latter must conform more rigidly to accepted

standards. Too great a departure from standard
would be revealed very quickly by the automatic
action of the weapon in which it is used, a compelling
factor in the production of reliable ammunition. It
is only fair to add that defects in the automatic
ammunition put out by makers of repute are few
and far between.

The " life " of ammunition is a matter which
merits the most careful attention, particularly when
we have to consider the needs of a service which is
obliged to have a large amount in constant use. In
some cases, too, complications arise from climatic
conditions and distance from source of supplies.

It is possible to keep ammunition in excellent
condition for a number of years provided that it is
not removed from its cartons and packing-cases and
that common-sense is used in the matter of storage.
Having in mind the needs touched upon in the
preceding paragraph, we prefer, however, not to trust
to reserve supplies kept in stock for a number of
years but to adopt instead what may be described
as a " revolving credit." The tables given in the
Appendix will convey our meaning more clearly, but
we may state here that two basic conditions influence
their construction, viz. :—

The undesirability of carrying ammunition in daily
use for more than four months.
The undesirability of keeping ammunition in stock
longer than two years.

From this as a starting point, quantities required on all counts can be estimated.

By means of this " revolving credit " system we are spared certain anxieties which would occur were reserve supplies to be kept in stock over a number of years. With our full supply expended in under two years, and replenished as necessary, we do not have to worry about such things as seasonal cracking or other forms of deterioration in the brass, deterioration of the smokeless powder charge, increased pressures due to that deterioration or, more important still, the reliability of the primers. We do not waste first-class ammunition on practice and training shoots, but use only that which we consider might be no longer reliable.

The reference to the reliability of the primers should be explained. We have in mind the modern non-fouling primer. It will be unnecessary for us to refer to its value in all circumstances, and particularly those in which the cleaning of weapons after firing has to be deferred longer than it should be. Up to date, however, it does not appear to last as long in adverse climatic conditions as the old rust-producing type. We admit that we are not quite sure of this, but while there is any doubt in the matter we prefer to take no more risks than we need, and this aspect is fully taken care of by the " revolving credit."

We think it will be helpful if our system of dealing

with the ammunition supply is closely linked with the armoury records which should be kept in respect of both ammunition and weapons.

Practice and training courses are invaluable in bringing to light any defective ammunition or pistols, which should be immediately withdrawn and sent to the armoury for examination.

If the examination reveals ammunition defects which are not due to ill-usage but to obvious faults in manufacture, the matter should be taken up with the makers, full records being kept. As regards the pistols, there should be a history sheet for each weapon and on it should be noted the attributed and actual causes of the defects (sometimes these differ widely), the repairs effected, the date returned to service and other appropriate data.

It is true that all this involves a certain amount of clerical work, but it is more than justified by the general efficiency which results and it sinks into insignificance when it is remembered what that efficiency may mean to men whose lives would otherwise be needlessly endangered.

CHAPTER VI

PRACTICAL PISTOL RANGES ·

DOUBTLESS most of us would prefer to do our pistol shooting out of doors. There is the pleasure of being in the fresh air, there are no powder fumes to contend with, and the noise is less trying than in an indoor range, where so many men find it necessary to plug their ears.

Apart, however, from these considerations, the value of an outdoor range is limited. It can only be used in daylight and in good weather. Further, though it may be a minor point, the equipment of an outdoor range is liable to deteriorate more rapidly than it would indoors. Influenced by the necessity to conduct pistol training regardless of weather and frequently after dark, our preference is for the indoor range. It gives us in addition greater facilities than would be reasonably possible out of doors for varying the lighting at will. We have in mind training courses which endeavour to reproduce as closely as possible the conditions which police the world over so often encounter in the course of duty. Criminals favour darkness or semi-darkness for the exercise of their talents, and a large proportion of the shooting affrays in which police are concerned take place under precisely those conditions. We venture

63

to suggest that every man who has to use a pistol in the course of duty should learn how to do so in the dark. It *can* be done, it is often necessary, and the acquisition of confidence in this respect is invaluable.

If circumstances dictate an outdoor range, select, if you can, a piece of ground on which a high bank or a hillside provides a natural stop butt. A disused quarry or gravel-pit usually answers the purpose admirably. If the only ground available is flat, the stop butt is best constructed of a steeply sloping bank of earth backed by a wall of brick, stone, concrete or heavy timber.

Reference to the plan (Fig. 19) of an indoor range will show the lay-out we suggest. The contents of the next paragraph apply equally to outdoor and indoor ranges.

Every precaution must be taken against ricochets. The earth of which the stop butt is built up must be thoroughly sifted to ensure the removal of all stones, large and small. It is a good plan to face the sloping front of the stop butt with turf. Every scrap of metal used in the construction and which is liable to

---

* Fig. 19.

Explanation—

1, 1, 1. Frames for three bobbing targets, full figure.
2. Track and frame for running target, half figure.
3. Track and frame for running target, full figure.
4. Track and frame for running target, full figure.
5, 5, 5, 5, 5. Frames for five bobbing targets, half-figure.
6, 6, 6, 6. Frames for four disappearing targets, head and shoulder.

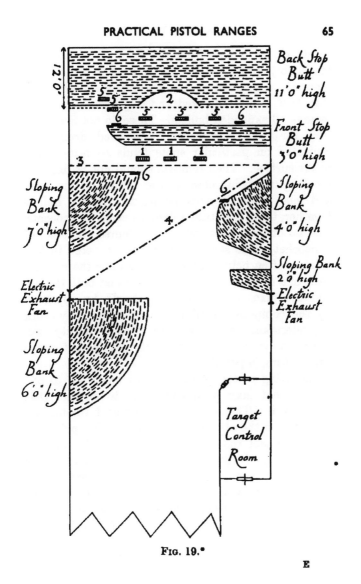

FIG. 19.*

E

be struck by bullets from the firing point must be thoroughly protected by earth or soft wood. At intervals, depending on the amount of shooting, the stop butt should be raked and dug over in order to remove all expended bullets. These do not penetrate very far in any case, and continued firing concentrated on particular spots tends to bring them to the surface. Their removal should not be deferred too long, for being close to the surface of the bank and most likely in agglomerations of many bullets together, they constitute a definite cause of ricochets. And no one can ever foretell the course (or force) of a ricochet. The sale of the metal recovered in this manner often helps materially to reduce the running costs of a range. Prudence suggests that both the site and the plans of construction should be approved by the competent local authority before any work is undertaken, and doubtless that authority will insist on an examination of the completed range before firing is permitted.

Reverting to the plan, we draw attention to one feature that may be unusual and to another that certainly is. The former is the Control Room, and the latter is the absence of any fixed firing point.

The control room houses the men who operate the targets. It provides them with perfect safety while firing is in progress, and from it they emerge at intervals to patch the targets. But they do not emerge until the Range Officer switches on a green light which shows high over the targets and is visible

to them. A red light is shown in the same place
while firing is actually in progress or about to take
place.

As stated, there is no fixed firing point nor is there
any barrier across the range. The range is not
divided into longitudinal sections, with booths for
individual shooters at the firing end. Such devices
would be impracticable for the training system
which we advocate, and this will be clear if we add
that we have to make provision for such widely
differing demands as two-handed shooting at 25 yards,
hip shooting at practically point-blank range, and
practices which entail running at full speed a certain
distance down the range in order to fire at several
suddenly appearing moving targets. Obviously there
is only room for one man at a time to shoot in safety
under such conditions. The only time when this
rule is permitted to be broken is in the initial recruit
practices at stationary targets, when three men may
sometimes shoot side by side, under the watchful
eye of the instructor. It might be inferred from the.
fact that, with the one exception mentioned, only
one man at a time can shoot, the proceedings would
be unduly slow. In actual practice, however, the
range illustrated and the system described have
shown their capacity for a number of years to take
care of the training and practice requirements of a
force of 6000 men, or, if we include auxiliaries who
also have to be trained, nearly 9000 men.

Freeing the range from all the obstacles that would

be constituted by fixed firing points also permits the staging on occasion of what we are pleased to call "mystery shoots." On these occasions the range, except for the targets, is transformed beyond all recognition, and it is astonishing what can be done in this respect in a building of very modest dimensions. To give an idea of what we mean, the range illustrated on p. 65 has more than once been made to represent the interior of a Chinese lodging-house harbouring, among other inmates, half a dozen bad characters who will resist arrest.

A screen hides all this from the men who are going to shoot. All they see from the outside is a wall with a door, through which, one by one, they will have to enter the lodging-house. No one knows what he will encounter inside, and the only instructions given are that innocent civilians are not to be "killed," such action being likely to impede promotion. The first man to shoot pushes in the door, closely followed by the range officer, and proceeds with caution or with reckless abandon, according to his nature, along a dark, narrow, twisting passage, kicks open a door at one point, descends a few steps, treads on floor-boards which give way under him, climbs some more steps and finds himself in a dimly lit room occupied by apparently harmless people (dummies) who vary from mere lodgers to dope fiends or stool-pigeons. He has to take in the situation in a flash, for his appearance is the signal for the fun to commence. A shot is fired at him (blank cartridge in the control room), and the criminals commence their " get-away " (" criminals " are life-size targets that bob up from nowhere and disappear as quickly, heads and shoulders that peer at him briefly round a corner, men running swiftly · across the room, possibly at an oblique angle, etc., all masked at some point in their careers by the " innocent bystanders," who must not be shot). There is no time to think, and anything resembling deliberate aim is a sheer impossibility.   Furniture and dummies impede his movements, and it is noticeable that he instinctively adopts the " crouch " and shoots as a rule with the arm in any position except fully extended.   His only course is to shoot quickly and keep on shooting till his magazine is empty, hoping that he is hitting the " criminals " and not the dummies.   Any ill-luck as regards the latter is rewarded, when the results are announced, by precisely the sort of comment that might be expected from the crowd.

This sort of thing is not mere play-acting.   It is done with the sole purpose of making practice as realistic as possible and of stimulating interest.   If the men are kept indefinitely at the same dull routine they *will* lose interest, and results suffer accordingly.

We should add now that the expenses of these productions are negligible if there are available a little imagination, a lot of willing help, some wood battens, straw, old clothes and hessian or old sacking. The steps referred to are easily arranged by having a pit in the floor, keeping it covered over when not required. The loose flooring only requires a very simple bit of mechanism, worked from the control room, to make it give way slightly when walked on.

Targets, always life-size, are drawn or printed on the cheapest paper and pasted on to a backing of hessian, old cloth or canvas ; anything will do. This backing is tacked on to frames which are slid into trolleys, or hung on wires which are designed to provide the runners, bobbers, charging men, etc. to which reference has been made. These devices are all very simple and only need a little ingenuity to work out for any requirements. The target frames do not merit anything but the cheapest wood and roughest workmanship since they very quickly get shot to pieces.

Special attention must be given to the ventilation of the range, and there cannot well be too many exhaust-fans to carry away the powder fumes. Continued exposure to powder fumes is liable to produce an affection of the eyes which is in all respects similar to and indeed difficult to distinguish from conjunctivitis (" pink-eye "). The persons most liable to suffer from this complaint are the control room operators who spend much of their time in patching targets, and that is just where the fumes collect most thickly when firing at the very short distances which we advocate. The first signs of any inflammation of the eyes should be the signal to re-examine the ventilating system of the range.

We have found that the most practical flooring for the range is beaten earth. We think, too, that an earthen floor helps to reduce noise, which of course is considerably more in an indoor than an outdoor range. Noise can be reduced further by the use of millboard on the sides of the building and by curtains suspended from the roof or ceiling. The matter is largely one of experiment, and experiments in this direction are likely to be well worth the trouble involved.

CHAPTER VII

STOPPING POWER

WE approach this subject with considerable diffidence. We regard it as essentially one in which theory should be discarded in favour of practice, but even practice, as evidenced in carefully noted records over a number of years, does not lead us to any finality in the matter. Instead, it provides us with so many contradictions that we feel that anything approaching dogmatism would be most unwise.

To clear the ground for discussion we can eliminate at once the ·22's and ·25's, leaving only the larger calibres available in modern revolvers and automatic pistols. Those will be calibres ·32, ·38 and ·45, or approximately those sizes.

We were brought up in the belief that a heavy bullet of soft lead, travelling in the leisurely manner of bygone days, could not be improved upon if it was desired to dispose of one's human foes in a decisive and clean-cut manner. We believed that such a bullet would mushroom, and that even if it did not do so, the impact of such a formidable mass of lead would infallibly do all that was required, including knocking the enemy clean off his feet.

We also believed that bullets of approximately equal weight, jacketed with cupro-nickel and

72

travelling at perhaps a greater velocity, provided penetration as opposed to shock and were therefore unsuited to their purpose ; and we had no faith whatever in light bullets driven at a much higher velocity, unless they could be so made as to secure effective expansion shortly after impact. Expanding bullets, however, are barred by the rules of the game as we have had to play it, so for practical purposes we must confine ourselves to solid bullets.

We are not so sure now of these beliefs. Perhaps the reasons for our doubts will be more easily apparent if we recount some actual experiences from the long list in our records. We shall make every effort to be impartial, and can assure our readers that in each case all data bearing on the subject was carefully sifted at the time and nothing has been preserved but actual facts.

We shall choose for our first instance one relating to the big lead bullet driven at a moderate velocity. On this occasion, a Sikh constable fired six shots with his ·455 Webley at an armed criminal of whom he was in pursuit, registering five hits. The criminal continued to run, and so did the Sikh, the latter clinching the matter finally by battering in the back of the criminal's head with the butt of his revolver. Subsequent investigations showed that one bullet only, and that barely deformed, remained in the body, the other four having passed clean through.

A very similar incident took place more recently —though it relates to a different weapon. A

European patrol-sergeant, hearing shooting and
shouts of " Ch'iang-Tao " (robber), rushed to a rice
shop which seemed to be the centre of the tumult,
and there saw an armed Chinese robbing the till.
The Chinese immediately opened fire on the sergeant
with an automatic pistol at about 6 yards, firing
several shots until his pistol jammed. Fortunately
none of the shots took effect, and meanwhile the
sergeant returned the fire swiftly and effectively with
a ·45 Colt automatic, commencing at about 10 feet
and firing his sixth and last shot at 3 feet as he rapidly
closed in on his opponent. Later, it was found that
of those six shots, four had struck fleshy parts of
the body, passing clean through, while one bullet
remained in the shoulder and another had lodged
near the heart. Yet, in spite of all this, the robber
was still on his feet and was knocked unconscious by
the butt of the sergeant's pistol as he was attempting
to escape by climbing over the counter. Here we
have two heavy jacketed bullets which did not
waste their substance on mere penetration, one of
them inflicting a wound which came near to being
fatal. In theory these two heavy bullets should have
stopped the man in his tracks, but the facts are as
related. Can anyone explain ?

    Descending in the scale of calibres and bullet
weights, the only record we have of a man dropping
instantly when shot relates to the performance of a
·380 Colt automatic (pocket model). In this instance
a single bullet penetrated from front to back, lodging

very near the spine. The victim nevertheless
recovered himself quickly and was able to get on his
feet again. We think this case is probably analogous
to the numerous instances that big-game hunters
will recall of animals dropping instantly to neck
shots that just miss the vertebra, only to get up
again a few moments after and disappear over the
horizon.

Turning now to the high velocity small calibre
weapons, we have seen terrible damage caused by a
Mauser automatic, calibre 7·63 mm., of military
pattern. We have in mind the case of a man who was
hit in the arm by a solid full-jacketed bullet from a
weapon of this type. Though he was in hospital
within half an hour of being shot, nothing could be
done to avoid amputation, so badly were the bone
and tissue lacerated. Perhaps " pulped " would
convey our meaning more exactly. Yet in theory at
least the bullet should have caused far less shock than
it obviously did. From what we have read, the
bullet had something of the effect that the latest
developments in ultra high velocity small-bore rifles
are reported to have on game animals. We might
add that in the particular service from whose records
we have been quoting, nothing is so feared, rightly
or wrongly, as the Mauser military automatic. The
mention of the word is sufficient, if there is trouble
afoot, to send men in instant search of bullet-proof
equipment.

We have tried to solve by experiment this question

of the knock-down blow, but there is no satisfactory way of doing it. The nearest we have come to it has been to allow ourselves to be shot at while holding a bullet-proof shield. The chief value of that experiment was a conclusive demonstration of the efficacy of the shield.

Nevertheless, it did enable us to form some idea of the disconcerting effect of the explosion when a pistol is fired at one at very short range. These experiments with bullet-proof shields amount to no more than the firing of various types of bullets at a very hard surface of considerable area, flexibly supported, *i.e.* by the arm. The shock of impact increased in proportion to the velocity of the bullets but in all cases was negligible, the supporting arm only recoiling minutely. The results to the bullets were exactly what might have been expected. Soft lead bullets at low velocity mushroomed perfectly, jacketed bullets at moderate velocity broke into sizable and greatly deformed fragments, while high velocity jacketed bullets practically disintegrated. But if the firing had been against a human body instead of a shield, it would not be wise to conclude either that the shock of impact would have been so slight or that the various bullets would have behaved exactly as they did.

Other tests, carried out by firing into wood of varied thickness and hardness, very rarely showed any appreciable deformation of bullets, even if they were of soft lead.

These little experiments left us, however, with a query which we have not been able to answer. How much, if anything, of deformation or disintegration is due to the sudden arrestation of the rotary motion when bullets are fired from a rifled barrel at objects hard enough to resist them effectively ?

To sum up, all that we have done in this chapter is to provide instances of how various types of weapons and their loads have not run true to form. Preconceived ideas, based on theory or perhaps hearsay, seem to have been upset. We say " seem " advisedly, for in spite of the length and variety of our records we do not consider that we have had, even yet, sufficient visual proof of the behaviour and effects of bullets fired into human targets to enable us to lay down any hard-and-fast rules.

We do not know that a big soft lead bullet will not have the knock-down effect generally claimed. All we can say is that we have never seen it. We do not know for certain, either, that a full-jacketed high-velocity small-calibre bullet will always have the effect described in the particular instance which we have given.

We incline to the belief that the human factor must influence to some extent the behaviour of bullets. A pugilist at the top of his form can stand vastly more punishment than a man who is " soft " and untrained. Capacity to resist shock and pain appears to be also a function of the nervous system, and marked differences occur in this respect as between

individuals of different races. Perhaps that partially
explains why some men are not knocked out by bullets
when they ought to be. Again, if a bullet caught a
man off balance, might not that aid in producing the
appearance of a knock-down blow ?

We have made no mention yet of an aspect of this
matter which we have observed time after time in
the course of years. A hit in the abdominal region
almost invariably causes a man to drop anything he
may have in his hands and to clutch his stomach
convulsively. We may add that such a hit almost
always has fatal results, and that is an excellent
reason for such equipment as effective bullet-proof
vests, at least for the use of police.

If the ideal to be attained is a weapon that, with a
body shot alone, will drop a man in his tracks with
absolute certainty, then there is something lacking
in the best of modern revolvers and automatics. It
could be done, doubtless, with a weapon of greatly
increased calibre and power, but the added weight
and size of such a weapon would almost certainly
render it unsuitable for average requirements. So
perhaps we shall have to make the best of such
weapons as are available to us.

Those readers who have had the patience to follow
us so far will most likely be justifiably irritated by
our inconclusiveness. We can imagine them saying,
" But there must be one or two kinds of pistol that
are better than all the others. Why on earth can't
they tell us what they are ? "

If that question is asked, we should reply that, for ourselves, we should choose the pistol which, while being easy to carry and convenient to use, would conform most nearly with the following requirements :—

(1) The maximum of stopping power.
(2) The maximum volume of fire.
(3) The maximum speed of discharge.

To attain the first requirement we should choose a cartridge that represents what we consider a safe middle course, *i.e.* with a bullet of reasonably large calibre and weight, driven at a very high velocity.

As regards the second requirement the reader will have gathered from Chapters III and IV on training that we have a preference for firing in " bursts " of two or more shots. We think that lack of stopping power inherent in the cartridge is compensated for in some degree by the added shock of two or more shots in very rapid succession. Medical evidence tends to confirm this belief, which is strengthened moreover by the evidences we have seen of the terribly destructive effects on human targets of submachine-guns of the Thompson type. Obviously, this belief of ours implies the necessity for a large volume of fire, quite apart from the desirability on other grounds of having as many rounds as possible at one's disposal without having to reload.

Throughout this book we have done our best to

emphasise the vital need for extreme rapidity of fire. For ourselves we can accomplish this, our third desideratum, most easily with an automatic. The more closely our own pistols resemble machine-guns the better we like it.

CHAPTER VIII

MISCELLANEOUS

Holsters.   Care and Cleaning of Pistols.

HOLSTERS for service men who are required to carry a pistol openly while in uniform must obviously be of a standard pattern, and there is little room for all the refinements that go to the making of a really good holster where individual requirements are the only consideration.

Nevertheless, the design of service holsters might well be given a little more thought than is often the case. It is not possible, perhaps, to combine service needs with the facilities for the lightning-quick draw which some special designs provide, but there are one or two things that can be done to help in the latter respect. The butt of the pistol should protrude from the holster sufficiently to allow the user to get it well into his hand as quickly as possible ; there should be no fumbling. If there is, there is something radically wrong with the design. The front of the holster should be cut away to allow the forefinger to enter the trigger-guard without resistance and without the stubbing of the finger-nail on the leather that is so often noticed. The gun can be secured in the holster either by a flap or a strap, both fastening on a metal stud. The strap is, of course, no wider

F

FIG. 20.

than it must be to effect its purpose. The flap offers better protection from the weather, and we do not think its greater width makes any real difference to the speed with which the pistol can be drawn. The bottom of the holster should be open so that in case of rain or accidental immersion, the water does not remain inside and the holster can dry out more quickly. The bottom of the holster cannot be entirely open if the design of the pistol is such that it will slip too far down, but it is always possible to leave an aperture or apertures of adequate size for draining.

There remains to be considered the position in which the holster should be worn. The writers have a preference for wearing the gun on the belt at the left side of the body. In that position (see Fig. 20) the wearer is able to draw his pistol at reasonable speed, and apart from those occasions when he is obliged to shoot, he can protect it with his left hand and forearm from attempts to snatch it from the holster. Policemen find that such attempts are by no means in- frequent in a crowd or on the part of " drunks " resisting arrest. To guard further against this danger (and it may well be serious), we recommend the use of a stout lanyard attached at one end to the swivel in the pistol butt. The other end should pass in a loop over the right shoulder, the shoulder strap of the uniform preventing the lanyard from slipping off. Never wear the lanyard round the neck, as we have sometimes seen it done, for needless to say, such a practice is liable to add to the danger very considerably.

Whatever the position in which the holster is worn, great care should be taken to ensure that its design and method of attachment to the belt provide the maximum of resistance when the pistol is drawn. To make our meaning clearer, the pistol should slip easily out of the holster, but the holster itself should remain as nearly immovable as possible. Otherwise, when the pistol is drawn, the holster has a tendency to accompany it, and the result is a slow and clumsy draw. With a holster worn on the right thigh, the necessary amount of resistance may have to be provided by a thong or string fastened to the bottom of the holster and tied round the leg. Though so far we have been referring solely to holsters to be worn openly when in uniform, it will be obvious that the necessity for resistance exists for all other holsters as well.

Turning now to holsters for other purposes, we strongly recommend the reader to be satisfied only with the best and to take any amount of trouble in order to get it.

Having provided yourself with the pistol of your choice, consider next how it will suit you best to carry it. Determine whether it is to be carried openly or concealed on the person. If the latter, do you prefer it under the left arm (Figs. 21 and 21A, pp. 85, 86) or around the waist (see Figs. 22, 22A, 22B, pp. 87, 88)? Having decided these points, get in touch with one of the reliable and well-known makers of holsters. If unable to visit him personally, provide him with such information as is appropriate to your require-ments. Depending on those requirements, such information might well consist of

The make and model of the pistol.
Your chest, waist and shoulder measurements.
Length of arm.
Size of hand and length and thickness of trigger-finger.
A photograph of yourself, showing the clothes usually worn.

With these particulars in his possession, the maker will be able to design a holster suited to your requirements in every way, including the correct angle at which to wear it. This latter is a most

Fig. 21.—Shoulder Holster.

FIG. 21A.—Shoulder Holster.

FIG. 22.—Belt-Holster and Pistol.

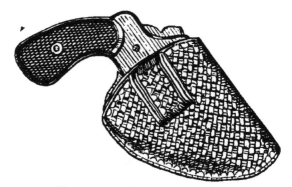

FIG. 22A.—Belt-Holster and Pistol.

FIG. 22B.—Cut-down Revolver.

important aid to a quick draw. Though the foregoing may appear to the uninitiated as unduly
meticulous, if not altogether too "finicky," it is
only in this way that you will be able to get the
utmost out of the pistol of your choice. That, we
presume, is your object, and that to attain it you will
be prepared to go to the necessary trouble and expense.

Supposing now that you have obtained a good
holster, do not put it away and forget it. Mere
possession is not sufficient. The best holster ever
made will not make you any quicker on the draw
without practice, and plenty of it. Nothing can excel
"dry" practice in front of a mirror, and a friend
with a stop-watch can often help you materially.

Though it is a safe general rule to seek the assistance of a manufacturer of repute, we should be the
first to admit that there are plenty of other ingenious
people capable of thinking out, designing and even
making extremely effective holsters for themselves.
One of the fastest holsters we have ever seen was
designed and made by an amateur for use when on
motor-cycle patrol. Fashioned from a cut-down
service holster and fastened on with pieces of string,
the finished product was not a thing of beauty,
but it was 100 per cent. practical. It hung slightly
below his belt in the centre of his body and enabled
him to drop his hand a few inches from the handle-
bar of the cycle on to the butt of the gun with
complete certainty and lightning speed. Moreover,
the holster held the gun securely even when riding

over very rough ground. Here is a case of a man who not only had sufficient ingenuity to make a holster which exactly met his particular requirements, but sufficient application to perfect himself in its use by assiduous " dry " practice.

Another instance of ingenuity on the part of an amateur, though it relates more nearly to a " gadget " than a holster, was furnished by a doctor whom one of the authors met in San Diego. This device was intended to cope with a " hold-up " when driving his motor-car. A slight flick of his hands and the next instant the doctor was grasping a pair of ·38 revolvers, all ready for instant action. The observer's impression was that the guns appeared from nowhere, and far too quickly to enable one to get any idea how it was done. Had the doctor been actually held up at the moment, it is more than likely that his assailant would have been completely beaten by the utter unexpectedness of the thing.

We should not attempt to describe the device even if we could. It is sufficient to say that it was the result of many weeks of planning, adjustment and " dry " practice, all of which the doctor found to be " well worth the trouble, and great fun besides."

On the same day, the author referred to was privileged to watch the Martin Brothers at quick-draw work with their famous front-draw holsters, one strapped down on each thigh, and he left firmly convinced that San Diego would be a very good town for bad men to keep away from.

CARE OF PISTOLS AND METHOD OF CLEANING

In one respect the pistol resembles the automobile engine or other piece of machinery in that it should be "run-in" and subsequently "tuned-up" to remove any small defects and asperities. This applies with greater force to automatics, and in their case the "running-in" process may well consist of fifty rounds of rapid fire. If all bearing-parts are then smoothed up by an armourer who knows his business, the pistols will not only be pleasanter to shoot with but will last much longer.

Where a number of men are engaged in cleaning their pistols at the same time, care must be taken that all parts which have been dismounted are reassembled on the right pistols. To this end, it is of great advantage if such parts are all stamped plainly with the numbers borne by the respective pistols to which they belong. This also ensures that pistols are correctly reassembled by the armourers after a general overhaul.

Cleaning in these days is a simple matter. Provide yourself with a celluloid-covered cleaning rod, the tip threaded to receive any of the following implements—a brass wire brush, a slotted jag, and a bristle brush. Provide yourself also with an aqueous solvent (of the nature of "Chloroil" or Young's ·303 Cleaner), some flannelette patches and a tube of gun grease.

If the pistol permits of it, dismantle it, to facilitate

the cleaning of the barrel. ' Attach the brass wire
brush to the rod, dip it into the solvent, and run it
through the barrel several times to loosen the fouling,
and more particularly, if your ammunition has the
older type of primer, to remove the potassium
chloride which in that case will have been deposited.
Then, using the slotted jag, run through several
patches soaked with the solvent, finishing with one
or two dry patches. The last dry patch should bear '
no traces of fouling. Finish with an application of
the gun grease on the bristle brush. There should be
no more grease than is necessary to coat the inside
of the barrel with a *very light film* and *neither breech
nor muzzle should be choked or clogged up.* If care is
exercised in these respects, the pistol may be fired
subsequently without having to wipe the barrel
out first.

Whenever the design of the pistol permits it,
always clean the barrel from the breech end.

All the foregoing remarks apply to barrels of
automatic pistols and barrels and cylinders of
revolvers.

Incidentally, nickel fouling due to jacketed bullets
does not appear to exist. If it does, it is so slight
as to be of no account.

The major part of the task is now finished. For
the rest, wipe over with a slightly greasy rag all other
metal parts, paying particular attention to the
breech face, and in the case of revolvers to the other
parts where fouling is apt to collect.

If the pistol is to be put away for any length of time, wipe dry and clean all metal parts other than the barrel (which has been attended to already), apply a film of gun grease (most easily done with the bristle brush) and wrap in greaseproof paper, making sure that you do not leave finger-marks on the metal. A pistol treated in this manner and put away in its box or case, if you have one, may be stored for a long time without attention. Never store in a holster ; the leather is susceptible to damp and will cause rusting of all metal in contact with it.

We do not favour the use of oil. If it is too thin it is not a good preservative, and if it is too thick it is liable to become gummy, to the detriment of moving parts. Almost invariably, too, its use is overdone, with the result that the pistol overflows with oil which cannot all be removed before firing. Firing, and more particularly rapid firing, is apt to cause the user to be bespattered with this excess of oil. It is neither useful nor pleasant and is best avoided altogether. Lubrication of such moving parts as can be seen is just as well accomplished by use of the gun grease, applied sparingly with the bristle brush. The grease does not melt, dry off or spatter. Lubrication of locks, etc., should be a matter for the armourer. Locks do not need much lubrication in any case, and are only liable to be gummed up from the usual practise of squirting oil into the interior of the mechanism through every available aperture.

AMMUNITION

"Revolving Credit" System, referred to
on p. 60.

THE unit quantities given in Table I are approximately those which have been found to answer our own purposes, but can be varied, of course, to suit different needs or the requirements of larger or smaller numbers of men. For greater simplicity, Table I is assumed to provide for a force of 1000 men.

TABLE I

Requirements over Twelve Months

		Rounds
To be carried in daily use by each man, 12 rounds . . .	× 1000 =	12,000
Practice and training, 36 rounds per man	× 1000 =	36,000
In reserve, 30 rounds per man .	× 1000 =	30,000
		78,000

An initial purchase is made of the total quantity indicated by Table I as required over a period of twelve months and, for added clarity, we shall assume that it is on hand at the end of December.

94

TABLE II
Disposal of Initial Purchase

	Rounds
1st January—	
Place to reserve . . .	30,000
Issue for daily use . .	12,000
Issue for training and practice	12,000
1st May—	
Withdraw 12,000 issued 1st January (for daily issue) and use for training and practice. Replace for daily use, by fresh issue of	12,000
1st September—	
Withdraw 12,000 issued 1st May (for daily use) and use for training and practice. Replace for daily use, by fresh issue of .	12,000
	78,000

In twelve months, therefore, 36,000 rounds have been actually expended in training and practice.

Meanwhile, a second but smaller purchase has been made and is on hand at the end of December, twelve months after the first purchase arrived, so that the stock of ammunition is as shown in the next table.

TABLE III

Stock at end of First Twelve Months	Rounds
In reserve	30,000
In daily use (issued 1st September) . .	12,000
Amount of second purchase	36,000
	78,000

We commence the second year with a stock of the same quantity as that with which we began originally and so are able to repeat exactly the processes of the first year.

There is one difference to be noted, however. The second purchase is not drawn on until the first is exhausted. Thus on 1st January of the second year, 12,000 rounds, issued for daily use at the beginning of the preceeding September, are withdrawn and issued for training and practice, their place being taken by 12,000 from reserve. The May issue, 12,000, and half the September issue, 6000, completely exhausted the 30,000 originally placed to reserve.

Our two basic conditions are therefore fulfilled, i.e. :

No ammunition in daily use longer than four months.

No ammunition in stock longer than two years.

As long as the programme is adhered to, the processes outlined are merely a matter of repetition year after year.

HANDS OFF!

By MAJOR W. E. **FAIRBAIRN**
AUTHOR OF THE FAMOUS BEST-SELLER ABOUT COMMANDO FIGHTING TACTICS "GET TOUGH!"

Self-Defense for Women

SELF-DEFENSE
for WOMEN

By *MAJOR W. E. FAIRBAIRN*

Author of
GET TOUGH!

Photographs by
MAJOR F. A. R. LEITAO
Shanghai Volunteer Corps

The Naval & Military Press Ltd

NOTE

There are many persons with an erroneous impression concerning the Art of Jiu-jitsu. Quite a number of them are under the impression that it is only necessary to take one or two lessons, after which they will be able to throw their opponents over their heads. There are others who believe that immediately a Jiu-jitsu expert catches hold of his opponent he will, by some secret Oriental method, throw him and break his arm or leg or render him unconscious. The reason for this being so generally believed is partly the fact that any two persons, without the slightest knowledge of any method of wrestling, could, with a few rehearsals, stage a demonstration that would easily deceive those not acquainted with the art, and partly the present day public demand for the spectacular.

THE AUTHOR

v

FOREWORD

It goes without saying that a woman should always know how to protect herself. In war time—in America at war—this is doubly so. Whether you carry on at home or in business, or whether you free a man for the front by taking his place on the assembly line or on the farm, the confidence you will gain from having learned to protect yourself, from knowing that you are the master of any unpleasant situation with which you may have to deal, will immeasurably increase your efficiency and value to the war effort. I hope that this book will be widely read, and I know that the result will be as I have said.

The basic methods of attack and defense in hand-to-hand fighting—described in my previous book, "Get Tough!"—were carefully worked out and developed during my many years service with the Shanghai Municipal Police. Those methods were designed primarily for use by men, though it is true that many of them are quite feasible for women. The methods of self-defense explained and illustrated in the present volume, however, have been especially selected for use by women, taking into account the usual disadvantages of weight, build, and strength. They are all practicable, and many are original, worked out in answer to the question: *What should I do were I to be attacked like this?*

It is to be expected that some of the more drastic measures advocated here will perhaps be considered distasteful and shocking. It is quite natural to feel this way, but a moment's consideration will, I am sure, convince the reader that any methods—so long as they be effective—are justifiable against a ruthless assailant.

In conclusion, a word about the handbag, handkerchief, or

vii

glove which are frequently mentioned as effective weapons of defense. In the hands of an expert, yes; but the average woman, as compared to a man, is handicapped far too much in weight and strength to rely upon disposing of her assailant by a flick in the eye with one of these articles. Such a measure would doubtless only enrage him. The twenty methods to follow are enough. Study them carefully, practice them diligently, and, if the time ever comes when you must use them, put them into effect suddenly and without restraint. To take the battle into your opponent's camp, to catch him off his guard, is seventy-five per cent of the battle won.

W. E. FAIRBAIRN

viii

CONTENTS

ix

HANDS OFF!

DEFENSE AGAINST VARIOUS HOLDS

No. I. Wrist Hold (One Hand)

Your assailant seizes your right wrist with his left hand, Fig. 1. To make him release his hold: bend your arm from the elbow, upwards and towards your body, then twist your wrist towards and over his thumb, Fig. 2.

Note: The above must be one continuous movement and carried out with speed.

Fig. I   Fig. 2

2

DEFENSE AGAINST VARIOUS HOLDS

No. 2. Wrist Hold (Two Hands)

Your assailant seizes you by both wrists, Fig. 3. To make him release his hold: bend your arms towards your body and twist your wrists in the direction of his thumbs.

Or: jerk your hands towards your body, at the same time hitting him in the face with the top of your head, Fig. 4.

Fig. 3

Fig. 4

3

Fig. 5   Fig. 6

DEFENSE AGAINST VARIOUS HOLDS

No. 3. Being Strangled (One Hand)

Your assailant seizes you by the throat with his right hand, forcing you back against a wall, Fig. 5.

1. With a sharp blow of your right hand strike his right wrist towards your left-hand side.

2. If necessary, knee him in the pit of the stomach with your right knee, Fig. 6.

Note: The position demonstrated in Fig. 5 (Forced back against a wall) was selected because it shows the only position where it would be possible, by means of a Strangle Hold, for an assailant to do you any harm. In the event of anyone attempting to strangle you with only one hand, and you are clear of a wall or other obstruction, all that is necessary to break the hold, is suddenly to step backwards or sideways in the direction of his thumb.

The best demonstration of defense against this One-Hand Hold is the position shown in Fig. 5—Against a Wall. Further, if your assailant puts all his strength and weight into the hold, so much the better. A sharp blow as in Fig. 6, with the palm of the right hand on the thumbside of his wrist, is all that is necessary to make him release his hold.

5

Fig. 7

Fig. 8

Fig. 9

DEFENSE AGAINST VARIOUS HOLDS

No. 4. How to Apply the "Chin Jab"

In Defense Holds No. 5, Being Strangled (Two Hands); No. 8, Waist Hold From the Front; and No. 10, Hair Hold (From Behind), it will be noted one of the methods is referred to as a "Chin Jab." This blow is struck with the base or heel of the palm of the hand at the "Point of the Chin," and, if applied correctly, is liable to render your assailant unconscious.

CAUTION: The "Chin Jab" should be used only when circumstances justify such drastic methods. Students are advised to practice at "Shadow Drill," not on their friends.

1. Bend the right arm from the elbow, turning the palm of the hand to the front, Fig. 7.

2. Bend the palm of the hand backwards as far as possible, extending the fingers and thumb, and keep them bent (Fig. 8) so that, in the event of your missing your assailant's chin, they will reach his eyes, should the situation justify such drastic action.

Note: The force of this blow does not depend upon the strength of the person applying it, but upon keeping the palm of the hand bent backwards. This permits one to deliver a "rock-crushing" blow with a follow-through from the shoulder and no possibility of hurting one's own hand when applying it.

3. The position of the hand in Fig. 8 was selected as the best to demonstrate the relative position of the fingers, thumb, and palm of the hand. Students will find that a position somewhat as in Fig. 9 will be a more practical position from which to start this blow.

7

Fig. 10

DEFENSE AGAINST VARIOUS HOLDS

No. 5. Being Strangled (Two Hands)

Your assailant seizes you by the throat with both hands, forcing you back against a wall, Fig. 10.

Note: In the event of being attacked in this manner, drastic methods are called for and are justifiable. We strongly recommend the application of the "Chin Jab."

1. Turn up the whites of your eyes to deceive your assailant and put him off his guard. Then suddenly shoot both your hands up inside his arms and strike him on the point of the chin—"Chin Jab."

2. Keep your fingers and thumbs extended and endeavour to reach his eyes with the points of your fingers or thumb of one of your hands. Simultaneously knee him in the pit of the stomach, Fig. 10.

9

DEFENSE AGAINST VARIOUS HOLDS

No. 6. "Bear Hug" (From in Front)

Your assailant, with both arms, seizes you around the body, imprisoning your arms, Fig. 11.

1. Kick him on the shins.
2. Knee him in the pit of the stomach.
3. Stamp on his feet.
4. Bump him in the face with your head.

Fig. 11

10

DEFENSE AGAINST VARIOUS HOLDS

No. 7. "Bear Hug" (From Behind)

Your assailant, with both arms, seizes you around the body, imprisoning your arms, Fig. 12.

1. Stamp on his feet.
2. Kick him on the shins.
3. Bump him in the face with the back of your head.

Fig. 12

11

Fig. 13

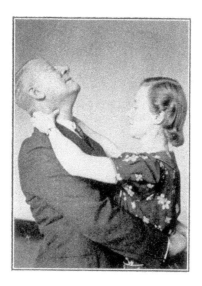

Fig. 14

DEFENSE AGAINST VARIOUS HOLDS

No. 8. Waist Hold (From in Front)

Your assailant seizes you around the body from in front, leaving your arms free.

1. Place your left hand around and in to the small of his back, simultaneously striking him on the point of the chin ("Chin Jab"). If necessary, knee him in the stomach, Fig. 13.

2. Seize his neck with both hands, fingers touching behind, thumbs in front, the points one on either side of the "Adam's apple." Force inwards and upwards with the points of your thumbs and towards you with the points of your fingers—then jerk his head sharply backwards, Fig. 14.

Note: The average person is very susceptible to the discomfort caused by this neck hold as shown in Fig. 14, and students are advised not to practice it on their friends.

13

Fig. 15

Fig. 15A

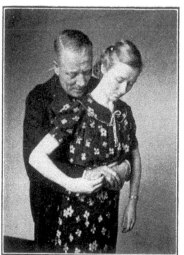

Fig. 16

Fig. 16A

DEFENSE AGAINST VARIOUS HOLDS

No. 9. Waist Hold (From Behind)

Your assailant seizes you around the waist from behind, leaving your arms free.

1. Strike the back of his hand a sharp blow with your knuckles, Figs. 15 and 15A.

2. Seize either of his little fingers and bend it backwards: if necessary, break it, Figs. 16 and 16A.

Note: It should be noted that the little-finger hold is the only hold on the fingers that is effective. There are many persons who could stand the pain of having one of their other fingers broken, but it is fairly safe to state that not more than one person in a hundred could stand the pain of having the little finger treated in the same way. Further, it is a sure method of making your assailant release his hold.

3. Stamp on his feet with the heel of your shoe simultaneously striking him in the face with the back of your head.

15

Fig. 17

Fig. 18

Fig. 19

DEFENSE AGAINST VARIOUS HOLDS

No. 10. Hair Hold (From Behind)

Your assailant seizes you by the hair, from behind, with his right hand.

1. Bend backwards and seize his hand from above, keeping a firm grip with your hands, force your head into his hand to prevent him letting go, Fig. 17.

2. Turn in towards your assailant; this will twist his wrist.

3. Force your head up and bend his wrist inwards, away from his elbow, Fig. 18.

Note: The success of this method depends mainly upon the speed with which it is completed and the continuous upward pressure of your head against his hand, combined with the firm grip on his hand by both of yours.

If, when you are in the position shown in Fig. 18, your assailant attempts to use his left hand against you, immediately release your hold with the right hand and strike him on the point of the chin ("Chin Jab"), Fig. 19.

17

Fig. 20

Fig. 21

Fig. 22

DEFENSE AGAINST VARIOUS HOLDS

No. 11. Coat Hold

Your assailant seizes you by the left shoulder with his right hand, Fig. 20.

1. Seize his right hand with your right hand and prevent him from releasing his hold.

2. Seize his right elbow with your left hand, your thumb to the left, Fig. 21.

3. With a circular upward and then downward motion of your left hand on the elbow, turn sharply outwards towards your right-hand side by pivoting on your right foot and stepping across his front with your left leg, Fig. 22.

4. Keep a firm grip with your right hand to prevent him releasing his hold and apply a downward pressure on his elbow with your left hand.

Note: It should be noted in Nos. 11 and 12, Coat Holds, and No. 13, Belt Hold, that your assailant having caught hold of your clothing, etc., has placed himself at a great disadvantage and it is for this reason that you should endeavour to prevent him from releasing his hold until you have effectively dealt with him.

19

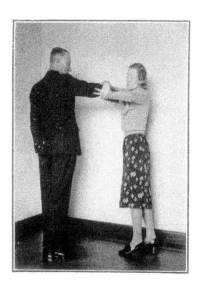

Fig. 23

Fig. 24

DEFENSE AGAINST VARIOUS HOLDS

No. 12. Coat Hold

Your assailant seizes you by the left shoulder with his right hand.

1. Seize his right elbow with your left hand from underneath; at the same time pass your right hand over the arm and seize the elbow with your right hand above your left, Fig. 23.

2. With a circular upward and downward motion of your hands on his elbow turn sharply outwards towards your right-hand side. This will bring you into the position shown in Fig. 24.

3. Force his elbow towards your body and push up with your left shoulder. This will prevent him from releasing his arm. If necessary, smash him in the face with your right knee.

21

Fig. 25

Fig. 26

DEFENSE AGAINST VARIOUS HOLDS

No. 13. Belt Hold

Your assailant seizes you by the belt with his right hand.

1. Seize his right hand from above with your right hand and prevent him from releasing his hold.

2. Seize his right elbow with your left hand from underneath, thumb to the left, Fig. 25.

Note: The success of the method depends upon the correct position of your left hand upon your assailant's right elbow, and special attention must be paid to the position of your left thumb.

3. With a circular upward and then downward motion of your left hand on the elbow, turn sharply towards your right-hand side by pivoting on your right foot, simultaneously stepping across his front with your left leg. Fig. 26.

Note: Providing you have prevented him from releasing his hold of your belt this will be found to be a very effective hold.

23

Fig. 27   Fig. 27A

Fig. 28   Fig. 28A

DEFENSE AGAINST VARIOUS HOLDS

No. 14. Simple Counters

(A) *Hand Shake:* It frequently happens that you meet a person who is very proud of his gripping powers and takes great pleasure, when shaking hands, in gripping your hand with all his strength, apparently with the idea of convincing you that he is a real "he-man," Fig. 27.

It is a very simple matter for you to take the conceit out of him—Place the *point* of your right thumb on the back of his hand between the thumb and index finger as in Fig. 27A.

Note: Only a very small amount of pressure with the point of your thumb is necessary to counteract his grip, and as the intention is to take the conceit out of him, do not make it obvious by applying more pressure than is necessary.

(B) *Against Being Lifted.* A person attempts to lift you up by catching hold of you under the arm-pits. To prevent this: force the points of your thumbs up and into his neck close alongside the jaw bone as in Figs. 28 and 28A. Push upwards and force his head slightly backwards, which will place him off balance, making it impossible for him to lift you.

25

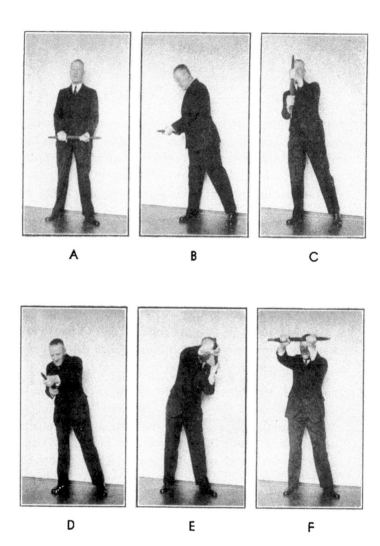

A   B   C

D   E   F

THE UMBRELLA AS A MEANS OF DEFENSE

No. 15. Umbrella Drill

The present-day umbrella, which is around 18 to 20 inches in length, is an ideal weapon for the purpose of defense against the more serious methods of attack, and students are advised to study and make themselves thoroughly acquainted with the application of the various blows, as demonstrated:

DRILL MOVEMENTS

A = Right hand above—left hand below.
Point of umbrella to the left-hand side.

B = Point, across the stomach.

C = Point up under the chin.

D = Point, down the face.

E = Handle, up across the face.

F = Up under the chin—aim to strike your opponent's Adam's apple with the center of the umbrella.

Note: In the following pages only one position of attack by an assailant has been shown. This is done so as not to confuse the student when learning. There are, of course, numerous other positions your assailant could adopt when attacking you, but, providing you make yourself proficient in the use of the umbrella, at least one or two of the "Drill Strokes," perhaps with a slight variation, will more than enable you to deal effectively with any assailant.

27

Fig. 29

Fig. 30

Fig. 31

Fig. 32

THE UMBRELLA AS A MEANS OF DEFENSE

No. 16. Being Held from in Front

CAUTION: Never attempt to strike your assailant over the head with your umbrella. The utmost injury that you could inflict with the handle of an umbrella would not be sufficient to make him release his hold, and would most likely only make him annoyed or angry with you. Further, a blow at the head, with any weapon such as a stick or umbrella, is in nine out of ten cases "telegraphed" that it is going to be given, with the result that it is a very simple matter to prevent its reaching its mark—see Fig. 29.

Having been "Held Up" as in Fig. 30, your assailant having hold of your shoulder or arms with one or both hands:

1. Hold your umbrella as in Fig. 31, right hand above, left hand below, with an interval of approximately six inches between your hands.

2. Strike your assailant with the point of the umbrella across the stomach, just below or above the belt line, by shooting your left hand forward and towards your right-hand side, simultaneously pulling the umbrella backwards with your right hand. This will bring your assailant to the position shown in Fig. 32.

[continued on page 31

29

Fig. 33

Fig. 34

Fig. 35

Fig. 36

THE UMBRELLA AS A MEANS OF DEFENSE

No. 16. Being Held from in Front (concl.)

3. Should your assailant still retain his hold (which is most unlikely), strike him under the chin with the point of the umbrella by jabbing upwards with both hands as in Fig. 33.

4. In the event of missing your assailant's chin with the point of the umbrella, strike at his face by hitting downwards with your left hand, simultaneously drawing back with your right hand as in Fig. 34.

5. Continue your defense by shooting your right hand forward and towards your left-hand side, striking your assailant across the face in the region of the nose with the handle of the umbrella as in Fig. 35.

6. If necessary, strike him under the chin as in Fig. 36.

31

Fig. 37   Fig. 38

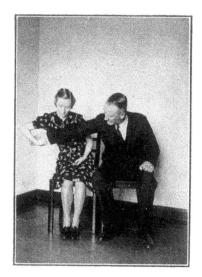

Fig. 39

A DEFENSE AGAINST WANDERING HANDS

No. 17. The Theatre Hold

1. You are sitting on a chair and a hand is placed on your left knee as in Fig. 37.

2. Catch hold of the hand with your right hand, passing your fingers and thumb under the palm of the hand as in Fig. 38. Although it is rather essential that the initial hold of the offending hand should be as near as possible to that shown, you should not have any difficulty in obtaining it, as the person concerned will most likely be under the impression that you are simply returning his caress.

3. Keeping a firm grip on the hand, lift it from your knee, pulling it across your body towards your right-hand side, Fig. 39.

[continued on page 35

33

Fig. 40

Fig. 41

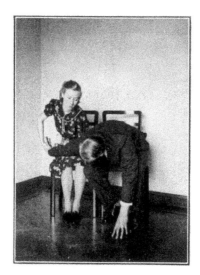

Fig. 42

A DEFENSE AGAINST WANDERING HANDS

No. 17. The Theatre Hold (concl.)

4. Twist the hand and arm away from you, simultaneously seizing his elbow from above, as in Fig. 40.

5. Force the arm downwards by pressing on the elbow with your left hand and twisting the arm with your right hand, until it is in the position shown in Fig. 41.

6. By your keeping a reasonable pressure on his elbow and a fairly firm grip of his hand, it is impossible for your opponent to move. An alternative method of holding your opponent is to apply pressure on his elbow with your left forearm as in Fig. 42.

Note: (A) For the purpose of clearness the various movements in The Theatre Hold have been demonstrated sitting in ordinary chairs in the front row. Had they been demonstrated as taking place in the second or back row, the opponent's head would have been smashed on to the backs of the front seats.

(B) Students should note that after their opponent's offending hand has been secured, as demonstrated in Fig. 38, all other movements of this hold are continuous. The amount of pain or discomfort inflicted on your opponent depends upon the speed with which the various movements are completed.

(C) If your opponent anticipates the application of this hold, it naturally follows that it might be difficult to apply. That being so—and the circumstances justifying it—we recommend the application of one of the Match-box. Defenses as demonstrated on pages 37 to 41.

35

Fig. 43

THE MATCHBOX DEFENSE

No. 18. Matchbox (Warning)

The use of the matchbox is one of the most drastic methods of defense that it is possible to employ and must only be used when the situation calls for drastic action. Further, students are warned to be extremely careful when testing the force of the blow on themselves (Fig. 43), otherwise it is quite possible for them to render themselves unconscious.

The advantage of using a matchbox, as compared with a stick or other weapon, lies in the surprise and complete unexpectedness of this form of attack. Any person not previously aware of this method of defense, seeing you take an ordinary matchbox out of a purse or pocket, would not be suspicious or on his guard.

There are several situations in which the use of a matchbox might easily be the only possible means of defense:

(A) You are driving a car and have picked up a hitch-hiker; he suddenly sticks a gun in your ribs. (See page 39.)

(B) You are unexpectedly stopped on a dark road with a demand "Give me a light" or "Hand over the bag." (see page 41.)

37

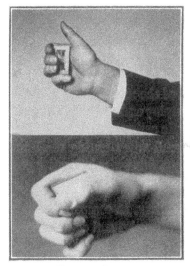

Fig. 44, Fig. 45   Fig. 46

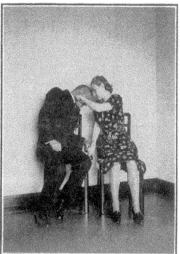

Fig. 47   Fig. 48

THE MATCHBOX DEFENSE

No. 19. Car "Hold-Up"

You are driving a car (left-hand drive), and have picked up a hitch-hiker. He suddenly sticks a gun in your ribs.

1. Take the matchbox and hold it as in Fig. 44, the top of the box being slightly below the finger and thumb, the box resting, if possible, on the little finger, Fig. 45.

2. Keeping the upper part of the left arm firmly against the left side of your body, with a circular upward motion of your left hand, pivoting your body from the hip (Fig. 46), strike your opponent on the jaw bone, anywhere between the ear and the point of the chin, Fig. 47. Simultaneously, seize the gun from above with your right hand, turning the muzzle away from your body as in Fig. 48. If you have struck your opponent correctly he will be "OUT."

Note: (A) Students must in practice check up against the fatal error, committed by most, of "telegraphing" their intentions by drawing back their striking hand. The blow starts from the original position of the hand when the matchbox was first put into position. The strength or force of the blow depends mainly upon the follow-through of the body, not in the strength of the arm.
(B) In the event of your opponent being on your left-hand side, take the matchbox in your right hand; the blow will be equally effective.

39

Fig. 49   Fig. 50

Fig. 51

THE MATCHBOX DEFENSE

No. 20. "Give Me a Light"

You are unexpectedly stopped on a dark road with a demand, "Give me a light" or "Hand over your bag."

The usual method of approach is for your assailant suddenly to step out of an alleyway or from behind a tree as you are about to pass, when your position would be somewhat as shown in Fig. 49.

1. Take the matchbox as in Fig. 50, the top of the box being slightly below the finger and thumb, the box resting, if possible, on the little finger.

2. It should be noted that the method of striking is somewhat different from that shown previously. In Fig. 51, your opponent being on his feet and very close to you, the blow must be delivered upwards. The force of the blow depends on the follow-through, which in this case is from the right hip, leg, and foot.

Note: An alternative method—if the situation is serious enough to justify such drastic action—is: take a matchbox with the heads of the matches on top—strike a match and set fire to the matches, immediately throwing it into your assailant's face.

[1]

41

SCIENTIFIC SELF-DEFENCE

W. E. Fairbairn

"Get tough, get down in the gutter, win at all costs.... I teach what is called 'Gutter Fighting.' There's no fair play, no rules except one: kill or be killed."

THE AUTHOR, WITH PROFESSOR OKADA
(Professor of Jui-jitsu, Second Pupil of the Mikado's
Personal Instructor), Shanghai, China, 1908

SCIENTIFIC
SELF-DEFENCE

by

W. E. FAIRBAIRN

*Superintendent, Shanghai Municipal Police,
Second Degree Black Belt of Kodokan
Jui-jitsu University, Tokyo, Japan*

PROFUSELY ILLUSTRATED

The Official Text Book for the Shanghai
Municipal Police and Hongkong Police

The Naval & Military Press Ltd

PREFACE

I do not know of any more interesting book to study than *Scientific Self-Defence*.

W. E. Fairbairn, the author, has a most extensive and practical knowledge of this art. I was forced to come to this conclusion when I attempted to grapple with him. Twenty-three years of association with the Shanghai Police Force has given him an experience which he could not get in any other city of the world.

In the early days of the cattle country, the six-shooter was the means of leveling all men to the same size. Now that the sale of the six-shooter is prohibited, every one should have some knowledge of the art of self-defence in cases of emergency.

I take great pleasure in commending this work to every one, and particularly those who have not had the good fortune to be born with great physical strength.

DOUGLAS FAIRBANKS

FOREWORD

This book is based upon an earlier work issued under the name of *Defendu* which was written for the police forces of the Far East. A second edition of *Defendu* was printed to meet the demand for copies from police and physical directors all over the world.

For this book the title *Scientific Self-Defence* has been selected as it conveys more clearly to the average man the contents of the work. At the same time it should be noted that every method shown in the present work has stood the criticism of police from practically every country in the world, including the Far East, which is the recognized home of jui-jitsu. A more exacting section of the community for criticizing a book on self-defence it would be almost impossible to find.

This system is not to be confounded with Japanese jui-jitsu, Chinese "boxing" or any other known method of defence and although some of the holds, trips, etc., are a combination of several methods, the majority are entirely original and no athletic effort is required to perform any of the exercises given.

After a long experience of methods of attack and defence, I am convinced that no methods that I have seen put into book form meet the requirements of the average man and present-day conditions. It should be realized that in boxing, wrestling and jui-jitsu competitions, etc., the competitors, in addition to having the spirit of fair-play ingrained in them from boyhood, are further protected from foul blows by the presence of a referee, but when dealing with street ruffians, burglars or armed robbers, one is faced by opponents or assailants who will recognize no bounds so long as their objective is attained and they can make good their escape.

The methods of defence explained and illustrated in this book have been specially selected for the man who requires quick knowledge of the best and easiest means of defending himself against almost every form of attack. It teaches a number of admittedly drastic and unpleasant forms of defences but all are justifiable and necessary if one is to protect himself against the foul methods

vii

that are used by a certain class. It further teaches how to protect certain vital parts of the body and it will be noted that the illustrations clearly emphasize this point.

W. E. FAIRBAIRN

Shanghai, China.

NOTE

It should be noted that the author has lived in Shanghai from 1907 to the present date. For years he was the Instructor in Self-Defence to the Shanghai Municipal Police and includes among his pupils, royalty and several of the highest jui-jitsu experts of Japan. He has made a scientific study of practically every known method of self-defence including the following:

Japanese jui-jitsu
> For which he holds the Second Degree BLACK BELT of Kodokan Jui-jitsu University, Tokyo, Japan.
> The author is the first foreigner living outside of Japan to be awarded a Black Belt Degree by Kodokan Jui-jitsu University.

Chinese "boxing"
> Studied under Tsai Ching Tung (now aged 83) who at one time was employed at the Imperial Palace, Peking, as an Instructor to Retainers of the late Dowager Empress.

CONTENTS

xi

CONTENTS

HOLDS THAT ARE EFFECTIVE

HOW TO THROW AN ASSAILANT

USE OF BATON, "NIGHT STICK" OR CLUB

xii

CONTENTS

HOW TO USE A WALKING STICK

HOW TO MAKE AN EFFECTIVE KNOT

MISCELLANEOUS ADVICE

xiii

SCIENTIFIC SELF-DEFENCE

No. 1.—WRIST HOLD.

(a) Your assailant seizes your right wrist with his left hand (Fig. 1). To make him release his hold:—Bend your arm towards your body and turn it in the direction of his thumb (Fig. 2).

FIG. 1

FIG. 2

2

No. 1.—WRIST HOLD.

(b) Your assailant seizes you by both wrists (Fig. 3).
To make him release his hold:—Bend your arms towards
your body and twist your wrists in the direction of his
thumbs. Or:—Jerk your hands towards your body, at the
same time hitting him in the face with the top of your head
(Fig. 4).

FIG. 4

FIG. 3

3

No. 2.—BEING STRANGLED.

(a) Your assailant seizes you by the throat with his right hand, forcing you back against a wall (Fig. 5).

1. With a sweeping blow of your right hand strike his right wrist towards your left-hand side.
2. If necessary, knee him in the testicles with your right knee (Fig. 6.)

FIG. 6

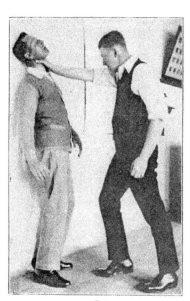

FIG. 5

4

No. 2.—BEING STRANGLED.

(b) Your assailant seizes you by the throat with both hands, forcing you back against a wall.

1. Bring your forearms up inside his arms and strike outwards.
2. If necessary, knee him in the testicles with your right knee (Fig. 7).

FIG. 7

5

No. 3.—"BEAR HUG." FROM IN FRONT.

Your assailant seizes you around the body and arms with both arms (Fig. 8).

1. Knee him in the testicles or stomach.
2. Kick him on the shins.
3. Stamp on his feet.
4. Bump him in the face with your head.
5. Seize him by the testicles with your right or left hand.

FIG. 8

6

No. 4.—"Bear Hug." From Behind.

Your assailant seizes you around the body with both arms (Fig. 9).

1. Kick him on the shins.
2. Stamp on his feet.
3. Bump him in the face with the back of your head.
4. Seize him by the testicles with your right or left hand.

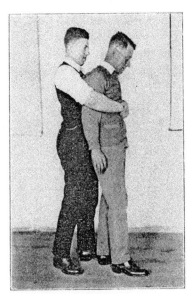

Fig. 9

7

DEFENCE AGAINST VARIOUS HOLDS

No. 5.—Waist Hold. From in Front.

Your assailant seizes you around the body from in front, leaving your arms free.

1. Strike his chin a hard upward jab with the heel of your right wrist (Fig. 10).
2. Seize his neck with both hands, fingers touching behind, thumbs in the front, one on each side of the "Adam's Apple." Force inwards with the point of your thumb and jerk his head sharply backwards (Fig. 11).
3. Seize the back of his neck between the thumb and the fingers of your right hand and force him to the ground (Fig. 12).
4. Kick him on the shins.
5. Knee him in the testicles or stomach.

8

No. 5.—Waist Hold. From in Front.

Fig. 10   Fig. 11

Fig. 12

9

No. 6.—WAIST HOLD. FROM BEHIND.

Your assailant seizes you around the waist from behind, leaving your arms free.

1. Strike the back of his hand with your knuckles (Fig. 13).

2. Seize either of his little fingers and bend it backwards; if necessary, break it (Fig. 14).

3. Stamp on his feet with the heel of your boot.

4. If your assailant has sufficiently long hair for you to get a good hold of it, reach over backwards with your left hand and seize it, bend suddenly forwards, pulling him by the hair over your back (Fig. 15).

10

No. 6.—Waist Hold. From Behind.

Fig. 13

Fig. 14

Fig. 15

11

No. 7.—Hair Hold. From Behind.

Your assailant seizes you by the hair, from behind, with his right hand.

1. Seize his hand with both of yours to prevent him letting go (Fig. 16).
2. Turn in towards your assailant; this will twist his wrist.
3. Force your head up and bend his wrist inwards, away from his elbow (Fig. 17).

12

No. 7.—HAIR HOLD. FROM BEHIND.

FIG. 16

FIG. 17

13

463

DEFENCE AGAINST VARIOUS HOLDS

No. 8.—Coat Hold.

Your assailant seizes you by the left shoulder with his right hand.

1. Seize his right hand with your right hand.
2. Seize his right elbow with your left hand, thumb to the right (Fig. 18).
3. With a circular upward and downward motion of your left hand on the elbow, turn sharply outwards towards your right-hand side (Fig. 19).
4. Keeping a firm grip with your right hand, which will prevent him from releasing his hold, force down on his elbow with your left hand.

Note.—An "Edge of the Hand Blow" given as shown in Figure 20 will be found to be very effective.

14

No. 8.—Coat Hold.

Fig. 18

Fig. 19

Fig. 20

15

No. 9—COAT HOLD.

Your assailant seizes you by the left shoulder with his right hand.

1. Seize his right elbow with your left hand from underneath; at the same time pass your right hand over the arm and seize the elbow with your right hand above your left (Fig. 21).
2. With a circular upward and downward motion of your hands on his elbow turn sharply outwards towards your right-hand side. This will bring you into the position shown in Fig. 22.
3. Force his elbow towards your body and push up with your left shoulder. This will prevent him from releasing his arm. If necessary, knee him in the face with your right knee.

16

No. 9.—Coat Hold.

Fig. 21

Fig. 22

17

No. 10.—COAT HOLD.

Your assailant seizes you by the lapel of your coat with his right hand.

1. Seize his right wrist with your right hand (Fig. 23).
2. Keeping a firm grip, turn rapidly towards your right-hand side by bringing your right leg to your right rear, simultaneously passing your left arm under his right arm, placing the palm of your left hand on his right thigh (Fig. 24).
3. Force down on the upper part of his right arm with your left shoulder.

Note.—Should your assailant attempt to step forward with his left leg release the hold with your right hand and seize his left ankle and pull it upwards; at the same time push him backwards with your left hand (Fig. 25).

18

No. 10.—Coat Hold.

Fig. 23   Fig. 24

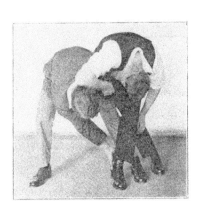

Fig. 25

19

No. 11.—BELT HOLD.

Your assailant seizes you by the belt with his right hand.

1. Seize his hand with your right hand to prevent him from releasing his hold.
2. Seize his right elbow with your left hand from underneath, thumb to the right (Fig. 26).
3. With a circular upward motion of your left hand force his elbow towards your right side, keeping a firm grip on his hand (Fig. 27).

Note.—Providing you have prevented him from releasing his hold of the belt, this will be found to be a very effective hold.

20

No. 11.—Belt Hold.

Fig. 26

Fig. 27

21

No. 12.—Neck Hold. From Behind.

Your assailant seizes you around the neck with his right arm from behind (Fig. 28).

1. Lean back on your assailant, seize his right wrist with your left hand and place your right forearm as in (Fig. 29).

2. Suddenly turn about, on your right heel, towards your right-hand side, simultaneously forcing his right wrist with a circular motion upward and downward of your left hand in the same direction as your body. This will force his right arm over your right arm and allow you to seize his wrist with your right hand above your left (Fig. 30).

3. Force the upper part of his right arm against your body and his elbow into your chest and jerk his wrist towards the ground.

22

No. 12.—Neck Hold. From Behind.

Fig. 28

Fig. 29

Fig. 30

23

No. 13.—Simple Counters.

1. It frequently happens that you meet a person who is very proud of his gripping powers and takes great pleasure when shaking hands in gripping your hand with all his strength and causing you to wince.

   To prevent this:—Force your right thumb into the back of his hand as in Fig. 31.

2. When walking you see two persons approaching you who intend to jostle you between them.

   To prevent this:—Place your hands on their shoulders, your forearms under their chins as in Fig. 32, and suddenly shoot your forearms outwards.

3. A person attempts to lift you up by catching hold of you under the armpits.

   To prevent this:—Force the points of your thumbs up into his neck, close alongside the jawbone, as in Fig. 33.

24

No. 13.—Simple Counters.

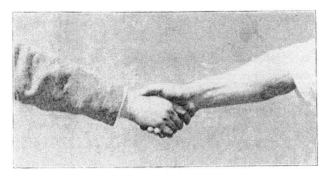

Fig. 31

Fig. 32

Fig. 33

25

METHOD OF DEALING WITH AN ARMED ASSAILANT

The "Defendu" method of dealing with an armed assailant may at first glance appear to be risky, but one will be surprised to discover how safe and simple this method is when put into practice by a person who has studied it and who has to cope with a man unacquainted with it.

The author, being aware that anything original is generally doubted, made it a point, when giving a demonstration, to have his assailant armed with a loaded air pistol, and at no time, even when the pistol was fired, did the pellet ever strike his body; in fact, in the majority of cases the opponent was disarmed before he could possibly fire.

It should always be borne in mind that a man who "holds" you "up" with a pistol or other weapon is, to use a slang term, "throwing a bluff" and is far too cowardly to commit murder; otherwise he would shoot on sight and rob you afterwards. He is aware that if a shot is fired it is liable to alarm the neighborhood, which is what he wants to prevent at all costs. Further, he is aware that a person carrying valuables might be armed, and for this reason he will be sure to make you hold your hands above your head so as to prevent you from drawing. Finally, in order to search you he must come within reach of your hands. The unexpectedness of finding that he is attacked by an apparently defenceless person will come as such a surprise to him that it will be the simplest thing possible to disarm him before he is aware what has happened.

The following is an extract from the *Over-Seas Daily Mail*, February 2, 1924.

26

DEALING WITH AN ARMED ASSAILANT

GIRL BANDIT'S COUPS

"HOLD YOUR HANDS UP NICELY"

The girl bandit with bobbed hair and a sealskin coat who within the last three weeks has robbed over a dozen New York shops reappeared at a provision merchant's establishment in Albany Avenue, Brooklyn.

She asked for a cake of soap. When the assistant handed her the article he found himself facing a pistol, while the sweet-voiced girl remarked, "Hold your hands up nicely; be a good boy, and go into the back room."

He did so, and the girl's customary male companion took $35 from his pocket and $55 from the till.

$20,000 JEWEL HAUL

Later the blonde girl undertook an excursion to Philadelphia in pursuit of a New York jeweler, Mr. Abraham Kaplan, who was carrying with him a suitcase containing $20,000 worth of jewels.

She accosted him as he was leaving Broad Street Station at Philadelphia and asked him the way to the post office. He told her he was unable to direct her, and, according to his story, she then drew a pistol from her handbag and ordered him to turn about. With the muzzle of her pistol pressed against his back, she forced him to walk into a narrow passage, where two men relieved him of his suitcase, a diamond scarf-pin, a watch, and $100 in cash.

"Holdups" of this description are of frequent occurrence in various parts of the world, and it is owing to this fact that the author is publishing the "Defendu" method of self-defence. Now, had this New York jeweler been acquainted with only a part of the "Defendu" method, it would have been a simple matter for him to have disarmed this girl bandit immediately she pressed the pistol against his back, and, what is of more importance, he would not, in doing so, have increased the risk that he ran of being shot.

27

No. 1.—Disarming a Person Found Pointing a Pistol at Another.

Should you find a man pointing with a pistol at another, and unaware of your presence:—

1. Seize his hand and pistol with your right hand from underneath, at the same time seizing his right elbow with your left hand (Fig. 34).
2. Jerk his hand upwards and backwards and force his elbow upwards with your left hand, simultaneously pivoting inwards on your left foot. This will break his trigger finger and cause him to release his hold on the weapon.
3. If necessary, knee him in the testicles with your right knee (Fig. 35).

28

DEALING WITH AN ARMED ASSAILANT

No. 1.—Disarming a Person Found Pointing a Pistol at Another.

Fig. 34

Fig. 35

29

No. 2.—Disarming an Assailant Holding You up with a Pistol. From in Front.

Your assailant gives the order, "Hands Up," and covers you by pointing a pistol at your stomach:

1. Hold up your hands above your head, keeping them as far apart as possible (Fig. 36).
2. Lead your assailant to suppose that you are scared to death.
3. With a swinging blow seize the pistol and hand with your right hand, simultaneously turning rapidly sideways towards your left-hand side. This will knock the pistol outwards past your body (Fig. 37).
4. Seize the pistol and hand from underneath with your left hand, knee him in the testicles, and letting go with your right hand seize his right elbow. Force his hand and pistol upwards and backwards with your left hand, and pull his elbow towards you (Fig. 38). If necessary, knee him in the testicles with your right knee.

Note.—The reason for keeping your hands held up as far apart as possible is that your assailant cannot look at two objects at one time. If he is watching your left hand, use your right; if the right, use the left; should he be looking at your body or face, use either. Should it be too dark for you to see which hand he is looking at, use which you think best; he will not be expecting any attack.

30

DEALING WITH AN ARMED ASSAILANT

No. 2.—Disarming an Assailant Holding You up with a Pistol. From in Front.

Fig. 36

Fig. 37

Fig. 38

31

No. 3.—Disarming an Assailant Holding You up with a Pistol. From in Front.

Having been "held up" as in Fig. 39, and while your assailant is watching your right hand, the following method should be applied:—

1. With a swinging blow seize your assailant's right wrist with your left hand, simultaneously turning rapidly sideways towards your right-hand side. This will knock the pistol inwards past your body (Fig. 40).

2. Seize the pistol and hand from underneath with your right hand, and with a circular backward and downward motion break his trigger finger and knee him in the testicles (Fig. 41).

32

No. 3.—Disarming an Assailant Holding You up with a Pistol. From in Front.

Fig. 39

Fig. 40

Fig. 41

33

No. 4.—Disarming an Assailant Holding You up with
a Pistol. From Behind.

Your assailant gives the order "Hands up" and covers
you by holding a pistol in the small of your back:

1. Hold up your hands above your head and exhibit the
   utmost terror (Fig. 42).
2. Turning rapidly inwards towards your left-hand side,
   passing your left arm over and around your assailant's
   right forearm, holding it with a firm grip of your left
   arm against the left side of your body, simultaneously
   knee him in the testicles with your right knee and
   "chin jab" him with your right hand (Fig. 43).

Note.—If you keep a fairly firm grip with your left arm on your
assailant's right arm it will be impossible for him to shoot
you or release his arm, and, as previously stated, the shock
from the blow on the testicles or even the "chin jab" will cause
him to immediately release his hold on the pistol.

34

DEALING WITH AN ARMED ASSAILANT

No. 4.—Disarming an Assailant Holding You up with
a Pistol. From Behind.

Fig. 42

Fig. 43

35

No. 5.—DISARMING AN ASSAILANT HOLDING YOU UP WITH
A PISTOL. FROM BEHIND.

Having been "held up" as in Fig. 44, and for some
reason or other not finding it convenient to turn towards
your left-hand side, the following method should be applied:

1. Turning rapidly outwards towards your right-hand
   side, lower your right hand and pass it under your
   assailant's right forearm and seize his arm above the
   elbow, lifting up his forearm with your right arm
   (Fig. 45).
2. Simultaneously seize the pistol underneath with your
   left hand and bend his wrist backwards. If necessary,
   knee him in the testicles (Fig. 46).

36

No. 5.—Disarming an Assailant Holding You up with a Pistol. From Behind.

Fig. 44

Fig. 45

Fig. 46

37

No. 6.—ARRESTING A MAN KNOWN TO CARRY FIREARMS.

Your opponent is coming towards you and you are aware that he will, if possible, shoot to avoid arrest.

When about 10 to 12 feet away from him give him the order to halt and "Hands Up," covering him with your weapon. Tell him to turn about and march in front of you with his hands held above his head; and whilst he is being searched, keep him covered from behind.

Note.—In no circumstances permit him to get within less than 10 feet of you previous to his having been handcuffed. Even if halted at a distance of 12 feet, a determined criminal may possibly endeavor to close on you by means of a "rolling dive" (Figs. 47, 48, 49, 50 and 51). Should this be attempted, a rapid leap to one side will get you into a position similar to your original one and well placed for delivering an effective shot.

Caution.—This fall must first be learnt as shown on page 141.

38

No. 6.—ARRESTING A MAN KNOWN TO CARRY FIREARMS.

FIG. 47

FIG. 48

FIG. 49

FIG. 50

FIG. 51

39

No. 7.—Disarming a Man Attacking You with a Knife. "Stage Style."

Your assailant rushes at you with a knife in his right hand:

1. Seize his right wrist with your left hand, bend his arm at the elbow towards him (Fig. 52).
2. Pass your right arm under the upper part of his right arm, seize his right wrist with your right hand above your left.
3. Force the upper part of his right arm against your body, and his elbow into your chest so that it will be at a right angle with your body.
4. Jerk his wrist towards the ground, and knee him in the testicles with your right knee (Fig. 53).

Note.—The above method will be found very effective should you ever be so fortunate as to be attacked in the above manner, but unfortunately, except on the stage, persons who carry a knife for the purpose of attack do not hold it as in Fig. 52.

It should be noted that the knife is held as in Fig. 54, edge of the blade uppermost. The part of the body usually aimed at is the pit of the stomach, with the intention of ripping it up. If attacked in this manner, and you are unarmed, there are only two methods of defense:—1st, RUN; or 2nd, with a lightning-like movement of either foot, kick your assailant in the testicles or stomach as in Fig. 55.

40

DEALING WITH AN ARMED ASSAILANT

No. 7.—Disarming a Man Attacking You with a Knife.

Fig. 52

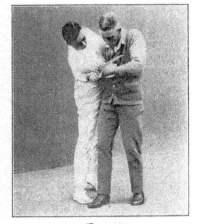

Fig. 53

Fig. 54

Fig. 55

41

HOLDS THAT ARE EFFECTIVE

No. 1.—Police Hold. ("Come Along" Grip.)

1. Stand facing your opponent.
2. Seize his right wrist with your right hand (Fig. 56).
3. Step in towards him with your left foot.
4. Pass your left arm over his right arm (above the elbow joint), catching hold of your right arm by the biceps with your left hand.
5. Keep your opponent's right arm straight and the knuckles downwards.
6. Stand upright and force your left forearm bone into the back muscles of his right arm by lifting upwards with your left arm and pressing downwards with right hand, towards your opponent's body, on his right wrist.
7. Apply the pressure until your opponent is standing on his toes (Fig. 57).

Note.—Should you, owing to the shortness of your forearm or for any other reason, find it difficult to catch hold of your biceps with your left hand (Fig. 57), seize the left lapel of your jacket instead. Never lean towards your opponent; by so doing you place yourself in a very cramped position. If your opponent attempts to throw himself forward or backwards, apply pressure with a jerk. This will strain the elbow joint and render his right arm useless for attack.

42

No. 1.—Police Hold. ("Come Along" Grip.)

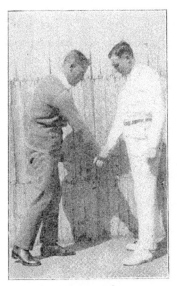

Fig. 56

Fig. 57

43

No. 2.—POLICE HOLD WITH TRIP.

Having secured the Police Hold (Fig. 57) :

1. Shoot your left leg across your opponent's legs, back of your leg to the front of his, your left foot flat on the ground and leg braced stiff (Fig. 58).

2. Bend forward and outwards from the waist, letting go with your left arm and pulling your opponent sharply towards your right-hand side by his right arm (Fig. 59).

Note.—The importance of keeping the leg braced stiff and the foot flat on the ground can be clearly seen from the following illustrations:

Fig. 60.—Leg and Foot, *Correct Position*—Leg capable of taking a strain of 300 to 400 pounds.

Fig. 61.—Leg and Foot, *Not Correct*—The leg in this position will not stand more than about a 30-pound strain.

44

HOLDS THAT ARE EFFECTIVE

No. 2.—Police Hold with Trip.

Fig. 58

Fig. 59

Fig. 60

Fig. 61

45

No. 3.—POLICE HOLD WITH FALL.

Having secured the Police Hold (Fig. 62), and having been tripped owing to your failure to keep sufficient pressure on his arm:—

1. Retain your hold with both hands.
2. Turn your head, keeping your chin down towards your left shoulder (Fig. 63), and let yourself fall— you cannot hurt yourself. Fig. 64 shows the position you would be in after the fall.

Note.—In practice care must be taken not to throw yourself forward when your opponent trips you, otherwise he is liable to be rendered unconscious by striking his head on the ground.

FIG. 62

46

No. 3.—Police Hold with Fall.

Fig. 63

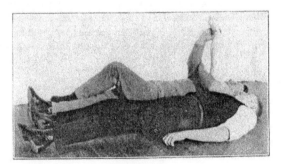

Fig. 64

47

No. 4.—HANDCUFF HOLD.

1. Stand facing your opponent.
2. Seize his right wrist with both of your hands—right hand above left (Fig. 65).
3. Swing his arm up high.
4. Pass under it by turning inwards with your back towards him (Fig. 66).
5. Step to his back with your left foot, and with a circular upward motion force his wrist well up his back.
6. Retain grasp on his wrist with your left hand and seize his right elbow with your right hand.
7. Bend his wrist towards his right shoulder and lift upwards with your right hand on his elbow.
8. Apply the pressure until your opponent is in the position shown in Fig. 67.

Note.—To throw your opponent:—Apply pressure with your left hand on his right (forward and towards the ground), at the same time lifting up his elbow.

All the above movements are one continuous swing of your opponent's right arm, and although from the positions shown in Figs. 65, 66 and 67, it may appear to the novice that your opponent could easily hit you with his disengaged hand or kick you with his feet, it will be found that it is almost impossible for him to do either. Should he, however, attempt to do so, and the circumstances justify it, "counter" as follows:—

While in the position shown in Fig. 65, release your hold with your left hand, pulling him towards you with your right hand, pass your left arm over his right arm and secure the Police Hold (Fig. 57), and apply pressure with a jerk.

While in the position shown in Fig. 66, shoot your left leg in front of his legs, simultaneously throwing yourself forward to the ground to your right front. This will throw him, with a smashing blow, on to his face, and, providing you have not allowed his wrist to turn in your hands, will probably dislocate his shoulders.

While in the position shown in Fig. 67, apply pressure on his wrist and elbow with a jerk and throw yourself forward to the ground. This will throw him on to his face and probably dislocate his wrist or shoulder.

48

No. 4.—HANDCUFF HOLD.

FIG. 65   FIG. 66

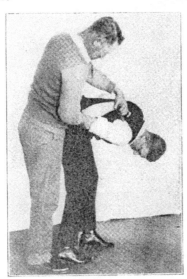

FIG. 67

49

No. 5.—HANDCUFF HOLD (FOR A SMALLER OPPONENT).

If your opponent is too small for you to pass under his arm, as in Fig. 68, apply the following hold:

1. Stand facing your opponent, slightly to his right-hand side.
2. Seize his right wrist with your left hand, your knuckles downwards and thumb to the left.
3. Seize his right elbow with your right hand, your knuckles towards your left-hand side (Fig. 69).
4. Force his hand up his back by pulling his elbow towards you and jerking his hand upwards. This will pull your opponent into the position shown in Fig. 70.

FIG. 68

50

No. 5.—HANDCUFF HOLD (FOR A SMALLER OPPONENT).

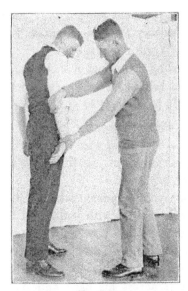

FIG. 69

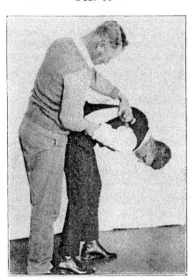

FIG. 70

51

No. 6.—Handcuff Hold (Handcuffing a Prisoner).

The reason for this hold being named the Handcuff Hold is that this is the only way one man can handcuff another, unless the latter is willing to submit.

When handcuffing a prisoner it should be done so that his hands are locked behind his back. This will handicap him in running should he attempt to get away.

To handcuff your opponent:

1. Secure the hold as in Fig. 70.
2. Throw your opponent, retaining the hold on his wrist and elbow.
3. Sit astride your opponent's back (Fig. 71), holding his elbow in position with your right thigh. This will allow you to release your hold with your right hand and snap the handcuff on his right wrist (Fig. 72.)
4. Reach over and seize his left wrist with your left hand and jerk it across his back and snap on the other handcuff.

Note.—Should you have any difficulty in securing your opponent's wrist, seize his chin from underneath with your right hand and the side of his head with your left hand. Jerk upwards with your right hand and push his head downwards with your left hand (Fig. 73).

An alternative method (if your opponent's hair is long enough for you to grip it) is to seize his hair as far forward as possible with your right hand, placing the left hand on the back of his neck and jerking upwards with your right hand and forcing downwards with your left (Fig. 74).

After a very little of either of the above methods your opponent will be quite willing to submit to being handcuffed.

Care should be taken not to break a person's neck by the above method.

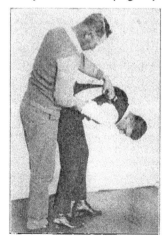

Fig. 70

52

No. 6.—HANDCUFF HOLD (HANDCUFFING A PRISONER).

FIG. 71

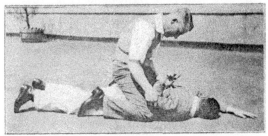

FIG. 72

FIG. 73

FIG. 74

53

No. 7.—ARM HOLD.

1. Stand level with your opponent on his right side and facing the same way.
2. Seize his right wrist with your right hand, back of your hand to the front, back of his hand downwards.
3. Raise his right arm with your right hand and at the same time pass your left arm under his right and place your left hand behind his neck (Fig. 75).
4. Straighten your left arm and pull downwards on his right arm with your right hand (Fig. 76).

Note.—Your left arm must be above your opponent's right elbow; otherwise you cannot obtain any leverage.

54

No. 7.—ARM HOLD.

FIG. 75

FIG. 76

55

No. 8.—BENT ARM HOLD.

You are facing your opponent and he raises his right hand as if about to deliver a blow.

1. Seize his right wrist with your left hand, bending his arm at the elbow, towards him (Fig. 77).
2. Pass your right arm under the upper part of his right arm, seizing his right wrist with your right hand above your left.
3. Force the upper part of his right arm against your body, and his elbow into your chest so that it will be at a right angle with your body.
4. Jerk his wrist towards the ground (Fig. 78).

56

No. 8.—Bent Arm Hold.

Fig. 77

Fig. 78

57

No. 9.—FRONT STRANGLE HOLD.

For defense against a right-handed punch to the head, or a downward swinging blow at the head with a stick, etc.

1. Duck your head to the left and rush in under your assailant's right arm to his right side (Fig. 79).
2. Pass your right arm around his neck, catching your right wrist with your left hand.
3. Apply pressure by pulling on your right wrist with your left hand, forcing his right arm up alongside his neck with your shoulder and head (Fig. 80).

Note.—Keep the fingers and thumb of your right hand rigid and force your right forearm bone into the muscle of his neck.

Bring your right hip into the small of his back and bend him backwards (Fig. 80).

58

No. 9.—Front Strangle Hold.

Fig. 79

Fig. 80

59

No. 10.—Front Strangle Hold with Throw.

Having secured the hold as in Fig. 81, and you want to throw your assailant:

1. Retain the hold with your right arm around his neck and place your left hand at the back of his right thigh (Fig. 82).
2. Lift upwards with your left hand, pulling downwards with your right arm, at the same time shooting your hip into the small of his back by straightening out your legs.
3. When your assailant is off his feet, bend forward from the waist and throw him over your shoulder (Fig. 83).

Note.—It is quite a simple matter for you to throw an assailant in the above manner, even if he should be twice your own weight, but care must be taken when practicing it to keep a firm grip with your right arm to prevent him from falling on his head.

Having decided to give your assailant a rather heavy fall, release your hold when in the position shown in Figure 83; this will throw him on his stomach, with his head towards you. Should your assailant be one of several who have made an unwarranted attack on you, release your hold with your right arm at the moment when he is in the position shown in Figure 84, and dislocate his neck.

Fig. 81

60

No. 10.—Front Strangle Hold with Throw.

Fig. 82

Fig. 83

Fig. 84

61

No. 11.—FRONT STRANGLE HOLD ON THE GROUND.

Having secured the hold as in Fig. 85, and you are tripped, or want to bring your assailant to the ground.

1. Retain the hold on your assailant's neck and arm, shoot both of your legs forward, letting your assailant take the force of the fall on his back.
2. Force your head down on to your assailant's right arm and head; at the same time force the weight of your body on to his chest, applying pressure by pulling up on your right wrist with your left hand (Fig. 86).

Note.—Should the circumstances justify, and it is necessary that you should release your hold, apply pressure sharply with your right arm on your assailant's neck until he faints (10 to 15 seconds).

It should be noted that your assailant while in this position (Fig. 86), cannot do you any injury whatever and providing you keep your left foot flat on the ground and your legs out of reach of his legs he cannot get up.

62

No. 11.—Front Strangle Hold on the Ground.

Fig. 85

Fig. 86

63

No. 12.—Back Strangle Hold.

1. Stand at your opponent's back.
2. Place your left arm around his neck, with your forearm bone bearing on his Adam's apple.
3. Place the back of your right arm (above the elbow) on his right shoulder and clasp your right biceps with your left hand.
4. Grasp the back of his head with your right hand.
5. Pull up with your left forearm and press forward on the back of his head with your right hand (Fig. 87).

Note.—If this hold is applied correctly it is impossible for your opponent to release himself; further, his neck can easily be dislocated and if pressure is applied for 10 seconds he will int owing to anæmia of the brain.

It should be noted that this is a drastic hold and would only be used against an opponent who would go to any extent to gain his freedom. Should.he attempt to seize you by the testicles, step back quickly, at the same time jolting his head forward with your right hand and dislocate his neck (Fig. 88).

64

HOLDS THAT ARE EFFECTIVE

No. 12.—Back Strangle Hold.

Fig. 87

Fig. 88

65

No. 13.—BACK STRANGLE HOLD APPLIED FROM THE FRONT.

1. Stand facing your opponent. Seize his right shoulder with your left hand and his left shoulder with your right hand (Fig. 89).
2. Push with your left hand (retaining the hold) and pull towards you with your right hand. If this is done suddenly your opponent will be turned completely around and your left arm will be in position around his neck.
3. Place the back of your right arm (above the elbow) on his right shoulder and clasp your right biceps with your left hand.
4. Grasp the back of his head with your right hand.
5. Pull up with your left forearm and press forward on the back of his head with your right hand (Fig. 90).

66

No. 13.—BACK STRANGLE HOLD APPLIED FROM THE FRONT.

FIG. 89

FIG. 90

67

No. 14.—WRIST AND ELBOW HOLD.

Your assailant seizes you by the throat with his right hand.

1. Seize assailant's right hand from above with your right hand, your fingers passing over the back of his hand to the palm.
2. Seize his right elbow with your left hand, thumb to the right (Fig. 91).
3. With a circular upward swing of your right hand towards your right-hand side, simultaneously turn inwards and press with your left hand on his elbow, bending his right wrist towards him (Figs. 92 and 92a).
4. To throw your assailant, jerk his right arm to the ground by falling forward on to your knees.

68

No. 14.—WRIST AND ELBOW HOLD.

Fig 91

Fig. 92

Fig. 92A

69

No. 15.—Wrist and Elbow Hold, Whilst Lying in Bed.

Your assailant seizes you by the throat with his right hand whilst you are lying in bed.

1. Seize his right hand from above, with your right hand, your fingers passing over the back of his hand to the palm.
2. Seize his right elbow with your left hand, thumb to the right (Figs. 93 and 93a).
3. Turn sharply to your right on to your stomach, pulling his right arm under your body, by pulling on the wrist and forcing towards your right-hand side with your left hand on his elbow. This will bring you and your assailant into the positions shown in Fig. 94.
4. Keeping his right arm straight, force down on his elbow with your left hand and twist his right wrist towards him by an upward motion of your right hand.

70

No. 15.—WRIST AND ELBOW HOLD, WHILST LYING IN BED.

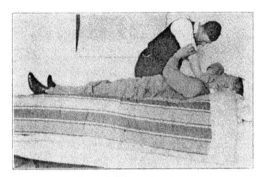

FIG. 93

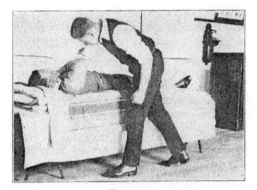

FIG. 93A

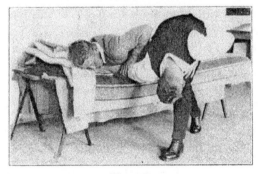

FIG. 94

71

No. 16.—Thumb and Elbow Hold.

Stand facing your opponent and slightly to his left.

1. Insert your right thumb between the thumb and forefinger of his left hand, palm of your right hand upwards, thumb to the right (Fig. 95).

2. Seize his left elbow with your left hand, knuckles to the right (Fig. 96).

3. Step in towards your opponent; at the same time turn your body so that you are facing in the same direction, simultaneously forcing his left forearm up across his chest and towards his left shoulder by pulling his elbow with your left hand over your right forearm and forcing upwards with your right hand.

4. Keeping a firm grip on the upper part of his left arm with your right arm, apply a slight pressure on the back of his hand towards your left-hand side with your right hand and you will be surprised to see how quickly your opponent will raise on his toes and shout for mercy (Fig. 97).

5. Should your opponent be a very powerful man and try to resist, a little extra pressure (3 to 4 lbs.) applied with the left hand on his elbow, as in Fig. 98, will be sufficient to convince him he has met his master, and he will be quite willing to submit to anything.

Note.—This is the most effective hold known, and I think I am correct in saying that only Japanese jui-jitsu experts (4th and 5th degree black belt) know how to apply it. Further, it should be noted that while all the other holds are very effective, and that it is not necessary to exert a great amount of strength to overcome your opponent, the fact remains that should it be necessary for you to have to take an opponent a distance of a mile or so, the strain, both mental and physical, would be so great that it would be very difficult for the average person to accomplish it, but if you have secured the hold as in Fig. 97, you would have no difficulty whatsoever in taking a very powerful opponent, even if he was resisting, as far as it is possible for you to walk.

72

HOLDS THAT ARE EFFECTIVE

No. 16.—Thumb and Elbow Hold.

Fig. 95

Fig. 96

Fig. 97

Fig. 98

73

No. 17.—HEAD HOLD.

Stand facing your opponent.

1. Strike your opponent on the left side of his neck with the inside of your right forearm (Fig. 99).
2. Pass your arm around his head, catching hold of your right wrist with your left hand and forcing his head down to your right (Fig. 100).
3. Force your right forearm bone into the right side of his face by pulling on your right wrist with your left hand and forcing downwards on the left side of his face with your body.

Note.—This hold is very painful for your opponent, and care must be taken in practice to apply the pressure gradually.

74

No. 17.—HEAD HOLD.

FIG. 99

FIG. 100

75

No. 18.—HEAD HOLD WITH THROW.

Having secured the hold as in Fig. 101, and you are about to be attacked by another opponent:

1. Retain the hold of your first opponent and turn sharply towards your left-hand side, straighten up your body and swing him by the neck off his feet (Fig. 102).

2. Keep turning until your opponent's feet are well clear of the ground; then suddenly release your hold. Immediately close with your second opponent and treat him likewise.

76

No. 18.—Head Hold with Throw.

Fig. 101

Fig. 102

77

No. 1.—WRIST THROW.

1. Stand facing your opponent and slightly to his right-hand side.

2. Lean forward and seize his right hand with your left, back of your hand towards your right-hand side, your fingers around his thumb towards the palm of his hand, your thumb forced in between the knuckle-joint of his first and second fingers (Fig. 103).

3. Raise his arm, by a circular motion, towards your left-hand side, at the same time seizing the little finger side of his right hand with your right. Turn his palm towards him; then force your thumbs into the back of his hand (Fig. 104).

4. Force his hand towards him. This will throw him on to his right-hand side (Fig. 105).

Note.—While Fig. 104 shows the thumbs forced into the back of the hand, it should be noted that it is not always possible to obtain this position quickly; but providing the palm of your opponent's hand is turned towards him, and pressure is applied with the thumbs on the back of his hand or fingers as in Fig. 106, this will be found to be nearly as effective.

If you have any difficulty in throwing your opponent, give his wrist a sharp turn to your left and pull downwards towards your left-hand side. Another method is to sink suddenly on to one knee and pull downwards towards your left-hand side.

Either of these will cause him to lose his balance and fall.

78

HOW TO THROW AN ASSAILANT

No. 1.—Wrist Throw.

Fig. 103

Fig. 104

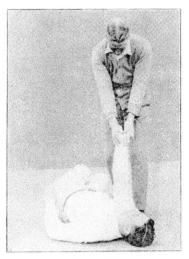

Fig. 105

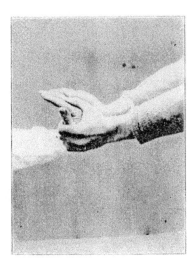

Fig. 106

79

No. 2.—WRIST THROW WITH LEG HOLD.

Having thrown your opponent as in Fig. 107, and you wish to hold him on the ground:

1. Retain the hold on his right wrist with both hands, step over his body with both feet, keeping his arm between your legs (Fig. 108).
2. Bend your legs from the knees and sit down as close to your opponent's body as possible (Fig. 109).
3. Pull on your opponent's wrist, to keep the arm straight, fall backwards and bend his arm the reverse way by resting the upper part of his arm on your right thigh and forcing his wrist towards the ground (Fig. 110).

Note.—Should your opponent attempt to pull his right arm away by the help of his left hand, force your left or right foot into the bend of his left arm and kick it away (Fig. 111).

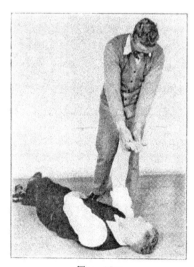

FIG. 107

80

No. 2.—Wrist Throw with Leg Hold.

Fig. 108

Fig. 109

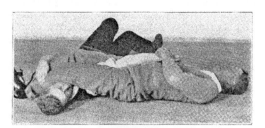

Fig. 110

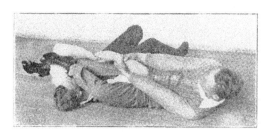

Fig. 111

81

No. 3.—ARM THROW.

1. Stand facing your opponent and slightly to his right-hand side.
2. Seize his right wrist with both of your hands, right above left (Fig. 112).
3. Swing his arm high up.
4. Pass under it by turning to your right (Fig. 113), keeping a firm hold on his wrist. This will cause his arm to twist as shown in Fig. 114.
5. When in this position sink slightly forward on the left knee, keeping your right leg firm and straight, pull down on your opponent's arm, by bending suddenly towards the ground bending from the waist.
6. This will cause him to fall on his back (Fig. 115).

Note.—This is a very dangerous throw, and great care must be taken when practicing it, otherwise you will dislocate your opponent's shoulder, or cause him to strike the back of his head on the ground.

82

HOW TO THROW AN ASSAILANT

No. 3.—Arm Throw.

Fig. 112

Fig. 113

Fig. 114

Fig. 115

83

No. 4.—HIP THROW.

Stand facing your opponent.

1. Seize both his arms above the elbows.
2. Turn your body sharply to your right and shoot your left leg to his left side. Take care that the back of your left leg is against his body and your left foot flat on the ground (Fig. 116).
3. Bend forward towards your right-hand side and jerk him sharply over your left hip, by pulling downwards with your right hand and pushing or lifting upwards with your left hand.
4. This will bring your opponent into the position shown in Fig. 117.

Note.—Having secured the hold as in Fig. 116, and you have difficulty in throwing your opponent, sink suddenly on to your right knee, pulling downwards with your right hand, and pushing or lifting upwards with your left hand (Fig. 118).

Care must be taken when applying this throw in the above manner, otherwise your opponent will be rendered unconscious through striking his head on the ground.

84

No. 4.—Hip Throw.

Fig. 116

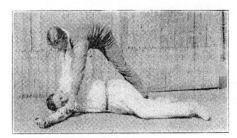

Fig. 117

Fig. 118

85

No. 5.—HIP THROW, WITH LEG HOLD.

Having secured throw as in Fig. 119:

1. Allow your right hand to slip up his left arm to his wrist and secure it with both hands, right above left. Step over his body with both feet, keeping his arm between your legs (Fig. 120).
2. Bend your legs from the knees and sit down as close to your opponent as possible.
3. Pulling on your opponent's wrist, to keep his left arm straight, fall backwards and bend his arm the reverse way, by resting the upper part of his arm on your left thigh and forcing his wrist towards the ground (Fig. 121).

Note.—Fig. 110 (Wrist Throw with Leg Hold, page 81) and Fig. 121 show that when the leg hold is applied your opponent's arm should be across the thigh which is nearest his body. By so doing you have a much better leverage and it becomes extremely difficult for him to pull his arm away.

86

No. 5.—HIP THROW, WITH LEG HOLD.

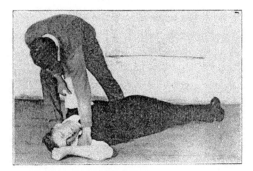

FIG. 119

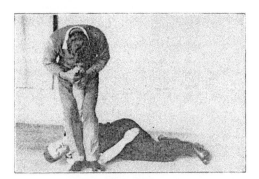

FIG. 120

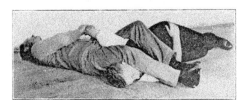

FIG. 121

87

No. 6.—Ankle Throw.

1. Stand facing your opponent.
2. Seize both his arms above the elbows.
3. Pull downwards with your right hand and lift upwards with your left (this will pull the weight of his body on to his left leg) ; at the same time strike his left ankle with the sole of your right foot without bending your leg (Fig. 122).

Note.—The blow of your right foot on your opponent's left ankle should be made with sufficient force to sweep his legs from under him.

88

No. 6.—Ankle Throw.

Fig. 122

89

No. 7.—INSTEP THROW.

1. Stand facing your opponent.
2. Seize him under the armpits with both hands, your toes turned outwards, and pull him towards you (Fig. 123).
3. Sinking from the knees, fall backwards, simultaneously pulling upwards with your hands and kicking his legs backwards as in Fig. 124.
4. This will throw your opponent over your head (Fig. 125).

Caution.—It should be noted that the Instep Throw is a very dangerous throw. Should your opponent be unacquainted with the "art of falling" he will probably meet with serious injury.

90

No. 7.—INSTEP THROW.

FIG. 123   FIG. 124

FIG. 125

91

No. 8.—Leg or Scissor Throw.

1. Stand on the right of your opponent (one to two feet away), facing in the same direction.
2. Seize the upper part of his right arm with your left hand (Fig. 126).
3. Jumping inwards, throw your left leg across the front of his legs and your right behind his knees (Fig. 127).
4. Almost simultaneously placing your right hand on the ground and turning your body to the rear, pulling him backwards by his right arm. This will bring him into the position shown in Fig. 128.

92

HOW TO THROW AN ASSAILANT

No. 8.—LEG OR SCISSOR THROW.

FIG. 126

FIG. 127

FIG. 128

93

No. 9.—Leg or Scissor Throw, with Leg Lock.

1. Having secured the throw as in Fig. 128, keep twisting your body towards your left, keep your legs straight and let go his right arm. This will turn your opponent over on to his stomach (Fig. 129).
2. Seize his right foot with your left hand and bend his leg from the knee, over your right leg (Fig. 130).

Note.—Should your opponent attempt to get up, force his right foot downwards and in the opposite direction to that in which he is trying to raise himself.

94

No. 9.—Leg or Scissor Throw, with Leg Lock.

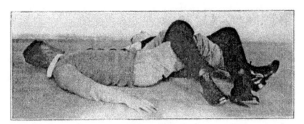

Fig. 128

Fig. 129

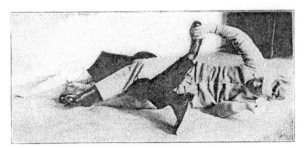

Fig. 130

95

EDGE OF THE HAND BLOWS.

It is not generally known that a person can hit with more force with the edge of the hand than with the clenched fist.

A person striking with his clenched fist distributes the force of the blow over a much larger surface than would be the case if he struck with the edge of his hand.

It stands to reason that a blow covering only one square inch of the body must be more painful than if it were distributed over four, providing that both blows are delivered with the same amount of force.

Further, an Edge of the Hand Blow, delivered in the manner shown in Fig. 131 ("Forearm Blow"), would break the forearm bone. This would be impossible with a blow from the clenched fist.

Note.—An "Edge of the Hand Blow" is given with the inner (*i.e.* little finger) edge of the palm, fingers straight and close together, thumb extended.

96

EDGE OF THE HAND BLOWS.

FOREARM

FIG. 131

97

EDGE OF THE HAND BLOWS

FOREARM   WRIST

Fig. 131   Fig. 132

BICEPS   NECK

Fig. 133   Fig. 134

98

EDGE OF THE HAND BLOWS

FACE

SHOULDER

Fig. 135

Fig. 136

NECK

NECK

Fig. 137

Fig. 138

99

EDGE OF THE HAND BLOWS

THIGH

SHIN

FIG. 139

FIG. 140

LEG

WAIST

FIG. 141

FIG. 142

100

KIDNEY

FIG. 143

SPINE

FIG. 144

101

No. 1.—Use of the Baton, "Night Stick" or Club.

Police clubs are provided with a leather thong or cord so that they can be secured to the hand. This prevents them from being snatched away. It is, in consequence, very important that all policemen should know the correct manner in which this thong or cord should be used.

For instance, if the thong were securely fixed around the wrist, and the club seized, it would be very difficult for its user to free himself, and he could easily be thrown to the ground by it.

To prevent this, the club should be held in the following manner:

1. Pass your right thumb through the loop (Fig. 145).
2. Pass the thong over the back of your hand to the palm (Fig. 146).

Note.—The thong or cord should be of sufficient length (but on no account longer) so that the head of the club will be in the center of the palm of the hand. By keeping a firm grip, it is impossible for an assailant to snatch it away. But should the club be seized, all that is necessary is to release the hold on the handle and the thong will slip off the thumb.

The blow with the club should be given in the same manner as a blow with a hammer, the wrist must be free. If the club is held as in Fig. 147 the wrist is partly locked and the force of the blow is checked. The above applies equally to loaded hunting crops when used as weapons of defense.

102

USE OF BATON, "NIGHT STICK" OR CLUB

No. 1.—Use of the Baton, "Night Stick" or Club.

Fig. 145

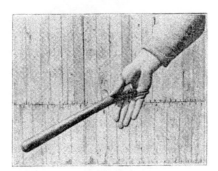

Fig. 146

Fig. 147

103

No. 2.—"CLUB BLOW."

1. To bring your assailant to the ground, hit him on the shin bone below the knee-cap (Fig. 148). This is more effective than a head blow.
2. To make your assailant release his hold of any weapon with which he may be armed, hit him on either the forearm or wrist.

FIG. 148

104

USE OF BATON, "NIGHT STICK" OR CLUB

No 3.—THE CLUB AS A PROTECTION.

To ward off a blow with a stick or similar weapon at your head:

1. Grasp the club with both hands near the ENDS, rush in as close as possible, taking the blow on the club (Fig. 149).
2. Release hold with your left hand and strike with club by a swinging blow at your assailant's shins. This will bring him to the ground.

Note.—It is to be noted that an assailant with a stick or other striking weapon can do little injury if you keep close to him.

FIG. 149

105

No. 4.—THE CLUB USED AS HANDCUFFS.

Having thrown your opponent, as in Fig. 150. (Handcuff Hold, page 53).

1. Pass the thong over his right wrist.
2. Seize his left wrist and pass it through the loop of the thong.
3. Twist the club until the thong cuts into the wrists.
4. Keeping hold of the club with your right hand, stand up and assist your opponent to rise (Fig. 151).

106

No. 4.—The Club Used as Handcuffs.

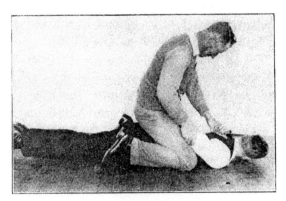

Fig. 150

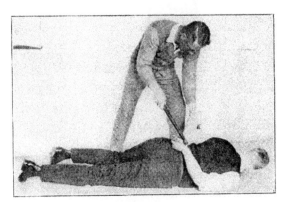

Fig. 151

107

No. 5.—Silk Cord v. Leather Thong.

It is recommended that a silk cord be used on police night sticks or clubs instead of a leather thong. The silk cord is much stronger and can be lengthened at will and used as a tourniquet in case of an accident (Fig. 152).

The cord should be of sufficient length (2-ft. 6-in.) to permit it being passed over any part of the thigh or arm, and should be secured to the club as in Fig. 153.

To shorten the cord to the correct length, so that the head of the club comes in the palm of the hand, make a number of "half hitches" and pass them over the head of the club (Fig. 154).

Fig. 152

108

No. 5.—Silk Cord v. Leather Thong.

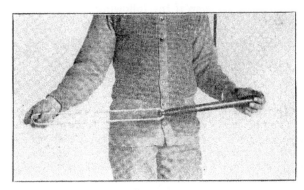

Fig. 153

Fig. 154

109

HOW TO USE A WALKING STICK

The art of usng a walking stick in attack or defence is not generally known, yet it is possible for anybody to master a very powerful man if the following instructions be carried out:

To bring your assailant to the ground, hit him on the shins, just below the knee-cap (Fig. 155), or jab him in the stomach with the point.

Note.—Never attempt to strike your assailant over the head, as this can be very easily guarded. In fact, it is almost impossible to strike a person over the head, if he is aware that you are about to do so. Further he would be sure to close with you, and the stick would prove a handicap in preventing you from securing an effective hold.

The best class of stick is a medium weight ash or a Malacca cane.

110

ATTACK AND DEFENCE WITH A WALKING STICK.

FIG. 155

111

HOW TO USE A WALKING STICK

No. 1.—Arm and Neck Hold, with-a Stick.

1. Holding your stick in the left hand, thumb to the left, stand level with your opponent on his right side, facing the same way.
2. Seize his right wrist with your right hand, back of your hand to the front, back of his hand downwards.
3. Raise his right arm with your right hand; at the same time pass the stick under the arm to the back of his neck (Fig. 156).
4. Pull downwards on his right arm and lift upwards with the stick (Fig. 157).

Note.—Care must be taken that the stick is above your opponent's right elbow, otherwise you cannot get any leverage on the arm.

112

No. 1.—ARM AND NECK HOLD, WITH A STICK.

FIG. 156

FIG. 157

113

No. 2.—ARM HOLD, WITH A STICK.

1. Holding your stick in the left hand, thumb to the handle, stand level with your opponent on his right-hand side, facing the same way.
2. Seize his right wrist with your right hand, back of your hand to the front, back of his hand downwards.
3. Pass the stick under his right arm, above the elbow, to his chest (Fig. 158).
4. Push forward on the stick with your left hand and pull his right backwards with your right hand (Fig. 159).

114

No. 2.—Arm Hold, with a Stick.

Fig. 158

Fig. 159

115

No. 3.—BACK STRANGLE HOLD, WITH A STICK.

1. Holding your stick in the right hand, thumb towards the handle, stand at your opponent's back.
2. Place the stick around his neck, from his left-hand side (Fig. 160).
3. Pass your left hand over your right arm and seize the stick close up to your opponent's neck.
4. Force your forearms into the back of his neck, and pull the stick towards you (Fig. 161).

Note.—This is a very severe hold and extra care must be taken in practicing it, otherwise you will cause unnecessary pain.

116

No. 3.—BACK STRANGLE HOLD, WITH A STICK.

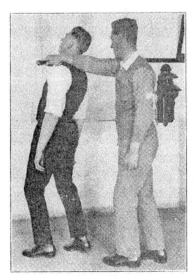

Fig. 160

Fig. 161

117

No. 4.—Crotch and Arm Hold, with a Stick.

1. Holding your stick in the left hand, thumb towards the handle, stand level with your opponent on his right side.

2. Pass the stick between his legs, seizing his right wrist with your right hand, back of your hand to the front, back of his hand downwards (Fig. 162).

3. Forcing the stick against the back of his left thigh, twist his wrist outwards and away from you with your right hand and pull it across your left leg, at the same time bringing the stick to the back of his right arm.

4. Holding his right arm straight, force downwards on the back of his right arm with the stick (Fig. 163).

118

No. 4.—Crotch and Arm Hold, with a Stick.

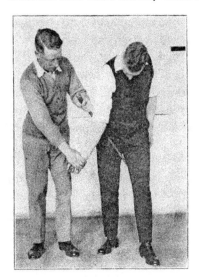

Fig. 162

Fig. 163

119

No. 5.—Neck Throw, with a Stick.

1. Holding your stick in the right hand, stand level with your opponent on his right side.
2. Pass the stick across your opponent's throat, grasp the other end with your left hand close up to the neck, simultaneously stepping behind him (Fig. 164).
3. Bending your arms from the elbows towards you, jerk him backwards to the ground (Fig. 165).

Note.—This throw is very severe and like No. 3 Back Strangle Hold, page 116, extra care must be taken in practicing it.

120

No. 5.—Neck Throw, with a Stick.

Fig. 164

Fig. 165

121

HOW TO MAKE AN EFFECTIVE KNOT

Practice tying the following knot on a stick, pole or anything similar:

Take a piece of cord or silk rope about a quarter of an inch in diameter, and from 5 to 7 yards in length. This can be carried or tied around the waist under the jacket.

1. Pass the cord behind the pole with, the *Short* end of the cord to the left and the *Long* end to the right (Fig. 166).
2. Pass the *Long* end of the cord, in a loop, over the pole and through the loop held in the left hand, then pull down on the *Short* end with the right hand (Fig. 167).
3. Pass the *Short* end of the cord, in a loop, over the pole and through the loop held in the left hand (Fig. 167), which will form the knot shown in Fig. 168.
4. Holding the loop in the left hand, pull down on the *Long* end of the cord, pass the left hand through the loop and pull on both *Ends* of the cord (Fig. 169).

Note.—For the purpose of illustrating clearly, rope was used instead of cord.

122

HOW TO MAKE AN EFFECTIVE KNOT

TYING AN EFFECTIVE KNOT.

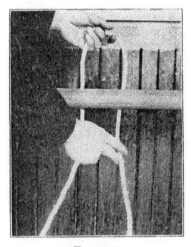

FIG. 166

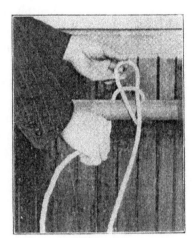

FIG. 167

FIG. 168

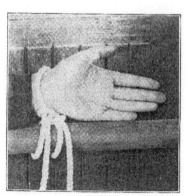

FIG. 169

123

Tying a Prisoner.

As is the case when using handcuffs, your prisoner is always more secure when his hands are fastened together behind his back: you would naturally compel him to precede you and you would then at once notice any attempt he might make to release his hands.

The knot shown on page 123 forms a very good substitute for a pair of handcuffs.

Tie the knot as shown in Fig. 170 on your prisoner's wrist, pass his other hand through the loop, held in the left hand and pull taut, then tie two half hitches to prevent slipping (Fig. 171).

124

TYING A PRISONER.

FIG. 170

FIG. 171

125

HOW TO SECURE AN OPPONENT

TYING UP AN OPPONENT.

Should it be necessary that you have to leave your opponent without a guard, the following method of securing him will be found very effective:

Secure his hands as in Fig. 171, throw him on the ground, pass the cord around his neck, pass the end under his hands. Bend his left leg backwards and tie two half hitches round his ankle (Fig. 172).

Note.—If your prisoner keeps still he will not hurt himself, but the more he moves the greater the discomfort he will suffer.

126

Tying up an Opponent.

Fig. 171

Fig. 172

127

To Lift a Man on to His Feet from the Ground.

Your opponent lies on his stomach on the ground and refuses to stand up.

1. Stand to one side or over your opponent.
2. Seize him round the neck with both hands, your fingers pressing into his neck alongside the "Adam's apple" (Fig. 173).
3. Force the points of your thumb into the hollows under the lobe of the ears and lift upwards (Fig. 174).

128

To Lift a Man on to His Feet from the Ground.

Fig. 173

Fig. 174

129

THE HANDKERCHIEF OR GLOVE AS AN AID TO SECURING A
HOLD OR THROW.

Under certain circumstances the pocket handkerchief is
a great aid in securing an effective hold or throw, such as
when a policeman is called into a building to eject a person.
Your opponent is standing and from all appearance is
about to resist being put out of the building.

1. Speak to him quietly but firmly and ask him to leave,
at the same time taking your handkerchief in your
hand.

2. Suddenly throw the handkerchief in his face, simultaneously closing with him. This will take him off
his guard and you should have no difficulty in applying one of the holds or throws demonstrated, in Figs.
57, 80, 100, 104, 116 and 122.

POLICE HOLD   STRANGLE HOLD

FIG. 57   FIG. 80

130

MISCELLANEOUS ADVICE

THE HANDKERCHIEF OR GLOVE AS AN AID TO SECURING A HOLD OR THROW.

HEAD HOLD

WRIST THROW

FIG. 100

FIG. 104

HIP THROW

ANKLE THROW

FIG. 116

FIG. 122

131

How to Deal with an Assailant Following You at Night.

It gives rise to a very uncomfortable feeling to realize that you are being followed, especially if it should happen to be on a dark night and the road a lonely one. The best thing to do under these circumstances is to carry the war into the enemy's camp rather than to wait for him to attack you. If you turn on him it will prove such a surprise to your assailant that you will have little difficulty in securing an effective hold or throw.

Having become aware that you are being followed:

1. Shorten your pace and allow your assailant to come within eight or ten paces.
2. Without losing a pace, suddenly turn around and walk towards him.
3. Apply one of the holds or throws shown on pages 130 and 131.
4. Should your assailant be armed with a stick or other striking weapon, close with him. Providing this is done quickly it will be very difficult for him to do you any injury.
5. If there should be two assailants, and they attempt to close in on you (a very old dodge), suddenly "Chin Jab" them both (Fig. 175).

Note.—Providing you have taken the precaution of turning up your coat collar and have not missed a pace whilst turning, your assailant, still hearing your footsteps, will on a dark night not be aware that you are coming towards him, until you have actually closed upon him.

132

How to Deal with an Assailant Following You at
Night.

Fig. 175

133

THE FARCE OF THE "FIREMAN'S LIFT."
(Raising and carrying an unconscious person, single-handed.)

It is not generally known that the method of picking up and carrying an unconscious person, commonly known as the "Fireman's Lift," which one sees demonstrated in nearly every book on First Aid, is an impossibility.

The instructions are usually as follows:

1. Turn the patient on to his face and then raise him to a kneeling position.
2. Place yourself under him, so that his stomach is on your right shoulder.
3. Pass your right arm between his thighs and behind his right thigh, grasping his right wrist with your right hand (Fig. 176).

To carry out the above, with a conscious subject, is easy enough, for the simple reason that when raised to a kneeling position he keeps his joints stiff. Were, however, the subject really unconscious he would not remain in a kneeling position, unless held there, but would collapse from the hips and fall sideways or forward (Fig. 177).

In addition, very few people, even when in a standing position, are strong enough to lift an unconscious body clear off the ground, and to attempt to do so from a kneeling position is an utter waste of time.

134

The Farce of the "Fireman's Lift."

Fig. 176

Fig. 177

135

THE ART OF FALLING

Japanese jiu-jitsu experts consider the art of falling correctly, *i. e.*, without hurting one's self, of more importance than the ability to secure an effective hold or trip, and it is owing to this that they are able to fall and be thrown about in competition in such a manner that, to a stranger, appears to be asking for a broken limb, yet they no sooner hit the ground than they are again on their feet.

The fact that falling backwards down a flight of stairs can be accomplished without the slightest injury by any one who has made a thorough study of this art, clearly demonstrates that a little practice at a few simple but very useful falls, etc., will well repay the student for his trouble.

Caution.—Students are warned that the fall, shown on pages 138 and 189 should first be practiced from the kneeling or crouching position as shown on the following pages.

The following is an extract from the *North China Daily News*, November 23, 1916.

THE LYCEUM THEATRE

"THE BREED OF THE TRESHAMS"

There was a gorgeous stage fight in the second act, with a stage fall downstairs by a man shot dead, such as we have never seen equalled.

From the *North China Daily News*, November 24, 1916.

Praise that is given unawares is the best praise of all, and in mentioning yesterday that the fall downstairs of a man shot dead was such as we have never seen equalled (referring to the second act of "The Breed of the Treshams" on Saturday night) the writer thought he was giving recognition to some good acting by a member of the Howitt-Phillips Company. The realistic fall of the dead man down a steep flight of stairs was done, not by an actor, but by a policeman, W. E. Fairbairn, the drill instructor of the Shanghai

136

Municipal Police, and although he had rehearsed the scene he had not rehearsed the actual fall. Such things come natural to policemen, especially to jiu-jitsu men. And beside Fairbairn, there were seven other Shanghai policemen in the show that night, so that the "guards" were real guards, with the result that the stage fight was as real as safety would allow.

137

SIDE FALL

FIG. 178

HAND SPRING

FIG. 179

"FLYING" DIVE

FIG. 180

138

STOMACH FALL

FIG. 181

CROUCH FALL

FIG. 182

FACE FALL

FIG. 183

139

No. 1.—"ROLLING DIVE."

(KNEELING POSITION.)

This must first be learnt in the following manner, and on no account must it be attempted from the standing position until the pupil is proficient, otherwise there is danger of injury to the head, neck and kidneys:

1. Kneel on the right knee, place the back of the right hand and forearm on the ground under the body (Fig. 184).

2. Place the left hand on the ground in front of the left shoulder, turning the head to the left-hand side (Fig. 185).

3. Throw yourself forward over the right shoulder on to your left side, bending the lower part of the left leg from the knee, towards the right-hand side, the right foot to be over the left leg and in the position shown in Fig. 186.

140

MISCELLANEOUS ADVICE

No. 1.—"Rolling Dive." (Kneeling Position.)

Fig. 184 Fig. 185

Fig. 186

141

No. 1.—"Rolling Dive."

(Crouching Position.)

When proficient from the kneeling position as demonstrated on page 141, it should be practiced from the crouching position as follows:

Bend forward from the waist, placing the back of the right hand on the ground, left hand and head to the left-hand side (Fig. 187). Then throw yourself forward over the right shoulder and carry on as from the kneeling position. Providing you have not forgotten to turn the head to the left-hand side and allowed the spine to bend when turning over, it should only be necessary to practice this dive from the crouching position a few times.

142

No. 1.—"ROLLING DIVE." (Crouching Position.)

FIG. 187

143

MISCELLANEOUS ADVICE

No. 1.—"ROLLING DIVE."

(Standing Position.)

1. Standing as in Fig. 188, turn the head to the left and throw yourself forward head-over-heels.
2. Fig. 189 shows the feet and hands ready to strike the ground a fraction of a second before the body reaches the position shown in Fig. 190.
3. Fig. 191 shows the position just before the completion of the "Dive."

Note.—All the above movements must be continuous, but should you wish to remain on the ground, hold your right foot as in Fig. 186, (page 141), which will prevent you from coming up on to the feet.

Fig. 188

144

No. 1.—"ROLLING DIVE." (Standing Position.)

FIG. 189

FIG. 190

FIG. 191
145

No. 2.—SIDE FALL.

This fall must first be practiced from the following position:

1. Crouch as in Fig. 192, throw yourself on to your right-hand side, striking the ground with the open palm of your right hand a moment before your body reaches the ground (Fig. 193), care being taken that the right arm is at an angle of 45 degrees from the body: this protects the elbow. At the same time bring the left foot over the right leg into the position shown in Fig. 194.

Note.—Placing the left foot in the above position turns the body on to the right side, with the results that kidneys and head are prevented from striking the ground. When proficient in the above it should be practiced from the standing position.

This fall is used when thrown by the "Hip Throw" and is also an old trick for a person wishing to fall himself, in order to get into a favourable position to throw his opponent. See Figs. 195 and 196, (page 149).

146

No. 2.—Side Fall.

Fig. 192

Fig. 193

Fig. 194

147

No. 3.—SIDE FALL, WITH THROW AND LEG LOCK.

Your opponent having thrown you by the Hip Throw, and you are in the position shown in Fig. 195:

1. Turn over sharply on to the left side, pass your right leg around and to the back of his knees, placing your left leg over his feet at the instep (Fig. 196).

2. Twist your body sharply towards your right-hand side at the same time striking his feet backwards with your left leg and striking his legs forward with your right leg at the back of his knees. This will bring you into the position shown in Fig. 197.

3. Seize his right foot with your left hand and bend his right leg, from the knee, over your left leg. Apply pressure by twisting your body sharply towards your right-hand side, simultaneously forcing his right foot downwards (Fig. 198).

Note.—All the above movements must be continuous.

148

No. 3.—Side Fall, with Throw and Leg Lock.

Fig. 195

Fig. 196

Fig. 197

Fig. 198

149

No. 4.—Front Fall.

This fall must first be practiced from the following position:

1. Kneeling on the knees, hands and arms held slightly in advance of the body, palm of the hands to the front, with fingers and thumbs as shown in Fig. 199.
2. Fall forward on to the forearms and hands as shown in Fig. 200.

Caution.—At the moment the forearms and hands touch the ground, raise on to the toes, bringing the knees and stomach clear of the ground and allow the arms to bend forward from the elbows to take the shock of the fall. When proficient, practice from the standing position.

Note.—This fall is used when there is insufficient room to do a "Rolling Dive."

150

No. 4.—Front Fall.

Fig. 199

Fig. 200

151

No. 5.—Getting Up from the Ground.

Having fallen or been thrown, as in Fig. 201:

1. Turn your body sharply towards your left-hand side, stomach to the ground, raising by the help of the right forearm and right knee to the position shown in Fig. 202.
2. Pushing with both hands, force yourself into the position shown in Fig. 203 and then stand up.

Note.—All the above movements must be one continuous roll or twist of the body. Further, having arrived at the position shown in Fig. 203, and your opponent is behind you, and you want to face him, turn sharply on your left foot, backwards towards your left-hand side, when you will be in the position shown in Fig. 204.

Fig. 201

152

No. 5.—Getting Up from the Ground.

Fig. 202

Fig. 203

Fig. 204
153

No. 6.—Getting Up from the Ground (Backwards).

Having fallen or been thrown as in Fig. 205:

1. Place your right arm at an angle of 90 degrees from the body, back of hand on the ground, head towards your left shoulder (Fig. 206).
2. Raise your legs from the waist and shoot them over your right shoulder (Fig. 207).
3. Allow your right arm and hand to turn with your body; then by bending the right leg from the knee you will be in the position shown in Fig. 208.
4. Press on the ground with both hands and force yourself up to a standing position.

Fig. 205

154

No. 6.—Getting Up from the Ground (Backwards).

Fig. 206

Fig. 207

Fig. 208

155

COMBINATION THROW, WITH A "COAT STRANGLE."

You and your opponents have hold of each other's clothing, as in Fig. 209, and you are thrown by the "Hip Throw" (Fig. 210).

1. Do not release your hold, and whilst falling, pull downwards with your right hand and push with your left, simultaneously twisting your body towards your right-hand side; this will pull your opponent right over you and on to his back, as in Fig. 211.

2. Retaining your hold, pull yourself into the position shown in Fig. 212.

Continued on page 158

FIG. 209

156

MISCELLANEOUS ADVICE

Combination Throw, with a "Coat Strangle."

Fig. 210

Fig. 211

Fig. 212

157

COMBINATION THROW, WITH A "COAT STRANGLE."

3. Release the hold with your right hand and seize the right lapel of his coat, the back of your hand inside the coat, the thumb outside, hand as near his neck as possible, at the same time passing your left hand under your right forearm and seize the left lapel of his coat as in Fig. 213.

4. Keeping a firm grip with both hands, apply pressure by forcing the little finger side of your right forearm under his chin and into his neck, squeezing his ribs with your thighs and forcing downwards with your body as in Fig. 214.

Note.—Should your opponent sink his chin into his chest in an attempt to prevent you from forcing your forearm into his neck, force your wrist bone on to the point of his chin and work it to and fro. This is very painful and will quickly make him raise his chin.

The alternative method is to fall sideways on to your back pulling your opponent over on top of you and in between your legs; you will then be in the position shown in Fig. 215. Lock your legs around his waist and apply pressure by pulling his neck towards you and forcing your forearm into his chin or neck, then shoot out your legs and squeeze his ribs (Fig. 216).

FIG. 213

158

COMBINATION THROW, WITH A "COAT STRANGLE."

FIG. 214

FIG. 215

FIG. 216

159

PHOTOGRAPHIC COPIES OF CERTIFICATES RECEIVED BY THE
AUTHOR FROM TOKYO JUI-JITSU UNIVERSITY (KODOKAN).

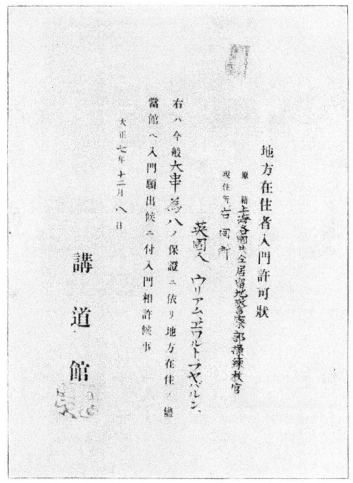

Translation of Certificate.
No. 217.   TOKIO JUI-JITSU UNIVERSITY (KODOKAN).
PERMISSION OF ENTRANCE.

The application for entrance of W. E. Fairbairn (resident in Foreign Country), a Drill Officer of the Police Force, Shanghai Municipal Council, having the guarantee of Tamehachi Ogushi, is hereby permitted on the Eighth Day of the Twelfth Moon in the Seventh Year of Taisho. (8th December, 1918).

(KODOKAN SEAL).

160

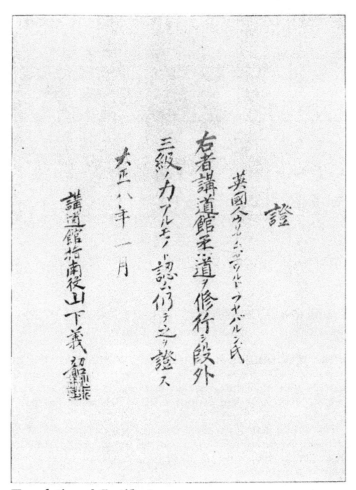

Translation of Certificate.

No. 218.   BROWN BELT, 3RD DEGREE.

This is to certify that W. E. Fairbairn, British Subject, having satisfactorily acquired the art of Kodokan Judo (Jui-jitsu), is awarded the Brown Belt, 3rd Degree (San Kyu), of the Tokyo Jui-jitsu University.

(Sd.) Y. YAMASHITA, Lodokan Judo Instructor.
First Moon in the Eighth Year
of Taisho (January, 1919).

(KODOKAN SEAL).

161

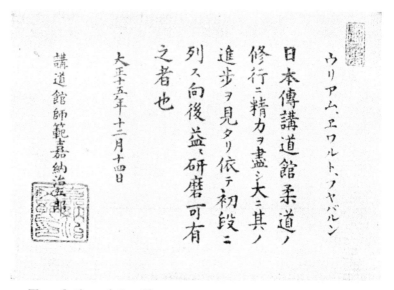

Translation of Certificate.

No. 219.   BLACK BELT, 1ST DEGREE

This is to certify that William Ewart Fairbairn has this day
been promoted to the rank of "First Degree" in the art of jui-jitsu
in recognition of his progress due to energetic and zealous study
and is hereby authorized to wear a Black Belt whilst engaged in
the art.

This institution highly appreciates the manner in which W. E.
Fairbairn has earned this honour and, while registering this record,
hopes that, in future, he will merit further honours by continuous
study and application.

(Signed & Sealed) JIGORO KANO,
President of the Kodokan
Jui-Jitsu Institution, Tokyo.
14th day of the 12th moon of the 15th year of Taisho.
(December 14, 1926).

162

PHOTOGRAPHIC COPIES OF CERTIFICATES RECEIVED BY THE
AUTHOR FROM TOKYO JUI-JITSU UNIVERSITY (KODOKAN).

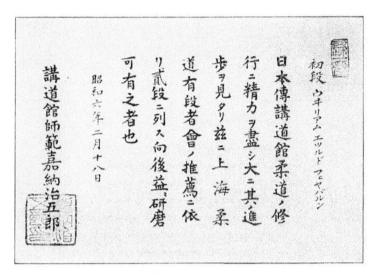

Translation of Certificate.

BLACK BELT, 2ND DEGREE

This is to certify that William Ewart Fairbairn who holds the
rank of "First Degree" has this day been promoted to the rank of
"Second Degree" in recognition of his further progress due to
energetic and zealous study and by the recommendation of the
Shanghai Jui-jitsu Association of Black Belt Holder.

This institution highly appreciates the manner in which W. E.
Fairbairn has earned this honour and while registering this record,
hopes that, in future, he will merit further honours by continuous
study and application.

(Signed & Sealed) JIGORO KANO,
President of the Kodokan
Jui-jitsu Institution, Tokyo.
18th day of the 2nd moon of the 6th year of Showa.
(February 18, 1931).

163

Shanghai Municipal Council.

POLICE FORCE.
(COMMISSIONER'S OFFICE.)

March 4, 1925.

The various forms of self-defence
have in recent years become an essential
factor in police training, and while
practical instruction at the hands of
an expert has been considered necessary
in acquiring a working knowledge, this
book, compiled by Inspector Fairbairn,
will in a great measure enable the reader
to teach himself. The admirable photographic
illustrations, the brief and clear instructions,
and the many orginal exercises described, are
a great advance on anything yet published.

As the most up-to-date comprehensive work
on defence against almost every form of attack,
this book, called ''Defendu,'' should form a portion
of the equipment of every police officer.

(sd.) K. J. McEUEN,

Commissioner of Police,
Shanghai,
China.

164

№ ...

Shanghai Municipal Council.

_____March 4,_____19 25.

TO CHIEF OFFICERS OF POLICE FORCES
AND OTHER INTERESTED PERSONS.

Sir,

This serves to introduce to you Inspector W.
Fairbairn, Drill Instructor of the Shanghai
Municipal Police who is proceeding home to England
on eight months furlough during which period it is
his intention to publish a book compiled by himself
on a system of self-defence known as ''Defendu.''

The methods contained in the book are
specially adopted for the use of policemen, are
simple and quite effective, as the bearer is quite
capable of demonstrating to any interested person.

I have much pleasure in recommending the book
to the careful consideration of the Chiefs of
Police Forces wishing to introduce an effective
method of defence against armed and other criminals.

Yours faithfully,

Commissioner of Police.

(1)

165

SCIENTIFIC
SELF-DEFENCE.

DEFENDU

By
W.E.Fairbairn

*"Get tough, get down in the gutter, win at all costs...
I teach what is called 'Gutter Fighting.' There's
no fair play, no rules except one: kill or be killed."*

The Author, with Professor Okada (Professor of Jui-jitsu,
2nd pupil of the Mikado's personal instructor).
Taken at Shanghai, China, 1908.

DEFENDU

(Scientific Self-Defence)

THE OFFICIAL TEXT BOOK FOR THE SHANGHAI
MUNICIPAL POLICE, HONGKONG POLICE AND
SINGAPORE POLICE

by

W. E. FAIRBAIRN

Instructor to the Shanghai Municipal Police,
Member of Tokyo Jui-jitsu University
(Kodokan)

(3rd Degree Brown Belt)

Photographs by

A. J. P. COGHLAN

The Naval & Military Press Ltd

FOREWORD

———•••———

In presenting a work on " Self-Defence " to the public, it may appear necessary, in view of the numerous books already published on the same subject, to say something in justification of such a venture.

First let it be said that I believe the " DEFENDU " system to be entirely new and original, and, further, it requires no athletic effort to perform any of the exercises given.

This system is not to be confounded with jui-jitsu or any other known method of defence, and although some of the holds, trips, etc. are a combination of several methods, the majority are entirely original.

After a long experience of methods of attack and defence I am convinced that none that I have yet seen put into book form meet the requirements of the average man and present-day conditions.

The " DEFENDU " system has been produced after considerable thought and several years spent in its preparation and is believed to be the most practical for the average man, who has neither the time nor the inclination to keep as physically fit as other methods require.

The methods of defence explained and illustrated in this book have been specially selected for the man who requires quick knowledge of the best and easiest means of defending himself against almost every form of attack. It teaches a number of drastic and admittedly unpleasant forms of defence and attack which have been found necessary to cope with the foul methods used by a certain class.

It further teaches you to protect certain vital parts of the body which are a target for the foul methods used by the bully or ruffian, and it will be noted that the illustrations clearly emphasize this point.

It should be realized that in boxing, wrestling and jui-jitsu competitions, etc., the competitors, in addition to having the spirit of fair-play ingrained in them from boyhood, are further protected from foul blows by the presence of a referee. But when dealing with the street ruffian, burglar or armed robber, one is faced by an opponent or assailant of a different stamp entirely. From reports all over the world, crime is on the increase, and most criminal methods recognize no bounds so long as the objective is attained and the perpetrators can make good their escape.

I am satisfied that every method herein illustrated is practical and complete in itself, and I feel sure that a new sense of security and confidence will be acquired after a short study of this system, which will amply compensate the reader for the time spent in studying it. In fact, after mastering a few of the holds, trips, etc., which require no great strength to perform, the reader will find himself in a position of security against almost any form of attack.

In conclusion, I wish to record my sincerest thanks to Captain E. I. M. Barrett, o.i.e., Messrs. W. Beatty, A. J. P. Coghlan, T. E. Wood and O. B. Perkins for their kindly encouragement, assistance and advice during the necessary lengthy and tedious stage of testing and selection of methods, before finally deciding on those considered to be the most simple and practical when put into use by the average untrained individual.

W. E. FAIRBAIRN.

Shanghai, China, 1925.

Shanghai Municipal Council.

March 4, 1925.

POLICE FORCE.
(COMMISSIONER'S OFFICE.)

The various forms of self-defence
have in recent years become an essential
factor in police training, and while
practical instruction at the hands of
an expert has been considered necessary
in acquiring a working knowledge, this
book, compiled by Inspector Fairbairn,
will in a great measure enable the reader
to teach himself. The admirable photographic
illustrations, the brief and clear instructions,
and the many orginal exercises described, are
a great advance on anything yet published.

As the most up-to-date comprehensive work
on defence against almost every form of attack,
this book, called ''Defendu,'' should form a portion
of the equipment of every police officer.

(sd.) K. J. McEUEN,

Commissioner of Police,
Shanghai,
China.

Shanghai Municipal Council.

March 4, 19 25.

POLICE FORCE.
(COMMISSIONER'S OFFICE.)

TO CHIEF OFFICERS OF POLICE FORCES
AND OTHER INTERESTED PERSONS.

Sir,

This serves to introduce to you Inspector W. Fairbairn, Drill Instructor of the Shanghai Municipal Police who is proceeding home to England on eight months furlough during which period it is his intention to publish a book compiled by himself on a system of self-defence known as ''Defendu.''

The methods contained in the book are specially adopted for the use of policemen, are simple and quite effective, as the bearer is quite capable of demonstrating to any interested person.

I have much pleasure in recommending the book to the careful consideration of the Chiefs of Police Forces wishing to introduce an effective method of defence against armed and other criminals.

Yours faithfully,

Commissioner of Police.

CONTENTS

CONTENTS.—*cont.*

CONTENTS.—*cont.*

DEFENCE AGAINST VARIOUS HOLDS

No. 1.—Wrist Hold.

(a) Your assailant seizes your right wrist with his left hand (Fig. 1). To make him release his hold:—Bend your arm towards your body and turn it in the direction of his thumb (Fig. 2).

Fig. 1

Fig. 2

12

No. 1.—Wrist Hold.

(*b*)   Your assailant seizes you by both wrists (Fig. 3).   To make him release his hold :—Bend your arms towards your body and twist your wrists in the direction of his thumbs.   Or :—
Jerk your hands towards your body, at the same time hitting him in the face with the top of your head (Fig. 4).

Fig.   3

Fig.   4

13

No. 2.—Being Strangled.

(a) Your assailant seizes you by the throat with his right hand, forcing you back against a wall (Fig. 5).

1. With a sweeping blow of your right hand strike his right wrist towards your left-hand side.

2. If necessary, knee him in the testicles with your right knee (Fig. 6).

Fig. 5

Fig. 6

14

No. 2.—Being Strangled.

(b) Your assailant seizes you by the throat with both hands, forcing you back against a wall.

1. Bring your forearms up inside his arms and strike outwards.
2. If necessary, knee him in the testicles with your right knee (Fig. 7).

Fig. 7

15

No. 3.—" Bear Hug." From in Front.

Your assailant seizes you around the body and arms with both arms (Fig. 8).
1. Knee him in the testicles or stomach.
2. Kick him on the shins.
3. Stamp on his feet.
4. Bump him in the face with your head.
5. Seize him by the testicles with your right or left hand.

Fig. 8

No. 4.--"Bear Hug." From Behind.

Your assailant seizes you around the body with both arms (Fig. 9).

1. Kick him on the shins.
2. Stamp on his feet.
3. Bump him in the face with the back of your head.
4. Seize him by the testicles with your right or left hand.

Fig. 9

17

No. 5.—Waist Hold. From in Front.

Your assailant seizes you around the body from in front, leaving your arms free.

1. Strike his chin a hard upward jab with the heel of your right wrist (Fig. 10).

2. Seize his neck with both hands, fingers touching behind, thumbs in the front, one on each side of the "Adam's Apple." Force inwards with the point of your thumb and jerk his head sharply backwards (Fig. 11).

3. Seize the back of his neck between the thumb and the fingers of your right hand and force him to the ground (Fig. 12).

4. Kick him on the shins.

5. Knee him in the testicles or stomach.

No. 5.—Waist Hold. From in Front.

Fig. 10

Fig. 11

Fig. 12

19

No. 6.—Waist Hold. From Behind.

Your assailant seizes you around the waist from behind, leaving your arms free.

1. Strike the back of his hand with your knuckles (Fig. 13).

2. Seize either of his little fingers and bend it backwards; if necessary, break it (Fig. 14).

3. Stamp on his feet with the heel of your boot.

4. If your assailant has sufficiently long hair for you to get a good hold of it, reach over backwards with your left hand and seize it, bend suddenly forwards, pulling him by the hair over your back (Fig. 15).

No. 6—Waist Hold. From Behind.

Fig. 13

Fig. 14

Fig. 15

21

No. 7.—Hair Hold.   From Behind.

Your assailant seizes you by the hair, from behind, with his right hand.

1. Seize his hand with both of yours to prevent him letting go (Fig. 16).

2. Turn in towards your assailant; this will twist his wrist.

3. Force your head up and bend his wrist inwards, away from his elbow (Fig. 17).

No. 7.—Hair Hold. From Behind.

Fig. 16

Fig. 17

No. 8.—Coat Hold.

Your assailant seizes you by the left shoulder with his right hand.

1. Seize his right hand with your right hand.

2. Seize his right elbow with your left hand, thumb to the right (Fig 18).

3. With a circular upward and downward motion of your left hand on the elbow, turn sharply outwards towards your right-hand side (Fig. 19).

4. Keeping a firm grip with your right hand, which will prevent him from releasing his hold, force down on his elbow with your left hand.

Note.—An " Edge of the Hand Blow " given as shown in Figure 20 will be found to be very effective.

24

No. 8.—Coat Hold.

Fig. 18

Fig. 19

Fig. 20

25

No. 9—Coat Hold.

Your assailant seizes you by the left shoulder with his right hand.

1. Seize his right elbow with your left hand from underneath; at the same time pass your right hand over the arm and seize the elbow with your right hand above your left (Fig. 21).

2. With a circular upward and downward motion of your hands on his elbow turn sharply outwards towards your right-hand side. This will bring you into the position shown in Fig. 22.

3. Force his elbow towards your body and push up with your left shoulder. This will prevent him from releasing his arm. If necessary, knee him in the face with your right knee.

26

No. 9.—Coat Hold.

Fig. 21

Fig. 22

27

No. 10.—Coat Hold.

Your assailant seizes you by the lapel of your coat with his right hand.

1. Seize his right wrist with your right hand (Fig. 23).

2. Keeping a firm grip, turn rapidly towards your right-hand side by bringing your right leg to your right rear, simultaneously passing your left arm under his right arm, placing the palm of your left hand on his right thigh (Fig. 24).

3. Force down on the upper part of his right arm with your left shoulder.

Note.—Should your assailant attempt to step forward with his left leg release the hold with your right hand and seize his left ankle and pull it upwards ; at the same time push him backwards with your left hand (Fig. 25).

28

DEFENCE AGAINST VARIOUS HOLDS

No. 10.—Coat Hold.

Fig. 23   Fig. 24

Fig. 25

29

No. 11.—Belt Hold.

Your assailant seizes you by the belt with his right hand.

1. Seize his hand with your right hand to prevent him from releasing his hold.

2. Seize his right elbow with your left hand from underneath, thumb to the right (Fig. 26).

3. With a circular upward motion of your left hand force his elbow towards your right side, keeping a firm grip on his hand (Fig. 27).

Note.—Providing you have prevented him from releasing his hold of the belt, this will be found to be a very effective hold.

No. 11.—Belt Hold.

Fig. 26

Fig, 27

31

No. 12.—Neck Hold.   From Behind.

Your assailant seizes you around the neck with his right arm from behind (Fig. 28).

1. Lean back on your assailant, seize his right wrist with your left hand and place your right forearm as in (Fig. 29).

2. Suddenly turn about, on your right heel, towards your right-hand side, simultaneously forcing his right wrist with a circular motion upward and downward of your left hand in the same direction as your body.   This will force his right arm over your right arm and allow you to seize his wrist with your right hand above your left (Fig. 30).

3. Force the upper part of his right arm against your body and his elbow into your chest and jerk his wrist towards the ground.

32

No. 12.—Neck Hold. From Behind.

Fig. 28

Fig. 29

Fig. 30

33

No. 13.—Simple Counters.

1. It frequently happens that you meet a person who is very proud of his gripping powers and takes great pleasure when shaking hands in gripping your hand with all his strength and causing you to wince.

   To prevent this:—Force your right thumb into the back of his hand as in Fig. 31.

2. Whilst walking you see two persons approaching you who intend to jostle you between them.

   To prevent this:—Place your hands on their shoulders, your forearms under their chins as in Fig. 32, and suddenly shoot your forearms outwards.

3. A person attempts to lift you up by catching hold of you under the arm-pits.

   To prevent this:—Force the points of your thumbs up into his neck, close alongside the jaw bone, as in Fig. 33.

34

No. 13.—Simple Counters.

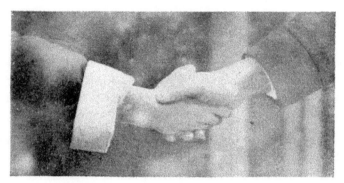

Fig. 31

Fig. 32   Fig. 33

35

METHOD OF DEALING WITH AN ARMED ASSAILANT

The " Defendu " method of dealing with an armed assailant may at first glance appear to be risky, but one will be surprised to discover how safe and simple this method is when put into practice by a person who has studied it and who has to cope with a man unacquainted with it.

The author, being aware that anything original is generally doubted, made it a point, when giving a demonstration, to have his assailant armed with a loaded air pistol, and at no time, even when the pistol was fired, did the pellet ever strike his body; in fact, in the majority of cases the opponent was disarmed before he could possibly fire.

It should always be borne in mind that a man who " holds" you " up " with a pistol or other weapon is, to use a slang term, " throwing a bluff " and is far too cowardly to commit murder; otherwise he would shoot on sight and rob you afterwards. He is aware that if a shot is fired it is liable to alarm the neighbourhood, which is what he wants to prevent at all costs. Further, he is aware that a person carrying valuables might be armed, and for this reason he will be sure to make you hold your hands above your head so as to prevent you from drawing, and for him to be able to search you he must come within reach of your hands. The unexpectedness of finding that he is attacked by an apparently defenceless person will come as such a surprise to him that it will be the simplest thing possible to disarm him before he is aware what has happened.

36

METHOD OF DEALING WITH AN ARMED ASSAILANT

Extract from the " Over-Seas Daily Mail," February 2, 1924.

GIRL BANDIT'S COUPS

"Hold Your Hands up Nicely"

" The girl bandit with bobbed hair and a sealskin coat who within the last three weeks has robbed over a dozen New York shops reappeared at a provision merchant's establishment in Albany Avenue, Brooklyn.

She asked for a cake of soap. When the assistant handed her the article he found himself facing a pistol, while the sweet-voiced girl remarked, " Hold your hands up nicely ; be a good boy, and go into the back room."

He did so, and the girl's customary male companion took $35 from his pocket and $55 from the till.

$20,000 JEWEL HAUL.

Later the blonde girl undertook an excursion to Philadelphia in pursuit of a New York jeweller, Mr. Abraham Kaplan, who was carrying with him a suitcase containing $20,000 worth of jewels.

She accosted him as he was leaving Broad Street Station at Philadelphia and asked him the way to the post office. He told her he was unable to direct her, and, according to his story, she then drew a pistol from her handbag and ordered him to turn about. With the muzzle of her pistol pressed against his back, she forced him to walk into a narrow passage, where two men relieved him of his suitcase, a diamond scarf-pin, a watch, and $100 in cash."

" Hold Ups " of this description are of frequent occurrence in various parts of the world, and it is owing to this fact that the author is publishing the " Defendu " method of self-defence. Now, had this New York jeweller been aquainted with only a part of the " Defendu " method, it would have been a simple matter for him to have disarmed this girl bandit immediately she pressed the pistol against his back, and, what is of more importance, he would not, in doing so, have increased the risk that he ran of being shot.

37

No. 1.—Disarming a Person found Pointing a Pistol at Another.

Should you find a man pointing with a pistol at another, and unaware of your presence :—

1.—Seize his hand and pistol with your right hand from underneath, at the same time seizing his right elbow with your left hand (Fig. 34).

2. Jerk his hand upwards and backwards, and force his elbow upwards with your left hand, simultaneously pivoting inwards on your left foot. This will break his trigger finger and cause him to release his hold on the weapon.

3. If necessary, knee him in the testicles with your right knee (Fig. 35).

No. 1.—Disarming a Person found Pointing a Pistol at Another.

Fig. 34

Fig. 35

39

No. 2.—Disarming an Assailant Holding you up with a Pistol. From in Front.

Your assailant gives the order, " Hands Up," and covers you by pointing a pistol at your stomach :

1. Hold up your hands above your head, keeping them as far apart as possible (Fig. 36).

2. Lead your assailant to suppose that you are scared to death.

3. With a swinging blow seize the pistol and hand with your right hand, simultaneously turning rapidly sideways towards your left-hand side. This will knock the pistol outwards past your body (Fig. 37).

4. Seize the pistol and hand from underneath with your left hand, knee him in the testicles, and letting go with your right hand seize his right elbow. Force his hand and pistol upwards and backwards with your left hand, and pull his elbow towards you (Fig. 38). If necessary, knee him in the testicles with your right knee.

Note.—The reason for keeping your hands held up as far apart as possible is that your assailant cannot look at two objects at one time. If he is watching your left hand, use your right; if the right, use the left; should he be looking at your body or face, use either. Should it be too dark for you to see which hand he is looking at, use which you think best ; he will not be expecting any attack.

40

No. 2.—Disarming an Assailant Holding you up with a Pistol. From in Front.

Fig. 36   Fig. 37

Fig. 38

41

No. 3.—Disarming an Assailant Holding you up with a Pistol. From in Front.

Having been " held up " as in Figure 39, and your assailant is watching your right hand, the following method should be applied :—

1. With a swinging blow seize your assailant's right wrist with your left hand, simultaneously turning rapidly sideways towards your right-hand side. This will knock the pistol inwards past your body (Fig. 40).

2. Seize the pistol and hand from underneath with your right hand, and with a circular backward and downward motion break his trigger finger and knee him in the testicles (Fig. 41).

42

No. 3.—Disarming an Assailant Holding you up with a Pistol. From in Front.

Fig. 39

Fig. 40   Fig. 41

No. 4.—Disarming an Assailant Holding you up with a Pistol. From Behind.

Your assailant gives the order " Hands up " and covers you by holding a pistol in the small of your back :

1. Hold up your hands above your head and exhibit the utmost terror (Fig. 42).

2. Turning rapidly inwards towards your left-hand side, passing your left arm over and around your assailant's right forearm, holding it with a firm grip of your left arm against the left side of your body, simultaneously knee him in the testicles with your right knee and " chin jab " him with your right hand (Fig. 43).

Note.—If you keep a fairly firm grip with your left arm on your assailant's right arm it will be impossible for him to shoot you or release his arm, and, as previously stated, the shock from the blow on the testicles or even the " chin jab " will cause him to immediately release his hold on the pistol.

44

No. 4.—Disarming an Assailant Holding you up with a Pistol. From Behind.

Fig. 42

Fig. 43

No. 5.—Disarming an Assailant Holding you up with a Pistol from Behind.

Having been " held up " as in Figure 44, and for some reason or other it is not convenient to turn towards your left-hand side, the following method should be applied :

1. Turning rapidly outwards towards your right-hand side, lower your right hand and pass it under your assailant's right forearm and seize his arm above the elbow, lifting up his forearm with your right arm (Fig. 45).

2. Simultaneously seize the pistol underneath with your left hand and bend his wrist backwards. If necessary, knee him in the testicles (Fig. 46).

46

No. 5.—Disarming an Assailant Holding you up with a Pistol. From Behind.

Fig. 44

Fig. 45

Fig. 46

47

DEALING WITH AN ARMED ASSAILANT

No. 6.—Arresting a Man Known to Carry Firearms.

Your opponent is coming towards you and you are aware that he will, if possible, shoot to avoid arrest.

When about 10 to 12 feet away from him give him the order to halt and " Hands Up," covering him with your weapon. Tell him to turn about and march in front of you with his hands held above his head ; and whilst he is being searched, keep him covered from behind.

Note.—In no circumstances permit him to get within less than ten feet of you previous to his having been handcuffed. Even if halted at a distance of 12 feet, a determined criminal may possibly endeavour to close on you by means of a "rolling dive" (Figs. 47, 48, 49, 50 and 51). Should this be attempted, a rapid leap to one side will get you into a position similar to your original one and well placed for delivering an effective shot.

Caution.—This Fall must first be learnt as shown on page 151.

No. 6.—Arresting a Man Known to Carry Firearms.

Fig. 47   Fig. 48

Fig. 49   Fig. 50

Fig. 51

49

No. 7.—Disarming a Man Attacking you with a Knife. " Stage Style."

Your assailant rushes at you with a knife in his right hand:

1. Seize his right wrist with your left hand, bend his arm at the elbow towards him (Fig. 52.)

2. Pass your right arm under the upper part of his right arm, seize his right wrist with your right hand above your left.

3. Force the upper part of his right arm against your body, and his elbow into your chest so that it will be at a right angle with your body.

4. Jerk his wrist towards the ground, and knee him in the testicles with your right knee (Fig. 53).

Note.—The above method will be found very effective should you ever be so fortunate as to be attacked in the above manner, but unfortunately, except on the " Stage," persons who carry a knife for the purpose of attack do not hold it as in Fig. 52.

It should be noted that the knife is held as in Fig. 54, edge of the blade uppermost. The part of the body usually aimed at is the pit of the stomach, with the intention of ripping it up. If attacked in this manner, and you are unarmed, there are only two methods of defence :— 1st, RUN ; or 2nd, with a lightning-like movement of either foot, kick your assailant in the testicles or stomach as in Fig. 55.

50

No. 7.—Disarming a Man Attacking you with a Knife. " Stage Style."

Fig. 52　　　　　　　　Fig. 53

Fig. 54　　　　　　　　Fig. 55

51

No. 1.—Police Hold. (" Come Along " Grip).

1. Stand facing your opponent.

2. Seize his right wrist with your right hand (Fig. 56).

3. Step in towards him with your left foot.

4. Pass your left arm over his right arm (above the elbow joint), catching hold of your right arm by the biceps with your left hand.

5. Keep your opponent's right arm straight and the knuckles downwards.

6. Stand upright and force your left forearm bone into the back muscles of his right arm by lifting upwards with your left arm and pressing downwards, towards your opponent's body, on his right wrist.

7. Apply the pressure until your opponent is standing on his toes (Fig. 57).

Note.—Should you, owing to the shortness of your forearm or for any other reason, find it difficult to catch hold of your biceps with your left hand (Fig. 57), seize the left lapel of your jacket instead. Never lean towards your opponent; by so doing you place yourself in a very cramped position. If your opponent attempts to throw himself forward or backwards, apply pressure with a jerk. This will strain the elbow joint and render his right arm useless for attack.

No. 1.—Police Hold. (" Come Along " Grip.)

Fig. 56

Fig. 57

53

No. 2.—Police Hold with Trip.

Having secured the Police Hold (Fig. 57):

1. Shoot your left leg across your opponent's legs, back of your leg to the front of his, your left foot flat on the ground and leg braced stiff (Fig. 58).

2. Bend forward and outwards from the waist, letting go with your left arm and pulling your opponent sharply towards your right-hand side by his right arm (Fig. 59).

N.B.—The importance of keeping the leg braced stiff and the foot flat on the ground can be clearly seen from the following illustrations:—

Fig. 60.—Leg and Foot, *Correct position*—Leg capable of taking a strain of 300 to 400 lbs.

Fig. 61.—Leg and Foot, *Not Correct*—The leg in this position will not stand more than about a 30 lb. strain.

HOLDS THAT ARE EFFECTIVE

No. 2.—Police Hold with Trip.

Fig. 58

Fig. 59

Fig. 60

Fig. 61

No. 3.—Police Hold with Fall.

Having secured the Police Hold (Fig. 62), and he has tripped you owing to your having failed to keep sufficient pressure on his arm :

1. Retain your hold with both hands.

2. Turn your head, keeping your chin down towards your left shoulder (Fig. 63), and let yourself fall—you cannot hurt yourself. Fig. 64 shows the position you would be in after the fall.

Note.—In practice care must be taken not to throw yourself forward when your opponent trips you, otherwise he is liable to be rendered unconscious by striking his head on the ground.

Fig. 62

No. 3.—Police Hold with Fall.

Fig. 63

Fig. 64

57

No. 4.—Handcuff Hold.

1. Stand facing your opponent.
2. Seize his right wrist with both of your hands—right hand above left (Fig. 65).
3. Swing his arm up high.
4. Pass under it by turning inwards with your back towards him (Fig. 66).
5. Step to his back with your left foot, and with a circular upward motion force his wrist well up his back.
6. Retain grasp on his wrist with your left hand and seize his right elbow with your right hand.
7. Bend his wrist towards his right shoulder and lift upwards with your right hand on his elbow.
8. Apply the pressure until your opponent is in the position shown in (Fig. 67.)

Note.—To throw your opponent .—Apply pressure with your left hand on his right (forward and towards the ground), at the same time lifting up his elbow.

All the above movements are one continuous swing of your opponent's right arm, and although from the position shown in Figs 65, 66 and 67, it may appear to the novice that your opponent could easily hit you with his disengaged hand or kick you with his feet, it will be found that it is almost impossible for him to do either. Should he, however, attempt to do so, and the circumstances justify it, " counter " as follows :—

Whilst in the position shown in Fig. 65, release your hold with your left hand, pulling him towards you with your right hand, pass your left arm over his right arm and secure the Police Hold (Fig. 57), and apply pressure with a jerk.

Whilst in the position shown in Fig. 66, shoot your left leg in front of his legs, simultaneously throwing yourself forward to the ground to your right front. This will throw him, with a smashing blow, on to his face, and, providing you have not allowed his wrist to turn in your hands, will probably dislocate his shoulders.

Whilst in the position shown in Fig. 67, apply pressure on his wrist and elbow with a jerk and throw yourself forward to the ground. This will throw him on to his face and probably dislocate his wrist or shoulder.

58

No. 4.— Handcuff Hold.

Fig. 65

Fig. 66

Fig. 67

No. 5.—Handcuff Hold (for a smaller opponent).

If your opponent is too small for you to pass under his arm, as in Fig. 68, apply the following hold.

1. Stand facing your opponent, slightly to his right-hand side.

2. Seize his right wrist with your left hand, your knuckles downwards and thumb to the left.

3. Seize his right elbow with your right hand, your knuckles towards your left-hand side (Fig. 69).

4. Force his hand up his back by pulling his elbow towards you and jerking his hand upwards. This will pull your opponent into the position shown in Fig. 70.

Fig. 68

60

No. 5.—Handcuff Hold (for a smaller opponent).

Fig. 69

Fig. 70

61

No. 6.—Handcuff Hold (Handcuffing a Prisoner).

The reason for this hold being named the Handcuff Hold is that this is the only way one man can handcuff another, unless the latter is willing to submit.

When handcuffing a prisoner it should be done so that his hands are locked behind his back. This will handicap him in running should he attempt to get away.

To handcuff your opponent :—

1. Secure the hold as in Fig. 70
2. Throw your opponent, retaining the hold on his wrist and elbow.
3. Sit astride your opponent's back (Fig. 71), holding his elbow in position with your right thigh. This will allow you to release your hold with your right hand and snap the handcuff on his right wrist (Fig. 72.)
4. Reach over and seize his left wrist with your left hand and jerk it across his back and snap on the other handcuff.

Note.—Should you have any difficulty in securing your opponent's wrist, seize his chin from underneath with your right hand and the side of his head with your left hand.

Jerk upwards with your right hand and push his head downwards with your left hand (Fig. 73).

An alternative method (if your opponent's hair is long enough for you to grip it) is to seize his hair as far forward as possible with your right hand, placing the left hand on the back of his neck and jerking upwards with your right hand and forcing downwards with your left (Fig. 74).

After a very little of either of the above methods your opponent will be quite willing to submit to being handcuffed.

Care should be taken not to break a person's neck by the above method.

Fig. 70

No. 6.—Handcuff Hold (Handcuffing a Prisoner).

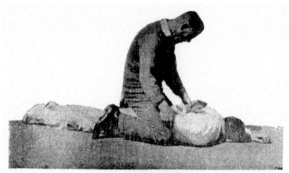

Fig. 71

Fig. 72

Fig. 73

Fig. 74

63

No. 7.—Arm Hold.

1. Stand level with your opponent on his right side and facing the same way.

2. Seize his right wrist with your right hand, back of your hand to the front, back of his hand downwards.

3. Raise his right arm with your right hand and at the same time pass your left arm under his right and place your left hand behind his neck (Fig. 75).

4. Straighten your left arm and pull downwards on his right arm with your right hand (Fig. 76).

Note.—Your left arm must be above your opponent's right elbow ; otherwise you cannot obtain any leverage.

64

No. 7.—Arm Hold.

Fig 75

Fig. 76

65

No. 8.—Bent Arm Hold.

You are facing your opponent and he raises his right hand as if about to deliver a blow.

1. Seize his right wrist with your left hand, bending his arm at the elbow, towards him (Fig. 77).

2. Pass your right arm under the upper part of his right arm, seizing his right wrist with your right hand above your left.

3. Force the upper part of his right arm against your body, and his elbow into your chest so that it will be at a right angle with your body.

4. Jerk his wrist towards the ground (Fig. 78).

No. 8.—Bent Arm Hold.

Fig. 77

Fig. 78

67

No. 9.—Front Strangle Hold.

For defence against a right-handed punch to the head, or a downward swinging blow at the head with a stick, etc.

1. Duck your head to the left and rush in under your assailant's right arm to his right side (Fig. 79).

2. Pass your right arm around his neck, catching your right wrist with your left hand.

3. Apply pressure by pulling on your right wrist with your left hand, forcing his right arm up alongside his neck with your shoulder and head (Fig. 80).

Note.—Keep the fingers and thumb of your right hand rigid and force your right forearm bone into the muscle of his neck.

Bring your right hip into the small of his back and bend him backwards (Fig. 80).

No. 9.—Front Strangle Hold.

Fig. 79

Fig. 80

No. 10.—Front Strangle Hold with Throw.

Having secured the hold as in Figure 81, and you want to throw your assailant,

1. Retain the hold with your right arm around his neck and place your left hand at the back of his right thigh (Fig. 82).
2. Lift upwards with your left hand, pulling downwards with your right arm, at the same time shooting your hip into the small of his back by straightening out your legs.
3. When your assailant is off his feet, bend forward from the waist and throw him over your shoulder (Fig. 83).

Note.—It is quite a simple matter for you to throw an assailant in the above manner, even if he should be twice your own weight, but care must be taken when practising it to keep a firm grip with your right arm to prevent him from falling on his head.

Having decided to give your assailant a rather heavy fall, release your hold when in the position shown in Figure 83; this will throw him on his stomach, with his head towards you. Should your assailant be one of several who have made an unwarranted attack on you, release your hold with your right arm at the moment when he is in the position shown in Figure 84, and dislocate his neck.

Fig. 81

70

No. 10.—Front Strangle Hold with Throw.

Fig. 82

Fig. 83

Fig. 84

71

No. 11.—Front Strangle Hold on the Ground.

Having secured the hold as in Figure 85, and you are tripped, or want to bring your assailant to the ground.

1. Retain the hold on your assailant's neck and arm, shoot both of your legs forward, letting your assailant take the force of the fall on his back.

2. Force your head down on to your assailant's right arm and head ; at the same time force the weight of your body on to his chest, applying pressure by pulling up on your right wrist with your left hand (Fig. 86).

Note.—Should the circumstances justify, and it is necessary that you should release your hold, apply pressure sharply with your right arm on your assailant's neck until he faints (10 to 15 seconds).

It should be noted that your assailant whilst in this position (Fig. 86), cannot do you any injury whatever and providing you keep your left foot flat on the ground and your legs out of reach of his legs he cannot get up.

No. 11.—Front Strangle Hold on the Ground.

Fig. 85

Fig. 86

73

No. 12.—Back Strangle Hold.

1. Stand at your opponent's back.

2. Place your left arm around his neck, with your forearm bone bearing on his Adam's apple.

3. Place the back of your right arm (above the elbow) on his right shoulder and clasp your right biceps with your left hand.

4. Grasp the back of his head with your right hand.

5. Pull up with your left forearm and press forward on the back of his head with your right hand (Fig. 87).

Note.—If this hold is applied correctly it is impossible for your opponent to release himself; further, his neck can easily be dislocated and if pressure is applied for 10 seconds he will faint owing to anæmia of the brain.

It should be noted that this is a drastic hold and would only be used against an opponent who would go to any extent to gain his freedom. Should he attempt to seize you by the testicles, step back quickly, at the same time jolting his head forward with your right hand and dislocate his neck (Fig. 88).

No. 12.—Back Strangle Hold.

Fig. 87

Fig. 88

75

No. 13.—Back Strangle Hold Applied from the Front.

1. Stand facing your opponent. Seize his right shoulder with your left hand and his left shoulder with your right hand (Fig. 89)

2. Push with your left hand (retaining the hold) and pull towards you with your right hand. If this is done suddenly your opponent will be turned completely around and your left arm will be in position around his neck.

3. Place the back of your right arm (above the elbow) on his right shoulder and clasp your right biceps with your left hand.

4. Grasp the back of his head with your right hand.

5. Pull up with your left forearm and press forward on the back of his head with your right hand (Fig. 90).

No. 13.—Back Strangle Hold Applied from the Front.

Fig. 89

Fig. 90

77

No. 14.—Wrist and Elbow Hold.

Your assailant seizes you by the throat with his right hand.

1. Seize assailant's right hand from above with your right hand, your fingers passing over the back of his hand to the palm.

2. Seize his right elbow with your left hand, thumb to the right (Fig. 91).

3. With a circular upward swing of your right hand towards your right-hand side, simultaneously turning inwards and pressing with your left hand on his elbow, bending his right wrist towards him (Figs. 92 and 92a).

4. To throw your assailant, jerk his right arm to the ground by falling forward on to your knees.

No. 14.—Wrist and Elbow Hold.

Fig. 91

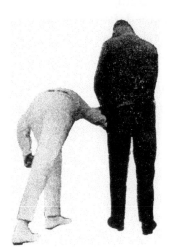

Fig. 92

Fig. 92A

79

HOLDS THAT ARE EFFECTIVE

No. 15.—Wrist and Elbow Hold, Whilst Lying in Bed.

Your assailant seizes you by the throat with his right hand whilst you are lying in bed.

1. Seize his right hand from above, with your right hand, your fingers passing over the back of his hand to the palm.

2. Seize his right elbow with your left hand, thumb to the right (Figs. 93 and 93A).

3. Turn sharply to your right on to your stomach, pulling his right arm under your body, by pulling on the wrist and forcing towards your right-hand side with your left hand on his elbow. This will bring you and your assailant into the position shown in Fig. 94.

4. Keeping his right arm straight, force down on his elbow with your left hand and twist his right wrist towards him by an upward motion of your right hand.

80

698

No. 15.—Wrist and Elbow Hold, Whilst Lying in Bed.

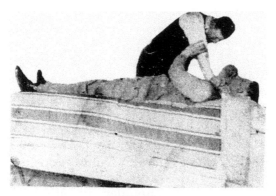

Fig. 93

Fig. 93A

Fig. 94

No. 16.—Thumb and Elbow Hold.

Stand facing your opponent and slightly to his left-hand side.

1. Insert your right thumb between the thumb and forefinger of his left hand, palm of your right hand upwards, thumb to the right (Fig. 95).

2. Seize his left elbow with your left hand, knuckles to the right (Fig. 96).

3. Step in towards your opponent; at the same time turn your body so that you are facing in the same direction, simultaneously forcing his left forearm up across his chest and towards his left shoulder by pulling his elbow with your left hand over your right forearm and forcing upwards with your right hand.

4. Keeping a firm grip on the upper part of his left arm with your right arm, apply a slight pressure on the back of his hand towards your left-hand side with your right hand and you will be surprised to see how quickly your opponent will raise on his toes and shout for mercy (Fig. 97).

5. Should your opponent be a very powerful man and try to resist, a little extra pressure (3 to 4 lbs.) applied with the left hand on his elbow, as in Figure 98, will be sufficient to convince him that he has met his master, and he will be quite willing to submit to anything.

Note.—This is the most effective hold known, and I think I am correct in saying that only Japanese Jui-jitsu experts (4th and 5th degree black belt) know how to apply it. Further, it should be noted that whilst all the other holds are very effective, and that it is not necessary to exert a great amount of strength to overcome your opponent, the fact remains that should it be necessary for you to have to take an opponent a distance of a mile or so, the strain, both mental and physical, would be so great that it would be very difficult for the average person to accomplish it, but if you have secured the hold as in Figure 97, you would have no difficulty whatsoever in taking a very powerful opponent, even if he was resisting, as far as it is possible for you to walk.

No. 16.—Thumb and Elbow Hold.

Fig. 95

Fig. 96

Fig. 97

Fig. 98

83

No. 17.—Head Hold.

Stand facing your opponent.

1. Strike your opponent on the left side of his neck with the inside of your right forearm (Fig. 99).

2. Pass your arm around his head, catching hold of your right wrist with your left hand and forcing his head down to your right thigh (Fig. 100).

3. Force your right forearm bone into the right side of his face by pulling on your right wrist with your left hand and forcing downwards on the left side of his face with your body.

Note.—This hold is very painful for your opponent, and care must be taken in practice to apply the pressure gradually.

No. 17.—Head Hold.

Fig. 99

Fig. 100

No. 18.—Head Hold with Throw.

Having secured the hold as in Figure 101, and you are about to be attacked by another opponent,

1. Retain the hold of your first opponent and turn sharply towards your left-hand side, straighten up your body and swing him by the neck off his feet (Fig. 102).

2. Keep turning until your opponent's feet are well clear of the ground ; then suddenly release your hold. Immediately close with your second opponent and treat him likewise.

No. 18.—Head Hold with Throw.

Fig. 101

Fig. 102

87

No. 1.—Wrist Throw.

1. Stand facing your opponent and slightly to his right-hand side.

2. Lean forward and seize his right hand with your left, back of your hand towards your right-hand side, your fingers around his thumb towards the palm of his hand, your thumb forced in between the knuckle-joint of his first and second fingers (Fig. 103).

3. Raise his arm, by a circular motion, towards your left-hand side, at the same time seizing the little finger side of his right hand with your right. Turn his palm towards him; then force your thumbs into the back of his hand (Fig. 104).

4. Force his hand towards him. This will throw him on to his right-hand side (Fig. 105).

Note.—Whilst Figure 104 shows the thumbs forced into the back of the hand, it should be noted that it is not always possible to obtain this position quickly; but providing the palm of your opponent's hand is turned towards him, and pressure is applied with the thumbs on the back of his hand or fingers as in Figure 106, this will be found to be nearly as effective.

If you have any difficulty in throwing your opponent, give his wrist a sharp turn to your left and pull downwards towards your left-hand side. Another method is to sink suddenly on to one knee and pull downwards towards your left-hand side.

Either of these will cause him to lose his balance and fall.

88

HOW TO THROW AN ASSAILANT

No. 1.—Wrist Throw.

Fig. 103

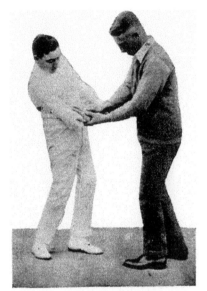

Fig. 104

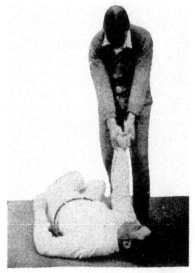

Fig. 105

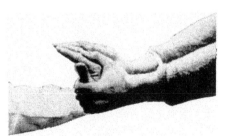

Fig. 106

89

No. 2.—Wrist Throw with Leg Hold.

Having thrown your opponent as in Fig. 107, and you wish to hold him on the ground,

1. Retain the hold on his right wrist with both hands, step over his body with both feet, keeping his arm between your legs (Fig. 108).

2. Bend your legs from the knees and sit down as close to your opponent's body as possible (Fig. 109).

3. Pull on your opponent's wrist, to keep the arm straight, fall backwards and bend his arm the reverse way by resting the upper part of his arm on your right thigh and forcing his wrist towards the ground (Fig. 110).

Note.—Should your opponent attempt to pull his right arm away by the help of his left hand, force your left or right foot into the bend of his left arm and kick it away (Fig. 111).

Fig. 107

90

No. 2.—Wrist Throw with Leg Hold.

Fig. 108

Fig. 109

Fig. 110

Fig. 111

91

No. 3.—Arm Throw.

1. Stand facing your opponent and slightly to his right-hand side.

2. Seize his right wrist with both of your hands, right above left (Fig. 112).

3. Swing his arm high up.

4. Pass under it by turning to your right (Fig. 113), keeping a firm hold on his wrist. This will cause his arm to twist as shown in Fig. 114.

5. When in this position sink slightly forward on the left knee, keeping your right leg firm and straight, pull down on your opponent's arm, by bending suddenly towards the ground, bending from the waist.

6. This will cause him to fall on his back (Fig. 115).

Note.—This is a very dangerous throw, and great care must be taken when practising it, otherwise you will dislocate your opponent's shoulder, or cause him to strike the back of his head on the ground.

No. 3.—Arm Throw.

Fig. 112

Fig. 113

Fig. 114

Fig. 115

No. 4.—Hip Throw.

Stand facing your opponent.

1. Seize both his arms above the elbows.

2. Turn your body sharply to your right and shoot your left leg to his left side. Take care that the back of your left leg is against his body and your left foot flat on the ground (Fig. 116).

3. Bend forward towards your right-hand side and jerk him sharply over your left hip, by pulling downwards with your right hand and pushing or lifting upwards with your left hand.

4. This will bring your opponent into the position shown in Fig. 117.

Note.—Having secured the hold as in Fig. 116, and you have difficulty in throwing your opponent, sink suddenly on to your right knee, pulling downwards with your right hand, and pushing or lifting upwards with your left hand (Fig. 118).

Care must be taken when applying this throw in the above manner, otherwise your opponent will be rendered unconscious through striking his head on the ground.

No. 4.—Hip Throw.

Fig. 116

Fig. 117

Fig. 118

95

No. 5.—Hip Throw, with Leg Hold.

Having secured throw as in Fig. 119,

1. Allow your right hand to slip up his left arm to his wrist and secure it with both hands, right above left. Step over his body with both feet, keeping his arm between your legs (Fig. 120).

2. Bend your legs from the knees and sit down as close to your opponent as possible.

3. Pulling on your opponent's wrist, to keep his left arm straight, fall backwards and bend his arm the reverse way, by resting the upper part of his arm on your left thigh and forcing his wrist towards the ground (Fig. 121).

Note.—Fig. 110 (Wrist Throw with Leg Hold, page 91) and Fig. 121 show that when the leg hold is applied your opponent's arm should be across the thigh which is nearest his body. By so doing you have a much better leverage and it becomes extremely difficult for him to pull his arm away.

No. 5.—Hip Throw, with Leg Hold.

Fig. 119

Fig. 120

Fig. 121

97

HOW TO THROW AN ASSAILANT

No. 6.—Ankle Throw.

1. Stand facing your opponent.

2. Seize both his arms above the elbows.

3. Pull downwards with your right hand and lift upwards with your left (this will pull the weight of his body on to his left leg) ; at the same time strike his left ankle with the sole of your right foot without bending your leg (Fig. 122).

Note.—The blow of your right foot on your opponent's left ankle should be made with sufficient force to sweep his legs from under him.

No. 6.—Ankle Throw.

Fig. 122

No. 7.—Instep Throw.

1. Stand facing your opponent.

2. Seize him under the arm-pits with both hands, your toes turned outwards, and pull him towards you (Fig. 123).

3. Sinking from the knees, fall backwards, simultaneously pulling upwards with your hands and kicking his legs backwards as in Fig. 124.

4. This will throw your opponent over your head (Fig. 125).

Caution.—It should be noted that the Instep Throw is a very dangerous throw. Should your opponent be unacquainted with the "art of falling" he will probably meet with serious injury.

No. 7.—Instep Throw.

Fig. 123

Fig. 124

Fig. 125

101

No. 8.—Leg or Scissor Throw.

1. Stand on the right of your opponent (one to two feet away), facing in the same direction.

2. Seize the upper part of his right arm with your left hand (Fig. 126).

3. Jumping inwards, throw your left leg across the front of his legs at the back of his knees (Fig. 127).

4. Almost simultaneously placing your right hand on the ground and turning your body to the rear, pulling him backwards by his right arm. This will bring him into the position shown in Fig. 128.

No. 8.—Leg or Scissor Throw.

Fig. 126

Fig. 127

Fig. 128

103

No. 9.—Leg or Scissor Throw, with Leg Lock.

1. Having secured the throw as in Fig. 128, keep twisting your body towards your left, keep your legs straight and let go his right arm. This will turn your opponent over on to his stomach (Fig. 129).

2. Seize his right foot with your left hand and bend his leg from the knee, over your right leg (Fig. 130).

Note.—Should your opponent attempt to get up, force his right foot down-wards and in the opposite direction to that in which he is trying to raise himself.

No. 9.—Leg or Scissor Throw, with Leg Lock

Fig. 128

Fig. 129

Fig. 130

105

Edge of the Hand Blows.

It is not generally known that a person can hit with more force with the edge of the hand than with the clenched fist.

A person striking with his clenched fist distributes the force of the blow over a much larger surface than would be the case if he struck with the edge of his hand.

It stands to reason that a blow covering only one square inch of the body must be more painful than if it were distributed over four, providing that both blows are delivered with the same amount of force.

Further, an Edge of the Hand Blow, delivered in the manner shown in Fig. 131 ("Forearm Blow"), would break the forearm bone. This would be impossible with a blow from the clenched fist.

Note.—An "Edge of the Hand Blow" is given with the inner (*i.e.* little finger) edge of the palm, fingers straight and close together, thumb extended.

Edge of the Hand Blows.

Forearm

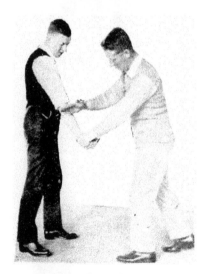

Fig. 131

107

EDGE OF THE HAND BLOWS

Wrist

Forearm

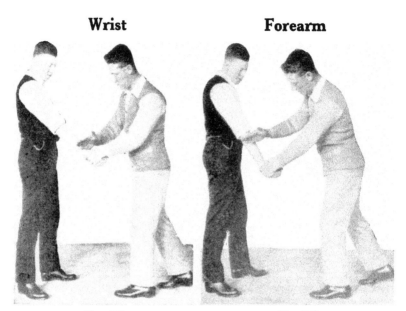

Fig. 131

Fig. 132

Biceps

Neck

Fig. 133

Fig. 134

108

Face

Fig. 135

Shoulder

Fig. 136

Neck

Fig. 137

Neck

Fig. 138

EDGE OF THE HAND BLOWS

Thigh

Fig. 139

Shin

Fig. 140

Leg

Fig. 141

Waist

Fig. 142

110

EDGE OF THE HAND BLOWS

Kidney

Fig. 143

Spine

Fig. 144

111

No. 1.—Use of the Baton, " Night Stick" or Club.

Police clubs are provided with a leather thong or cord so that they can be secured to the hand. This prevents them from being snatched away. It is, in consequence, very important that all policemen should know the correct manner in which this thong or cord should be used.

For instance, if the thong were securely fixed around the wrist, and the club seized, it would be very difficult for its user to free himself, and he could easily be thrown to the ground by it.

To prevent this, the club should be held in the following manner :—

1. Pass your right thumb through the loop (Fig. 145).

2. Pass the thong over the back of your hand to the palm (Fig. 146).

Note.—The thong or cord should be of sufficient length (but on no account longer) so that the head of the club will be in the centre of the palm of the hand. By keeping a firm grip, it is impossible for an assailant to snatch it away. But should the club be seized, all that is necessary is to release the hold on the handle and the thong will slip off the thumb.

The blow with the club should be given in the same manner as a blow with a hammer, the wrist must be free. If the club is held as in Fig. 147 the wrist is partly locked and the force of the blow is checked. The above applies equally to loaded hunting crops when used as weapons of defence.

112

No. 1.—Use of the Baton, " Night Stick" or Club.

Fig. 145

Fig. 146

Fig. 147

113

No. 2.—" Club Blow."

1. To bring your assailant to the ground, hit him on the shin bone below the knee-cap (Fig. 148). This is more effective than a head blow.

2. To make your assailant release his hold of any weapon with which he may be armed, hit him on either the forearm or wrist.

Fig. 148

114

No. 3.—The Club as a Protection.

To ward off a blow with a stick or similar weapon at your head,

1. Grasp the club with both hands near the ENDS, rush in as close as possible, taking the blow on the club (Fig. 149).

2. Release hold with your left hand and strike with club by a swinging blow at your assailant's shins. This will bring him to the ground.

Note.—It is to be noted that an assailant with a stick or other striking weapon can do little injury if you keep close to him.

Fig. 149

115

No. 4.—The Club Used as Handcuffs.

Having thrown your opponent, as in Fig. 150. (Handcuff Hold, page 63).

1. Pass the thong over his right wrist.

2. Seize his left wrist and pass it through the loop of the thong.

3. Twist the club until the thong cuts into the wrists.

4. Keeping hold of the club with your right hand, stand up and assist your opponent to rise (Fig. 151).

No. 4.—The Club Used as Handcuffs.

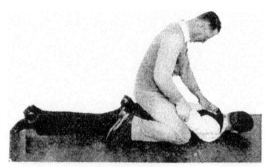

Fig. 150

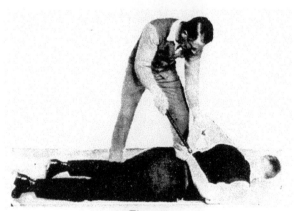

Fig. 151

117

No. 5.—Silk Cord v Leather Thong.

It is recommended that a silk cord be used on police night sticks or clubs instead of a leather thong. The silk cord is much stronger and can be lengthened at will and used as a tourniquet in case of an accident (Fig. 152).

The cord should be of sufficient length (2-ft. 6-in.) to permit it being passed over any part of the thigh or arm, and should be secured to the club as in Fig. 153.

To shorten the cord to the correct length, so that the head of the club comes in the palm of the hand, make a number of " half hitches " and pass them over the head of the club (Fig. 154).

Fig. 152

118

No. 5.—Silk Cord v Leather Thong.

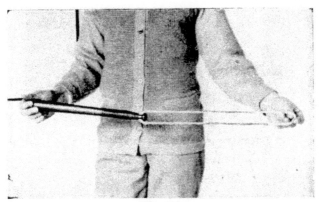

Fig. 153

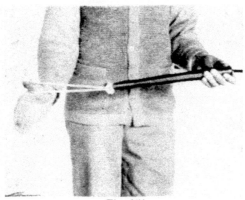

Fig. 154

119

Attack and Defence with a Walking Stick.

The art of using a walking stick in attack or defence is not generally known, yet it is possible for anybody to master a very powerful man if the following instructions be carried out.

To bring your assailant to the ground, hit him on the shins, just below the knee-cap (Fig. 155), or jab him in the stomach with the point.

Note.—Never attempt to strike your assailant over the head, as this can be very easily guarded. In fact, it is almost impossible to strike a person over the head, if he is aware that you are about to do so. Further he would be sure to close with you, and the stick would prove a handicap in preventing you from securing an effective hold.

The best class of stick is a medium weight ash or a Malacca cane.

Attack and Defence with a Walking Stick.

Fig. 155

121

No. 1.—Arm and Neck Hold, with a Stick.

1. Holding your stick in the left hand, thumb to the left, stand level with your opponent on his right side, facing the same way.

2. Seize his right wrist with your, right hand, back of your hand to the front, back of his hand downwards.

3. Raise his right arm with your right hand ; at the same time pass the stick under the arm to the back of his neck (Fig. 156).

4. Pull downwards on his right arm and lift upwards with the stick (Fig. 157).

Note.—Care must be taken that the stick is above your opponent's right elbow, otherwise you cannot get any leverage on the arm.

No. 1.—Arm and Neck Hold, with a Stick.

Fig. 156

Fig. 157

123

No. 2.—Arm Hold, with a Stick.

1. Holding your stick in the left hand, thumb to the handle, stand level with your opponent on his right-hand side, facing the same way.

2. Seize his right wrist with your right hand, back of your hand to the front, back of his hand downwards.

3. Pass the stick under his right arm, above the elbow, to his chest (Fig. 158).

4. Push forward on the stick with your left hand and pull his right backwards with your right hand (Fig. 159).

No. 2.—Arm Hold, with a Stick.

Fig. 158

Fig. 159

125

No. 3.—Back Strangle Hold, with a Stick.

1. Holding your stick in the right hand, thumb towards the handle, stand at your opponent's back.

2. Place the stick around his neck, from his left-hand side (Fig. 160).

3. Pass your left hand over your right arm and seize the stick close up to your opponent's neck.

4. Force your forearms into the back of his neck, and pull the stick towards you (Fig. 161).

Note.—This is a very severe hold and extra care must be taken in practising it, otherwise you will cause unnecessary pain.

126

No. 3.—Back Strangle Hold, with a Stick.

Fig. 160

Fig. 161

127

No. 4.—Crotch and Arm Hold, with Stick.

1. Holding your stick in the left hand, thumb towards the handle, stand level with your opponent on his right side.

2. Pass the stick between his legs, seizing his right wrist with your right hand, back of your hand to the front, back of his hand downwards (Fig. 162).

3. Forcing the stick against the back of his left thigh, twist his wrist outwards and away from you with your right hand and pull it across your left leg, at the same time bringing the stick to the back of his right arm.

4. Holding his right arm straight, force downwards on the back of his right arm with the stick (Fig. 163).

128

No. 4.—Crotch and Arm Hold, with Stick.

Fig. 162

Fig. 163

129

No. 5.—Neck Throw, with a Stick.

1. Holding your stick in the right hand, stand level with your opponent on his right side.

2. Pass the stick across your opponent's throat, grasp the other end with your left hand close up to the neck, simultaneously stepping behind him (Fig. 164).

3. Bending your arms from the elbows towards you, jerk him backwards to the ground (Fig. 165).

Note.—This throw is very severe and like No. 3. Back Strangle Hold, Page 126, extra care must be taken in practising it.

No. 5.—Neck Throw, with a Stick.

Fig. 164

Fig. 165

131

HOW TO MAKE AN EFFECTIVE KNOT

Tying an Effective Knot.

Practice tying the following knot on a stick, pole or anything similar.

Take a piece of cord or silk rope about a quarter of an inch in diameter, and from 5 to 7 yards in length. This can be carried or tied around the waist under the jacket.

1. Pass the cord behind the pole with, the *Short* end of the cord to the left and the *Long* end to the right (Fig. 166).

2. Pass the *Long* end of the cord, in a loop, over the pole and through the loop held in the left hand, then pull down on the *Short* end with the right hand (Fig. 167).

3. Pass the *Short* end of the cord, in a loop, over the pole and through the loop held in the left hand (Fig. 167), which will form the knot shown in Fig. 168.

4. Holding the loop in the left hand, pull down on the *Long* end of the cord, pass the left hand through the loop and pull on both *Ends* of the cord (Fig. 169).

Note.—For the purpose of illustrating clearly, rope was used instead of cord.

132

HOW TO MAKE AN EFFECTIVE KNOT

Tying an Effective Knot.

Fig. 166

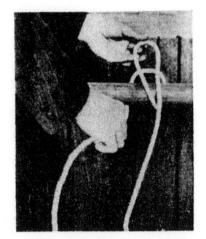

Fig. 167

Fig. 168

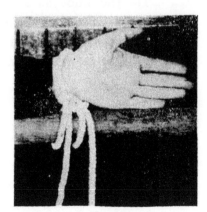

Fig. 169

133

Tying a Prisoner.

As is the case when using handcuffs, your prisoner is always more secure when his hands are fastened together behind his back : you would naturally compel him to precede you and you would then at once notice any attempt he might make to release his hands.

The knot shewn on page 133 forms a very good substitute for a pair of handcuffs.

Tie the knot as shown in Figure 170 on your prisoner's wrist, pass his other hand through the loop, held in the left hand and pull taut, then tie two half hitches to prevent slipping (Fig. 171).

Tying a Prisoner.

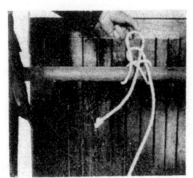

Fig. 170

Fig. 171

135

Tying up an Opponent.

Should it be necessary that you have to leave your opponent without a guard, the following method of securing him will be found very effective.

Secure his hands as in Fig. 171, throw him on the ground, pass the cord around his neck, pass the end under his hands. Bend his left leg backwards and tie two half hitches round his ankle (Fig. 172).

Note:—If your prisoner keeps still he will not hurt himself, but the more he moves the greater the discomfort he will suffer.

136

Tying up an Opponent.

Fig. 171

Fig. 172

137

To Lift a Man on to his Feet from the Ground.

Your opponent lies on his stomach on the ground and refuses to stand up.

1. Stand to one side or over your opponent.

2. Seize him round the neck with both hands, your fingers pressing into his neck alongside the " Adam's apple " (Fig. 173).

3. Force the points of your thumb into the hollows under the lobe of the ears and lift upwards (Fig. 174).

138

To Lift a Man on to his Feet from the Ground.

Fig. 173

Fig. 174

139

The Handkerchief or Glove as an Aid to Securing a Hold or Throw.

Under certain circumstances the pocket handkerchief is a great aid in securing an effective hold or throw, such as when a policeman is called into a building to eject a person.

Your opponent is standing and from all appearance is about to resist being put out of the building.

1. Speak to him quietly but firmly and ask him to leave, at the same time taking your handkerchief in your hand.

2. Suddenly throw the handkerchief in his face, simultaneously closing with him. This will take him off his guard and you should have no difficulty in applying one of the holds or throws demonstrated, in Figs. 57, 80, 100, 104, 116 and 122.

Police Hold   **Strangle Hold**

Fig. 57   Fig. 80

140

The Handkerchief or Glove as an Aid to Securing a Hold or Throw.

Head Hold

Wrist Throw

Fig. 100

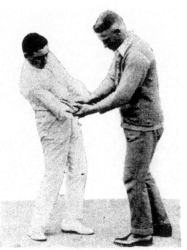

Fig. 104

Hip Throw

Ankle Throw

Fig. 116

Fig. 122

141

How to Deal with an Assailant Following You at Night.

It gives rise to a very uncomfortable feeling to realize that you are being followed, especially if it should happen to be on a dark night and the road a lonely one. The best thing to do under these circumstances is to carry the war into the enemy's camp rather than to wait for him to attack you. If you turn on him it will prove such a surprise to your assailant that you will have little difficulty in securing an effective hold or throw.

Having become aware that you are being followed,

1. Shorten your pace and allow your assailant to come to within eight or ten paces.

2. Without losing a pace, suddenly turn around and walk towards him.

3. Apply one of the holds or throws shown on pages 140 and 141.

4. Should your assailant be armed with a stick or other striking weapon, close with him. Providing this is done quickly it will be very difficult for him to do you any injury.

5. If there should be two assailants, and they attempt to close in on you (a very old dodge), suddenly " Chin Jab " them both (Fig. 175).

Note.—Providing you have taken the precaution of turning up your coat collar and have not missed a pace whilst turning, your assailant, still hearing your footsteps, will on a dark night not be aware that you are coming towards him, until you have actually closed upon him.

How to Deal with an Assailant Following You at Night.

Fig. 175

143

The Farce of the " Fireman's Lift."

(Raising and carrying an unconscious person, single handed).

It is not generally known that the method of picking up and carrying an unconscious person, commonly known as the " Fireman's Lift," which one sees demonstrated in nearly every book on First Aid, is an impossibility.

The instructions are usually as follows :—

1. Turn the patient on to his face and then raise him to a kneeling position.

2. Place yourself under him, so that his stomach is on your right shoulder.

3. Pass your right arm between his thighs and behind his right thigh grasping his right wrist with your right hand (Fig. 176).

To carry out the above, with a conscious subject, is easy enough, for the simple reason that when raised to a kneeling position he keeps his joints stiff. Were, however, the subject really unconscious he would not remain in a kneeling position, unless held there, but would collapse from the hips and fall sideway or forward (Fig. 177).

In addition, very few people, even when in a standing position, are strong enough to lift an unconscious body clear of the ground, and to attempt to do so from a kneeling position is an utter waste of time.

144

The Farce of the " Fireman's Lift."

Fig. 176

Fig. 177

145

The Art of Falling.

Japanese jiu-jitsu experts consider the art of falling correctly, *i.e.*, without hurting one's self, of more importance than the ability to secure an effective hold or trip, and it is owing to this that they are able to fall and be thrown about in competition in such a manner that, to a stranger, appears to be asking for a broken limb, yet they no sooner hit the ground than they are again on their feet.

The fact that falling backwards down a flight of stairs can be accomplished without the slightest injury by any one who has made a thorough study of this art, clearly demonstrates that a little practice at a few simple but very useful falls, etc., will well repay the student for his trouble.

Caution :—Students are warned that the fall, shown on Page 148 and 149 should first be practiced from the kneeling or crouching position as shown on the following pages.

The Art of Falling.

Extract from "North China Daily News," 23rd November, 1916.

THE LYCEUM THEATRE.

THE BREED OF THE TRESHAMS.

"There was a gorgeous stage fight in the second act, with a stage fall downstairs by a man shot dead, such as we have never seen equalled."

Extract from "North-China Daily News," 24th November, 1916.

"Praise that is given unawares is the best praise of all, and in mentioning yesterday that the fall downstairs of a man shot dead was such as we have never seen equalled" (referring to the second act of "The Breed of the Treshams" on Saturday night) the writer thought he was giving recognition to some good acting by a member of the Howitt-Phillips Company. The realistic fall of the dead man down a steep flight of stairs was done, not by an actor, but by a policeman, W. E. Fairbairn, the drill instructor of the Shanghai Municipal Police, and although he had rehearsed the scene he had not rehearsed the actual fall. Such things come natural to policemen, especially to jiu-jitsu men. And beside Fairbairn, there were seven other Shanghai policemen in the show that night, so that the "guards' were real guards, with the result that the stage fight was as real as safety would allow."

147

Side Fall

Eig. 178

Hand Spring

Fig. 179

"Flying" Dive

Fig. 180

148

Stomach Fall

Fig. 181

Crouch Fall

Fig. 182

Face Fall

Fig. 183

149

No. 1.—" Rolling Dive."

(Kneeling Position).

This must first be learnt in the following manner, and on no account must it be attempted from the standing position until the pupil is proficient, otherwise there is danger of injury to the head, neck and kidneys :—

1. Kneel on the right knee, place the back of the right hand and forearm on the ground under the body (Fig. 184).

2. Place the left hand on the ground in front of the left shoulder, turning the head to the left-hand side (Fig. 185).

3. Throw yourself forward over the right shoulder on to your left side, bending the lower part of the left leg from the knee, towards the right-hand side, the right foot to be over the left leg and in the position shown in Fig. 186.

150

No. 1.—" Rolling Dive." (Kneeling Position).

Fig. 184

Fig. 185

Fig. 186

151

No. 1.—" Rolling Dive."

(Crouching Position).

When proficient from the kneeling position as demonstrated on page 151, it should be practiced from the crouching position as follows :—

Bend forward from the waist, placing the back of the right hand on the ground, left hand and head to the left-hand side (Fig. 187). Then throw yourself forward over the right shoulder and carry on as from the kneeling position. Providing you have not forgotten to turn the head to the left-hand side and allowed the spine to bend when turning over, it should only be necessary to practice this dive from the crouching position a few times.

No. 1.—" Rolling Dive." (Crouching Position).

Fig. 187

153

No. 1.—" Rolling Dive."

(Standing Position).

1. Standing as in Fig. 188, turn the head to the left and throw yourself forward head-over-heels.

2. Fig. 189 shows the feet and hands ready to strike the ground a fraction of a second before the body reaches the position shown in Fig. 190.

3. Fig. 191 shows the position just before the completion of the " Dive."

Note.—All the above movements must be continuous, but should you wish to remain on the ground, hold your right foot as in Fig. 186, (page 151), which will prevent you from coming up on to the feet.

Fig. 188

154

No. 1.—" Rolling Dive." (Standing Position).

Fig. 189

Fig. 190

Fig. 191

155

No. 2.—Side Fall.

This fall must first be practised from the following position :—

1. Crouch as in Fig. 192, throw yourself on to your right-hand side, striking the ground with the open palm of your right hand a moment before your body reaches the ground (Fig. 193), care being taken that the right arm is at an angle of 45 degrees from the body : this protects the elbow. At the same time bring the left foot over the right leg into the position shown in Fig. 194.

Note.—Placing the left foot in the above position turns the body on to the right side, with the results that kidneys and head are prevented from striking the ground. When proficient in the above it should be practised from the standing position.

This fall is used when thrown by the " Hip Throw " and is also an old trick for a person wishing to fall himself, in order to get into a favourable position to throw his opponent. See Figs. 195 and 196, (page 159.)

No. 2.—Side Fall.

Fig. 192

Fig. 193

Fig. 194

157

No. 3.—Side Fall, with Throw and Leg Lock.

Your opponent having thrown you by the Hip Throw, and you are in the position shown in Fig. 195,

1. Turn over sharply on to the left side, pass your right leg around and to the back of his knees, placing your left leg over his feet at the instep (Fig. 196).

2. Twist your body sharply towards your right-hand side at the same time striking his feet backwards with your left leg and striking his legs forward with your right leg at the back of his knees. This will bring you into the position shown in Fig. 197.

3. Seize his right foot with your left hand and bend his right leg, from the knee, over your left leg. Apply pressure by twisting your body sharply towards your right hand side simultaneously forcing his right foot downwards (Fig. 198).

Note :—All the above movements must be continuous.

No. 3.—Side Fall, with Throw and Leg Lock.

Fig. 195

Fig. 196

Fig. 197

Fig. 198

159

No. 4.—Front Fall.

This fall must first be practised from the following position :—

1. Kneeling on the knees, hands and arms held slightly in advance of the body, palm of the hands to the front, with fingers and thumbs as shown in Fig. 199.

2. Fall forward on to the forearms and hands as shown in Fig. 200.

Caution :—At the moment the forearms and hands touch the ground, raise on to the toes, bringing the knees and stomach clear of the ground and allow the arms to bend forward from the elbows to take the shock of the fall.

When proficient, practice from the standing position.

Note :—This fall is used when there is insufficient room to do a " Rolling Dive."

No. 4.—Front Fall.

Fig. 199

Fig. 200

161

No. 5.—Getting Up from the Ground.

Having fallen or been thrown, as in Fig. 201,

1. Turn your body sharply towards your left-hand side, stomach to the ground, raising by the help of the right forearm and right knee to the position shown in Fig. 202.

2. Pushing with both hands, force yourself into the position shown in Fig. 203 and then stand up.

Note.—All the above movements must be one continuous roll or twist of the body. Further, having arrived at the position shown in Fig. 203, and your opponent is behind you, and you want to face him, turn sharply on your left foot, backwards towards your left hand side, when you will be in the position shown in Fig. 204.

Fig. 201

162

No. 5.—Getting Up from the Ground.

Fig. 202

Fig. 203

Fig. 204

163

No. 6.—Getting Up from the Ground (Backwards).

Having fallen or been thrown as in Fig. 205,

1. Place your right arm at an angle of 90 degrees from the body, back of hand on the ground, head towards your left shoulder (Fig. 206).

2. Raise your legs from the waist and shoot them over your right shoulder (Fig. 207).

3. Allow your right arm and hand to turn with your body ; then by bending the right leg from the knee you will be in the position shown in Fig. 208.

4. Press on the ground with both hands and force yourself up to a standing position.

Fig. 205

164

No. 6.—Getting Up from the Ground (Backwards).

Fig. 206

Fig. 207

Fig. 208

165

Combination Throw, with a " Coat Strangle "

You and your opponents have hold of each other's clothing, as in Fig. 209, and you are thrown by the "Hip Throw" (Fig. 210).

1. Do not release your hold, and whilst falling, pull downwards with your right hand and push with your left, simultaneously twisting your body towards your right hand side; this will pull your opponent right over you and on to his back, as in Fig. 211.

2. Retaining your hold, pull yourself into the position shown in Fig. 212.

Contd: Next Page

Fig. 209

166

Combination Throw, with a " Coat Strangle "

Fig. 210

Fig. 211

Fig. 212

167

Combination Throw, with a " Coat Strangle "—Contd.

3. Release the hold with your right hand and seize the right lapel of his coat, the back of your hand inside the coat, the thumb outside, hand as near his neck as possible, at the same time passing your left hand under your right forearm and seize the left lapel of his coat as in Fig. 213.

4. Keeping a firm grip with both hands, apply pressure by forcing the little finger side of your right forearm under his chin and into his neck, squeezing his ribs with your thighs and forcing downwards with your body as in Fig. 214.

Note.—Should your opponent sink his chin into his chest in an attempt to prevent you from forcing your forearm into his neck.

Force your wrist bone on to the point of his chin and work it to and fro. This is very painful and will quickly make him raise his chin.

The alternative method is to fall sideways on to your back, pulling your opponent over on top of you and in between your legs ; you will then be in the position shown in Fig. 215. Lock your legs around his waist and apply pressure by pulling his neck towards you and forcing your forearm into his chin or neck, then shoot out your legs and squeeze his ribs (Fig. 216).

Fig. 213

168

Combination Throw, with a "Coat Strangle"—Contd.

Fig. 214

Fig. 215

Fig. 216

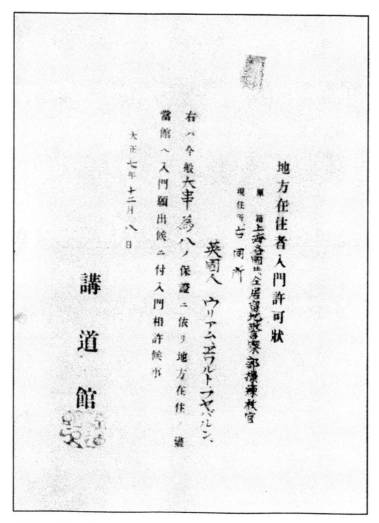

Translation of Certificate.

No. 217. **Tokyo Jui-jitsu University (Kodokan).**
Permission of Entrance.

The application for entrance of W. E. Fairbairn (resident in Foreign Country), a Drill Officer of the Police Force, Shanghai Municipal Council, having the guarantee of Tamehachi Ogushi, is hereby permitted on the Eighth Day of the Twelfth Moon in the Seventh Year of Taisho. (8th December, 1918).

(KODOKAN SEAL).

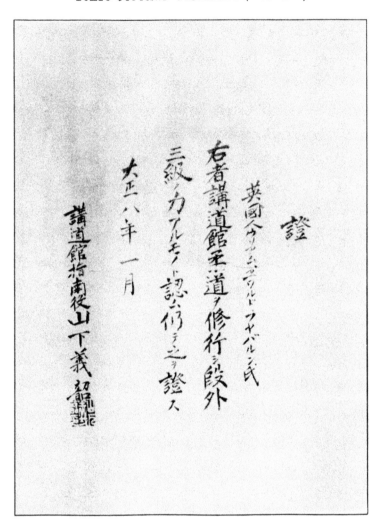

Translation of Certificate.

No. 218.   **Brown Belt, 3rd Degree.**

This is to certify that W. E. Fairbairn, British Subject, having satisfactorily acquired the art of Kodokan Judo (Jui-jitsu), is awarded the Brown Belt, 3rd Degree (San Kyu), of the Tokyo Jui-jitsu University.

             (Sd.) Y. YAMASHITA, Kodokan Judo Instructor.
First Moon in the Eighth Year of Taisho, (January, 1919).

                         (KODOKAN SEAL).

171

www.ingramcontent.com/pod-product-compliance
Ingram Content Group UK Ltd.
Pitfield, Milton Keynes, MK11 3LW, UK
UKHW021357291224
3880UKWH00017B/105

9 781783 317042